Believing in *Magic*

Believing in *Magic*

The Psychology of Superstition

Stuart A. Vyse

OXFORD UNIVERSITY PRESS

New York   Oxford   1997

Oxford University Press

Oxford   New York
Athens   Auckland   Bangkok   Bogotá   Bombay
Buenos Aires   Calcutta   Cape Town   Dar es Salaam
Delhi   Florence   Hong Kong   Istanbul   Karachi
Kuala Lumpur   Madras   Madrid   Melbourne
Mexico City   Nairobi   Paris   Singapore
Taipei   Tokyo   Toronto

and associated companies in
Berlin   Ibadan

Published by Oxford University Press, Inc.,
198 Madison Avenue, New York, New York 10016

Library of Congress Cataloging-in-Publication Data
Vyse, Stuart A.
Believing in magic : the psychology of superstition / Stuart A. Vyse
p. cm.   Includes bibliographical references and index.
ISBN 0-19-507882-9
1. Superstition.   I. Title.
BF1775.V97   1997
133.4'3'019—dc20   96-28082

1 3 5 7 9 8 6 4 2

Printed in the United States of America
on acid-free paper

To my students,
from whom I have learned so much

Preface

For at least twenty-five years I have wanted to write a book, but until recently I could not have imagined that it would be this book. The idea emerged rather suddenly, but once adopted, made perfect sense. Superstition and belief in the paranormal are common features of modern life, and they appear to be in no danger of extinction. The topic is inherently interesting to many people, and in my case, it was stimulating enough to sustain me through several years of writing. But more important, this book has given me the opportunity to say something new about the origins of superstitious beliefs and actions, and to share some of my views about human behavior and society.

In undertaking this project, I concentrated on three goals. First, I provided a psychological account of superstitious behavior—how people acquire it and why it persists. There have been a few previous books on this and related subjects, but they did not benefit from the wealth of contemporary research on these topics.[1] Second, I used superstition as a vehicle to introduce readers to the science of psychology. Psychology is well known as a profession devoted to the treatment of behavioral and emotional problems, but fewer people are familiar with psychology as the science of everyday, nonpathological behavior. While addressing my first goal, I introduced several fields of the science of human behavior to demonstrate what that science can do when researchers focus their attention on a feature of our common experience. Finally, I describe the role of superstition in the contemporary world and offer some thoughts about how we should respond to it.

With these goals in mind, I adopted three strategies in constructing this volume. First, to accommodate a wide range of readers, I chose a style of writing that I hope is clear, entertaining, and stripped of most psychological jargon. Second, I deliberately deemphasized psychological theory. Psychological researchers often approach their investigations from a particular theoretical viewpoint, which affects the questions they ask and the conclusions they draw. Rather than involve the reader in theoretical disputes that do not aid in understanding the psychology of superstition, I limited my discussions of theory and tried to give a balanced presentation of material from a variety of theoretical traditions. Third, I included all the sources and supporting evidence required for an academic volume, but this material is hidden away in notes that can be safely ignored. Psychologists, students, and other interested readers in search of more advanced material and references to the primary sources will find them at the end of the book.

For a brief time, years before I began my career as a psychologist, I had the good fortune to be a student of the American novelist John Gardner. It was the early 1970s, and at that time, I was nurturing my dream of being a writer as a graduate student in English. Gardner was a brilliant, driven man who was said to have entire rooms of his house filled with manuscript pages. When he spoke to us about writing, he would adopt an imploring tone, and he often repeated one phrase that I have never forgotten: "Write as if the fate of the world depended upon it—it does."

I always wondered how he could say this with a straight face. It was, of course, the end of the Vietnam era, and outside the classroom we were testing the strength of our convictions on a daily basis. But, as talented and successful as he was, I could never understand how he might believe that his novels could save the world. Later he wrote a book of criticism entitled *On Moral Fiction*,[2] and I began to understand. He simply meant that writers must avoid the nihilistic and self-indulgent treatments of trivial topics that are so common in contemporary fiction and make their writing moral—not in the sense of presenting some social or religious message—but in the sense of testing our beliefs and values in the interest of human betterment. The medium of Melville and Joyce was too important to be mere entertainment.

Scientists and academics face a similar challenge. To the general public, much of their work seems arcane and insignificant. Professional and technical vocabularies render scientific writing inaccessible to the untrained reader, and the object of study often appears to have little or no practical value. Of course, most of the time this is not the case. The topics studied are often of great social relevance, but those closest to the subject sometimes find it difficult to convey the larger meaning of their work to people outside the research community. This book is a modest effort to do just that.

July 1996   S.A.V.
Westerly, Rhode Island

Acknowledgments

Writing is a solitary enterprise, but as I worked on this book I benefited from the assistance of many friends and more than a few strangers. Several Connecticut College faculty colleagues reviewed sections of the manuscript or recommended material, including Kenneth Bleeth, John Burton, Ann Sloan Devlin, Eugene Gallagher, Donald Peppard, and Jefferson Singer. My students David Albert, Susan Dutton, Michelle Hylan, Denise Nelligan, and Gail Sulser served as research assistants, and Ruth Heltzer, Adair Kendrick, Benjamin Tuck, Alan Tuerkheimer, and Craig Wilkinson collaborated on research related to superstition. A number of people supplied valuable material for the book or assisted me in gathering material, including Ed Duckworth of the *Providence Journal-Bulletin,* Norma Vyse Richards, Mark Simon, editor of the *Thoroughbred Times,* Linda Souyack, librarian for the *Daily Racing Form,* Susan Tien, Arthur F.

Vyse III, Keith R. Vyse, and Stephen Weiner. I would also like to thank Nancy MacLeod for her help on a multitude of things.

Connecticut College has supported this effort in a variety of ways, but I am particularly grateful for two sabbaticals and several R. F. Johnson Faculty Development Grants.

A book of this kind could not be written without the use of libraries, and in recognition of all those who work to maintain these wonderful institutions, I wish to acknowledge the libraries I used. While on sabbatical at Harvard University I worked in both the Psychology Library in William James Hall and Widener Library, and I also used Adams Library at Rhode Island College. I found sources in a number of public libraries, including municipal libraries in New London, Connecticut, Providence, Rhode Island, and Westerly, Rhode Island. I also used both the Main and Performing Arts branches of the New York Public Library. Of course, most of the work was done at Connecticut College's Shain Library, and although I was assisted by many staff members, interlibrary loan librarians Helen Aitner and Ashley Powell Hanson, special collections librarian Brian Rogers, and audiovisual coordinator Peter Berris deserve special thanks.

From the beginning Joan Bossert, my editor at Oxford University Press, has been an enthusiastic supporter, and her skillful editing significantly improved the quality of this volume. Oxford copy editor Christine Cipriani further refined the final product. Any clinkers that remain are my own responsibility.

Finally, I want to thank my family and friends for their support. Special thanks go to my wife Judith and my children Graham and Emily for their patience and encouragement during this lengthy process.

Contents

Believing in *Magic*

1

Believing in Magic

Conceptions of the *mana* [magical] type are so frequent and so widespread that we should ask ourselves if we are not confronted with a permanent and universal form of thought which, being a function of a certain situation of the mind in the face of things, must appear each time this situation is given.

—Claude Lévi-Strauss

When it comes to hitting, Wade Boggs is an expert. The New York Yankees third baseman has won the American League batting title five times, and he is the only player in this century to get two hundred hits in seven consecutive seasons.[1] At the plate, Boggs is one of baseball's most methodical workmen. Firmly rooted in the left-hand batter's box, he leans in, anticipating the pitch, and fixes the mound with a hardened stare. His bat is cocked tightly behind his left shoulder, vibrating more rapidly as the pitcher begins his motion. When the ball finally comes to the plate, a translucent streak on a field of green, he measures its path with instantaneous accuracy and adjusts his stance and swing to meet it. He rarely swings at a bad pitch, and never at the first pitch, good or bad. Down in the count at 1-and-2 or 2-and-2, he can foul off a dozen pitches before finding one to put in play. And when he hits (on average, approximately every third trip to the plate), he can place the ball at will: launching a flare into an unprotected patch of short right center or drilling it down the line to disappear into a shadowy corner of left field. Destined to join the hallowed figures of baseball history, Boggs is one of the greatest hitters ever to play the game.

One might expect this future Hall of Famer to project an air of confidence. To understand what forces control the motion of the ball, and to be a clear-thinking master of what Ted Williams calls the Science of Hitting.[2] Surprisingly, this is not the case. Like many in his profession, Wade Boggs's life is filled with superstition. Believing that he hits better after eating chicken, he has eaten chicken every day for at least twenty years. Indeed, he is so knowledgeable about preparing chicken that he published his favorite recipes in a cookbook.[3] Having eaten, Boggs begins a pregame ritual that takes five hours to complete and includes such eccentricities as ending his grounder drill by stepping on third, second, and first base, taking two steps in the first-base coaching box, and jogging to the dugout in exactly four strides. He never steps on the foul line when running onto the field and always steps on it on his way back to the dugout. At precisely 7:17 P.M. he runs wind sprints in the outfield, and when he finally steps into the batting box he draws the Hebrew letter *chai* in the dirt with his bat.[4] Boggs has explained the motivation for his elaborate routines by saying, "I don't like surprises. I face enough of the unexpected when I'm hitting; I don't need any others."[5]

• • •

Like Wade Boggs, we all live in a world of uncertainty. Some of the most critical events in our lives are completely unpredictable and, when they do occur, utterly unexpected. Consider the problem of disease. Despite substantial advances in our understanding of most common ailments, everyone is a potential victim. Heart disease is the most common killer at 33 percent of all deaths, followed by cancer at 24 percent, and strokes at 7 percent.[6] By keeping abreast of the current research findings, we can learn the "risk factors" associated with each disease; we can even improve our chances for continued health. But many important variables remain beyond our control. Heart disease, for example, is partly a function of genetics; if one of your parents has had a heart attack, you are more likely to have one yourself. You can strengthen your heart through exercise and keep your blood vessels clean by maintaining a healthy diet, but you can never remove that fraction of increased risk created by your genetic inheritance.

The multiple causes of disease, some known and some unknown, make it impossible to predict the medical fate of any particular individual. Many of us have friends who are overweight, loathe exercise, and continue to indulge their passions for fatty foods, cigarettes, and alcohol while living to an enviable age. Conversely we have heard of ascetics who, like author and running enthusiast Jim Fixx, die of heart attacks in what appears to be the full bloom of health.[7] And disease is only one example of the uncertainty of our daily lives. We assume various risks when we drive our cars, make financial investments, change jobs, or fall in love. The consequences of our actions may be joyful, sad, or neither, but they are rarely predictable.

Uncertainty is an inescapable feature of the human experience, and people approach it in different ways. Some seem to crave it. Drawn to the thrill of taking chances, they gamble, drive fast, skydive, or take drugs. Others are crippled by uncertainty. Our failure to accommodate the random happenings of life can lead to a variety of psychological problems, including substance abuse, phobia, and depression. But most of us fall somewhere between these two extremes. We manage to survive the unpredictable and uncontrollable aspects of our lives by avoiding those risks we can avoid and finding ways to cope with those we cannot. Some achieve this feat with relative ease. These rationalists and fatalists seem constitutionally equipped to prevail over the indeterminacy of daily events. They neither seek external support for life's slings and arrows nor show visible signs of wounding. Still others find explanations in religious faith or personal philosophy. But some people, many of whom are quite sensible about other aspects of their lives, respond to uncertainty with superstitious beliefs or actions.

The superstitions of baseball players are legendary, as much a part of their peculiar subculture as rosin bags and chewing tobacco. They fear the jinx, wear lucky socks, and place faith in the power of "rally caps."[8] But superstitions are not unique to athletes. Many people—most of us, in fact—hold beliefs that are irrational and superstitious. For example, it is widely thought that the position of the stars at the time and place of one's birth helps determine one's health, physical characteristics, personality, and future destiny. Although evidence does not support the validity of astrology, millions of Americans believe in it.[9] Furthermore, many people carry good-luck charms or engage in simple acts, such as knocking on wood or crossing fingers, that they hope will ward off bad fortune and bring on good. In our scientifically advanced Western society, this behavior seems paradoxical. Our understanding of the natural world tells us that these signs and gestures cannot possibly affect the events at which they are directed, yet superstition is extremely common, if not universal.

This popular form of irrational behavior presents a challenge for contemporary psychology. Why is superstitious behavior so prevalent? How is this behavior established and maintained? Is there a superstitious personality? Often, the phenomena of the psychological laboratory are far removed from the uncontrolled complexity of the outside world, and in this case, the gap seems particularly wide. While no simple psychological truth can account for such diverse practices as numerology, psychokinesis, and the use of good-luck charms, modern psychology can account for many of our common superstitions. In the following chapters we will see that superstitions are not abnormal. They are, in fact, a largely predictable outcome of the processes that control human learning and cognition. Indeed, some of the characteristics that have led to our emergence as the dominant species on Earth are the very ones that make us superstitious. We will also learn that, although superstition is a normal part of human nature, it is avoidable. In many cases, we can, and should, take more reasoned action. It is my hope that this book will help readers understand their own irrationality and nudge them along a truer course.

Superstition and Culture

Before examining the psychological factors responsible for the development and persistence of superstitious behavior, I would like to place this topic in a broader context. Although psychologists began to study superstition before the turn of the century, they made little progress before the 1950s. Long before this, anthropologists struggled to identify the origins of superstition (or what they more often call *magic*) and to distinguish it from religion, on the one hand, and science, on the other. Although the methods of ethnology and social anthropology are quite different from those of experimental psychology, these efforts represent the first steps toward an understanding of the psychology of superstition.

Magic and Religion

Almost from their beginnings, magic and religion have been intermingled. The shaman is often both a spiritual leader and the person who brings rain when it is needed.[10] The earliest priests of ancient Egypt, Rome, and Greece used magic to inspire the faith of the masses. They made statues weep and caused lamps to burn perpetually in the tombs of holy men. The Bible recounts the story of the Hebrew prophet Aaron, who "cast down his rod before the Pharaoh and before his servants, and it became a serpent."[11]

In the United States, the elimination of disease or disability through "faith healing" is associated with fundamentalist Christian groups, but it has a much longer tradition in the Roman Catholic church. Ailing pilgrims have often traveled to a variety of locations in Europe and North America where they believed miracle cures could be achieved. One of the most famous sites is the shrine at Lourdes, France, where thousands have come to be bathed in the healing spring waters. To date, sixty-five miraculous cures have been certified by the Church.[12] Moreover, when evaluating candidates for canonization, the Vatican requires potential saints to have performed some miracle, usually an unexplained cure.[13] This commingling of the magical and the spiritual has made it particularly difficult for anthropologists to distinguish between the two, in part because there has been little agreement on terms.

When we speak of magic, we usually mean stage illusions or *legerdemain*. The magician's act is made up of "tricks," and there is an understanding between the performer and the audience that nothing supernatural is involved. No one is more aware of this tacit agreement than the professional stage magician. Although the members of this unique group guard their secrets jealously, most clearly identify themselves as entertainers, not priests. Indeed, professional magicians such as James "The Amazing" Randi have been among the most outspoken critics of psychics and others who claim to possess personal supernatural abilities.[14] The magics studied by anthropologists, however, are sorcery, witchcraft, and conjuring, and in those cultures where magic plays a role, its power is real.

Magic as a Product of the "Primitive" Mind

In 1890, Scottish classicist Sir James Frazer published the first extensive study of magic, myth, and religion in his twelve-volume work *The Golden Bough*. This influential investigation described a wide range of beliefs and practices shared in similar forms by cultures throughout the world. Frazer identified two broad categories of magic based on opposing motivations: positive magic or sorcery, which aims to bring about desirable events, and negative magic or taboo, which aims to avoid unwanted ends. In addition, Frazer described two important principles of sympathetic magic: *homeopathy*, or magic based on the law of similarity, and *contagion*, or contagious magic.

Homeopathic magic is founded on the notion that "like produces like." Thus, an American Ojibway employs homeopathic magic to harm an enemy by striking or stabbing a doll-like image of her.[15] A vestige of this form of magic remains in the practice of burning a hated foe in effigy. Similarly, a magical taboo in Madagascar forbade soldiers from eating the knee of an ox, lest the soldier acquire the ox's weak knees and be unable to march.

The magical principle of contagion holds that there is a lasting connection between things that were once in contact. For example, some cultures give special significance to the treatment of the placenta and umbilical cord after the birth of a child. In Laos it is believed that if the afterbirth is placed in the highest branch of a tree, it will be eaten by spirits who will prepare the child for a happy life. Even today, couples who are recent southeast Asian immigrants to the United States often ask delivery-room doctors and nurses if they may keep the placenta. Similarly, natives of the Marshall Islands throw a boy's umbilical cord into the sea to make him a good fisherman. Another example of contagious magic involves the relationship between a footprint and its maker. In Mecklenberg, Germany it was once believed that you could render a person lame by driving a nail into her footprint. Another German tradition held that if the dirt of a footprint was tied up in cloth and hung to dry in chimney smoke, its maker would wither away or her foot would shrivel up.

Frazer believed that magic could be distinguished from religion in two ways. First, magic is sympathetic. It makes use of the principles of homeopathy and contagion in a way that religious rites do not. Second, magic is a form of direct action. Spells and rituals are aimed directly at a specific end, whereas prayer, for example, involves the persuasion of an intermediate figure. Furthermore, Frazer believed that both primitive religion and magic were faulty attempts at understanding and controlling life events.[16] As a scholar in the post-Darwinian era, Frazer had come to reject the Presbyterianism of his youth in favor of a Victorian rationalism that held religion to be an outgrowth of intellectual immaturity. The powerful influence of Darwin's theory of evolution led many early anthropologists to organize cultures hierarchically, with the "lower races" below and European society above. Consequently, Frazer attributed both the magical and religious practices he reported to the workings of a lower form of human intelligence. These "primitive" cultures possessed a psychology that was less highly evolved than his own; thus they developed less-reasoned responses to a bewildering world.

Most modern anthropologists have abandoned the ethnocentrism of their predecessors in favor of a more egalitarian stance. The beliefs and practices of various cultures are now described without implication that some are superior to others; hence, Frazer's view of a savage mentality has not survived. In fact, the error of Frazer's ethnocentrism has been dramatically demonstrated in a series of experiments showing that American college students acquire disgust for foods through a process that closely resembles sympathetic magic. In a study published in 1986, University of Pennsylvania psychologist Paul Rozin and his colleagues found that students were reluctant to eat sugar that had been labeled "sodium cyanide," even when the students had watched it being poured from a Domino brand box and had arbitrarily placed the label on the container themselves.[17] In addition, Rozin's subjects were not averse to eating fudge when it had been pressed into the shape of a disk, but they were extremely reluctant to eat it when molded into the shape of animal feces. Thus, the attitudes of "sophisticated" American college students toward foods were affected by the magical principle of similarity: the image is the object.

Magic as a Social Institution

Frazer's work was praised for its demonstration of the universality of many myths and religious beliefs, but he was soon criticized for oversimplification. In *The Elementary Forms of the Religious Life*, French sociologist Émile Durkheim accused Frazer of failing to recognize the "profoundly religious character" of many of the beliefs and rites he described. Alternatively, Durkheim proposed a method for distinguishing between religion and magic based on the social function of each.[18] He began by rejecting the common notion that religion and magic can be distinguished from other domains by their supernatural character. The use of the term *supernatural* assumes an opposing concept: "the *natural* order of things," consisting of laws that describe everyday phenomena.[19] *Unsupported objects fall to earth. Animals must breath to sustain life.* Natural laws of this type provide us with useful expectations for the physical world, and they make it possible to distinguish the natural from the supernatural. But, as Durkheim pointed out, not all cultures distinguish between these two domains. Rites performed to make the soil rich or bring on rain may have the same validity and logical status as the methods used to prepare food.

As an alternative to the natural/supernatural distinction, Durkheim suggested that within each culture, objects and activities can be separated into two categories: the "sacred" and the "profane." Anything can be sacred—rocks, trees, and words as well as gods and spirits—but sacred things are held in higher regard and have nothing in common with the profane. Religion is made up of "beliefs," statements about the nature of sacred things, and "rites," or rules of conduct with respect to sacred things. Furthermore, religion has a unique social function. Its beliefs and practices are common to a specific group united by their faith. Durkheim called this a church, and argued that "in all history, we do not find a single religion without a church."[20]

According to this scheme, magical things are also sacred. They are placed in a higher category and give rise to beliefs and rites similar to those surrounding religious objects. But Durkheim believed that magic and religion fulfill different social functions: whereas religion serves the group, magic serves the individual. Belief in magic may be widespread, yet it does not unite those who believe in it: *"there is no Church of magic."*[21] He acknowledged that, on occasion, magical societies have appeared, such as "assemblies of witches," but that such organizations are not essential to the use of magic. In contrast, religion, Durkheim maintained, could not exist without a community of believers.

Although Durkheim and his followers helped place magic and religion in their social contexts, other writers soon rejected this sociological analysis, arguing, for example, that profoundly religious experiences often occur in solitude. In many religions, believers periodically turn away from the group and engage in individual prayer or contemplation, and because these experiences can have a powerful effect on an individual's religious faith, Durkheim's critics asserted that these solitary experiences contradict the view that religion exists to serve society.[22] Moreover, Durkheim's theory does not move us toward an understanding of the psychology of superstition.

Magic as a Response to Uncertainty

As a graduate student in chemistry at the University of Cracow, Bronislaw Malinowski read Frazer's *Golden Bough* in preparation for a foreign-language examination, and this single experience forever changed the direction of his life. After receiving his Ph.D., Malinowski went on to London to study anthropology and soon emerged as an important contributor to the field of ethnology.[23] Among other things, Malinowski was praised for the depth of his fieldwork. Whereas earlier scholars, including Frazer and Durkheim, had remained in Europe and obtained their ethnographic data from the reports of missionaries and travelers, Malinowski was one of a new generation of anthropologists who believed it was essential to live among the people they studied. Only by functioning within a culture could one make a balanced analysis of its customs. Thus, motivated by this belief and, in part, by a desire to escape internment during World War I, Malinowski lived from 1914 to 1918 among the Trobriand Islanders of Melanesia, off the coast of New Guinea.

In his 1925 essay "Magic, Science, and Religion," Malinowski presented a psychological analysis of magic that stands in contrast to Durkheim's sociological interpretation.[24] In particular, Durkheim and his followers, most notably Marcel Mauss[25] and Lucien Lévy-Bruhl, believed that cultures in which magic plays a role are prescientific; they have not yet adopted the methods of modern science. Reliance on magic belies a "primitive" inability to benefit from experience and a generally mystical and superstitious approach to the world. But Malinowski's observations of the Trobrianders convinced him that their culture combined magical beliefs and rituals with practical and genuinely scientific knowledge. Furthermore, although these two realms were kept separate, they were often rallied to the same end. For example, the Trobrianders were skilled gardeners who showed great knowledge of soil types and planting methods; yet they also performed magical rites over their gardens to insure success. The community magician often supervised both the daily management of the garden and all magical ceremonies, but it was understood that these were different kinds of activities. No work was done in the garden the day a magical rite was performed.

Malinowski believed that when important events fell outside the reaches of the islanders' scientific knowledge, magic was employed as a hedge against uncertainty. The strongest support for this notion was found in Trobriand fishing practices. Malinowski observed that those who plied the calm inner waters of the lagoon employed only highly standardized and reliable fishing methods. But fishing on the open sea was dangerous and unpredictable, and Malinowski noted that deep-sea fishermen performed elaborate magical rituals to insure a safe trip and good results. He summarized the relationship between magic and uncertainty as follows:

> We find magic wherever the elements of chance and accident, and the emotional play between hope and fear have a wide and extensive range. We do not find magic wherever the pursuit is certain, reliable, and well under the control of rational methods and technological processes. Further, we find magic where the element of danger is conspicuous.[26]

For Malinowski, religion was distinguished from magic by its unique psychological function. Whereas magic was directed at future events, religious rites helped the community surmount a current crisis. The customs surrounding death provide the best example. The death of a close friend or loved one brings conflicting feelings of sadness, fear, and anger. For those left behind, this emotional challenge is accompanied by the distasteful practical problem of disposing of a lifeless body. By ritualizating the activities of mourning and burial, religion helps to standardize the emotional responses of loss and suffering and provides alternatives to the mourner's more destructive impulses. Other ceremonies surrounding birth, initiation, and marriage ritualize additions to the community and important changes in status. These are "self-contained acts, the aim of which is achieved in their very performance" (Malinowski, 1972/1948, p. 52).

Magic as a Failure of Confidence

A different view of magic and religion was proposed by British historian Keith Thomas. In his 1971 volume, *Religion and the Decline of Magic*, he examined magical beliefs and practices in England from 1500 to 1700 and the factors that led to their diminished popularity. During the sixteenth and much of the seventeenth century, religious objects were the source of much magic. To encourage converts to a new religious order, the priests of the medieval church in England had found it necessary to incorporate a large measure of pagan supernaturalism. Anglo-Saxons had commonly worshiped wells, trees, and stones; eventually a wide variety of powers were attributed to the consecrated objects of the church.

Holy water was a particularly versatile agent. To avail themselves of its reputed curative powers, parishioners often drank it, sprinkled it in children's cradles or on ailing cattle, and splashed it on their houses to ward off evil spirits and protect against lightning. Other supernatural powers were attributed to soil from the churchyard, friars' coats, the key to the church, coins from the offertory, and the Host. Belief in the magic of consecrated objects was so ardent and so widespread that the clergy were forced to take elaborate precautions to prevent theft. According to Thomas, after conducting mass, priests were required to "swallow the remaining contents of the chalice, flies and all if need be, and to ensure that not a crumb of the wafer was left behind," and to place the Eucharist, holy oil, and holy water under lock and key.[27]

Sickness and premature death were a much greater concern in the sixteenth and seventeenth centuries than they are today. Thomas described the situation this way:

> Even among the nobility, whose chances are likely to have been better than those of other classes, the life expectation at birth of boys born in the third quarter of the seventeenth century was 29.6 years. Today it would be around 70. A third of these aristocratic infants died before the age of five . . . . In London, conditions were particularly bad. The first English demographer, John Graunt, estimated in 1662 that, of every hundred live children born in the metropolis, thirty-six died in their first six years and a further twenty-four in the following ten years.[28]

Given the insecurity of life, it is not surprising that so many popular supernatural beliefs had as their object the cure of illness or the maintenance of health. One of the most important of these beliefs involved the healing power of the royalty. It was widely believed that the monarch's touch could cure a variety of ailments. Typically, a special religious service was conducted for this purpose.

Patients approached one by one and knelt before the monarch, who lightly touched them on the face while a chaplain read aloud from St. Mark: "They shall lay hands on the sick and they shall recover." They then retired and came forward again so that the King might hang around their necks a gold coin strung on a white silk ribbon.[29] This ceremony was so popular that, according to the King's Healing Register, Charles II touched 8,577 people between May 1682 and April 1683. The gold coin hung around the sufferer's neck was thought to be a talisman with its own medicinal powers; those who received it were urged not to remove the coin lest their disease return and overtake them.

Alchemy, astrology, conjuring, and witchcraft were also widely practiced during this period, but by the eighteenth century they had become much less acceptable. This waning influence of the supernatural occurred at a time of rapid scientific and technological development. The magical arts were severely threatened by advances in the natural sciences, such as Boyle's descriptions of the behavior of gases and Newton's theory of gravitation. In addition, improvements in communication reduced the isolation of small communities and improved access to information. Literacy in England had made great strides during the seventeenth century, and by 1700, newspapers were widely read. Other developments increased the security of life. Deposit banking became more popular, and by the end of the seventeenth century, underwriters had begun to offer life and fire insurance. Finally, Pascal, Bernoulli, and other European mathematicians introduced theories of probability that provided alternative explanations for misfortune and helped to objectify the interpretation of everyday events.

Although these changes were concurrent with the decline of magic in the latter half of the seventeenth century, Thomas maintained that supernaturalism was not defeated by the march of progress. He disputed Malinowski's notion that magic appears whenever the limits of science and technology are reached. In support of his view, Thomas pointed out that magical beliefs about disease and death were rejected before medical science had provided an adequate replacement. For example, in 1616, William Harvey presented his theory of the blood's circulation throughout the body, yet this important development did not immediately lead to life-saving therapies. These and other scientific advances weakened the appeal of supernatural theories of disease without providing alternative forms of treatment.

As a result, Thomas suggested that magic was supplanted not by technological advances, but by a change in the popular psyche. England in the eighteenth century was marked by "the emergence of a new faith in the potentialities of human initiative."[30] The construction of new hospitals decreased reliance on amateur physicians and local magicians. Agriculturists encouraged fertilization and discouraged fertility rites, and in general, there was an increased commitment to experimentation in farming and other endeavors. Thus, in Thomas's view, magic was defeated not by new technology, but by new aspirations and a spirit of self-help.

• • •

These anthropological studies of magic provide an excellent point of departure for the investigation of superstition in contemporary American society. Frazer's work reveals the breadth and variety of magical beliefs while identifying their many common features. Durkheim makes the important point that superstition must be placed in a social context, taking into account the cultural status of science and technology. Malinowski's theory provides a truly psychological account of superstition and magic as motivated by the reduction of anxiety produced by conditions of risk and uncertainty. (This view of Trobriand magic does not account for many of the common superstitions observed in our own culture, yet superstitious behavior is still more likely when an important future outcome is unknown. Furthermore, these magical acts often do reduce the anxiety associated with uncontrollable events.) Finally, Thomas suggests that other factors may cause the historical ebb and flow of magical thinking, including a culture's collective psychology. But contrary to Thomas's view, even a casual examination of contemporary American culture reveals that superstition and magical thinking abound. As a group, contemporary Americans may be less superstitious than Britains of the sixteenth and seventeenth centuries, but science and reason have yet to defeat the forces of the paranormal. Indeed, many recent victories have been on the side of superstition.

The Prevalence of Superstition

Although everyday experience suggests that superstitious beliefs and behavior are widespread, it is probably impossible to determine accurately the extent of their popularity. Undoubtedly, many believers are reluctant to confess their superstitions for fear of ridicule. Furthermore, some superstitions are exercised infrequently or in private, making it difficult to observe them directly. Nevertheless, there are some existing data to suggest the dimensions of this phenomenon.

Indirect Indicators

Over the last three decades, several important social trends have helped to popularize a variety of superstitious and paranormal beliefs. Particularly in the 1970s and 1980s, but continuing to this day, the New Age movement has rejected Western science, technology, and orthodox religion, given new life to old superstititions, and introduced new ones. Some adherents visit "channelers," who claim to speak the wisdom of alien beings or people from centuries past; others advocate nontraditional medical treatments, such as magic crystals and a contemporary version of healing by therapeutic touch. Belief in reincarnation, astrology, numerology, and extrasensory perception (ESP) are also common. Several New Age magazines are in print, and it has been estimated that the number of New Age bookstores doubled between the years of 1982 and 1987, reaching a national total of 2,500.[31] Finally, actress Shirley McLaine, who has emerged as a leading spokesperson for the movement, has written five spiritual books that together have sold over eight million copies.

A more recent trend has been the increased popularity of religious spiritualism, including the belief that angels exist and can affect events on Earth, belief in religious miracles, and belief in faith healing. There has been a rise in the number of sightings of Jesus's image on walls, windows, and other unexpected locations, and several recent reports of crying or bleeding pictures or paintings of Jesus.[32] Although some of these ideas are purely religious and thus not properly labeled supersititious, others conflict directly with accepted scientific knowledge and are at least examples of paranormal belief.

Finally, it appears that Americans are increasingly anxious about their world and suspicious of the media. Conspiracy theories are growing in popularity and have fostered an increasing belief in unidentified flying objects (UFOs) and in alien abduction. (Belief in widespread visitation of creatures from other planets typically requires the assumption that the government has always known about such visits but has maintained a conspiracy of silence.) In his 1994 book *Abduction*, Harvard psychiatrist John Mack promoted the idea that "several hundred thousand to several million Americans may have had abduction or abduction-related experiences,"[33] in most cases, without their knowledge. He suggested that these experiences had important and undesirable psychological effects on the people involved, and he described his treatment of several patients who believed they had been abducted. Belief in UFOs and alien abductions also represent paranormal rather than superstitious beliefs, but all of these movements reflect a willingness to accept ideas that are not supported by scientific facts.

The effects of these cultural trends can be seen in a number of areas of the news and entertainment media. Psychologist James Alcock reported that the number of titles listed in *Books in Print* under the subject "occult and psychic" grew from 131 in 1965 to 1,071 in 1975.[34] By 1990, this number listed under similar categories had grown to 2,150 titles, and in 1994 it was 2858.[35] Furthermore, approximately 1,200 of the nation's 1,750 daily newspapers carry astrological columns.[36] Although some of those who read these publications may not be true believers, it is safe to assume that many others are, and the increasing production of books on the occult suggests a growing acceptance of magic and superstition. Recently, a number of prime-time television programs devoted to the unskeptical presentation of paranormal phenomena have emerged on the major networks, including "Unsolved Mysteries," "The X Files," "Sightings," and "Encounters," and many popular films have featured paranormal forces, including *Ghost*, the fifteenth-highest-grossing film ever, and *The Exorcist*.[37] As this book was going to press in the summer of 1996, two of the season's most popular films were *Independence Day*, a science fiction thriller about an alien invasion, and *Phenomenon*, the story of a man who acquires paranormal powers.

Gallup Polls

More objective studies of the prevalence of superstitious and paranormal beliefs have taken the form of surveys of students enrolled in college psychology courses or surveys of the general public. The best of these are three Gallup polls conducted in 1978, 1990, and 1994.[38] In each case, over 1,000 adults were interviewed about a wide range of topics. The results presented in Table 1.1 indicate that large numbers of Americans believe in various paranormal religious ideas, such as angels, miracles, and the devil; but nonreligious phenomena such as ESP, *déjà vu*, and ghosts are also widely endorsed. Of the nine beliefs that were surveyed more than once, only two—ESP and astrology—show a decreasing trend. The other beliefs are all on the rise, with some showing substantial increases (e.g., the devil, communication with the dead, and ghosts). Although these findings indicate that belief in the paranormal is strong and increasing, the most dramatic result was that when presented with a list of eighteen such phenomena, only 7 percent of the 1990 respondents said they did not believe in any of them.[39]

Table 1.1   Percentage of Americans Who Believe in Various Paranormal Phenomena[a]

	1978	1990	1994
Extrasensory perception	51	47	—
Angels	—	—	72
Miracles	—	—	79
The Devil	39	55	65
Reincarnation	—	21	27
Déjà vu	30	55	—
Astrology	29	25	23
Clairvoyance	24	26	—
Communication with the dead	—	18	28
Ghosts	11	25	—
Witches	10	14	—

[a] Questions were worded differently in the 1978 and 1990 surveys.

Fewer people have had personal experiences with these phenomena, but according to the 1990 poll, direct contact with the paranormal is surprisingly common. The most frequently mentioned experiences are presented in Table 1.2.

Finally, the 1990 poll asked respondents about their belief in traditional superstitions. Forty-four percent of Americans said they were at least a little superstitious, and 18 percent admitted to being somewhat or very superstitious. Table 1.3 presents a list of the most popular superstitions.

Although these figures suggest a more moderate level of belief in superstition, they probably underestimate the true degree of acceptance. Psychologists have long recognized that research participants are sometimes motivated by a fear of negative evaluation. Even when they reply anonymously, as in the case of the Gallup polls, survey respondents may imagine that the interviewers are forming judgments about them. This fear makes

Table 1.2   Percentage of Americans Who Have Had Various Paranormal Experiences[a]

Had a feeling of déjà vu	56
Received a message without using the traditional five senses	25
Felt in touch with someone who was already dead	17
Consulted a fortuneteller	14
Been in a house you felt was haunted	14
Communicated with the Devil	10
Seen or been in the presence of a ghost	9
Felt that you were here on Earth in a previous life	8
Seen someone moving or bending an object with mental energy	7
Consulted an astrologer	6

[a] In some cases I have abbreviated the wording of the questions asked in the original survey.

Table 1.3   *Percentage of Americans Who Endorse Various Superstitions* [a]

Black cat crossing path	14
Walking under a ladder	12
Numbers/Friday the 13th/Bad things happening in threes	9
Breaking a mirror	5
Wearing lucky clothing/dressing in a certain order/avoiding some colors	2
Speaking ill or well of a person or event making it happen	2
Picking up pennies/coins	1
Following horoscope	1
Knocking on wood	1
Evil/the Devil	1
Telepathy/ESP	1
Other	11
None	2
No opinion	52

[a] Values are percentages of respondents who reported being at least a little superstitious. The percentages add to more than 100 percent due to multiple responses.

some people reluctant to reveal their true feelings on questions involving unconventional beliefs or behavior. Reports of traditional superstitions are thus particularly vulnerable to bias caused by apprehension about being evaluated. Although belief in the paranormal is decidedly unorthodox, a number of factors promote its acceptance by the general public. Self-proclaimed psychics, astrologers, and "authorities" on the paranormal appear frequently in radio and television interviews to assert the genuineness of a variety of supernatural occurrences. Others describe personal experiences with spiritual healing or sightings of extra-terrestrial beings. Finally, it is impossible to prove many of these beliefs conclusively true or false. For example, it has been suggested that sometime in the distant past, the Earth was visited by beings from another planet. At this time, there is no clear proof of either the existence or the nonexistence of extraterrestrial beings, and visitation in ancient times would be particularly difficult to establish. As a result, acceptance is a question of faith rather than evidence; personal philosophy rather than objective science. Believers often portray themselves as "open-minded" and democratic in their acceptance of a broad range of ideas and skeptics as traditional, critical, and prejudicial.

In contrast, none of these influences promote the social acceptance of superstition. There are no priests of superstition appearing on television urging people to avoid black cats and ladders. In conventional use, the word *superstition* has a distinctly negative flavor, and superstitious people are often thought to be primitive and ignorant. Unlike belief in the paranormal, belief in superstition is thoroughly unfashionable. As a result, it is likely that belief in these traditional superstitions is more common than the Gallup poll results suggest. It is easier to be superstitious than to admit it.

What Is Superstition?

We have come this far without establishing a definition of the topic, but we can delay no longer. Unfortunately this, too, is an all-but-impossible assignment. The word *superstition* has so many attendant connotations that it defies use as an objective scientific term. Our challenge is to encircle those pieces of meaning that are free of pejorative flavor and do not imply a particular origin or cause. A number of definitions of superstition have been proposed. The *Random House Dictionary of the English Language* defines superstition as "a belief or notion, not based on reason or knowledge, in or of the ominous significance of a particular thing, circumstance, occurrence, proceeding, or the like."[40] This circuitous phrase is both too broad and too limiting for our purposes. Our definition cannot be restricted to beliefs regarding "ominous" things. When a gambler uses the digits of his daughter's birthday to play the numbers, there is no "ominous significance" in his belief. He is not fearful of losing; indeed, he is undoubtedly quite familiar with loss. Instead, the gambler is hoping to increase his odds of winning something that has positive significance: money. Many dictionary definitions of superstition suggest that it is motivated by fear, but although this is a familiar notion—not unlike Malinowski's idea that superstition reduces anxiety—it is clear that many superstitious acts are not motivated by fear. Moreover, not all irrationality is superstition. Murder and schizophrenia[41] are irrational, but they are not superstitious. Thus our definition must be narrowed to include only certain forms of irrational behavior encountered in sane, law-abiding people.

In a 1956 essay, psychiatrist Judd Marmor proposed a definition of superstition that, with some fine-tuning, may meet our needs: "beliefs or practices groundless in themselves and inconsistent with the degree of enlightenment reached by the community to which one belongs."[42] This version has two advantages. First, it avoids cultural and historical prejudice by placing superstitious behavior in its social context. In twentieth-century America, belief in alchemy is genuinely irrational because it contradicts established principles of physics and chemistry, but in tenth-century Persia, the idea that base metals could be transformed into silver or gold was not inconsistent with the science of the day.[43] Second, this interpretation is relatively objective, avoiding any inferred motivation, such as fear.

But there is one difficulty. How do we establish *the degree of enlightenment reached by the community*? In our Western culture, the most acceptable response to illness is to visit a physician, yet most of those who do have little understanding of the medicines and treatments they receive. They go because they trust that the doctor is a reputable authority. If, instead, a person consults a witch doctor, should we call this superstitious? The methods of either practitioner can appear magical to the untrained observer. In these cases, we must base our test of the community's enlightenment on the views of accepted experts. The physician is trusted, in part, because her practices are endorsed by scientific and educational organizations, as well as government public-health agencies. Where scientific consensus combines with the acceptance of the general public, we can safely identify a set of beliefs or practices as endorsed by the community.

Unfortunately, the opinions of experts are often in dispute. The scientific community may reach a consensus while other groups disagree. For example, Darwin's theory of evolution is widely accepted by biologists and educators, but some fundamentalist Christians reject it in favor of what they call "Scientific Creationism." In other areas, the experts themselves disagree. Many important mental disorders are still incompletely understood, and various professionals have proposed radically different views of cause, diagnosis, and treatment for them. In the case of schizophrenia, few mental-health experts believe that it is caused by demonic possession, but some would say that a Freudian interpretation is equally as superstitious. This lack of scientific consensus on mental disorders has led both jurists and the general public to be skeptical of psychological and psychiatric expert testimony.[44] Thus we must limit our definition of superstition to those topics on which scientists and the general public agree.

Narrowing the Field

Superstitious behavior is as widespread and various as humanity itself, so our discussion will be made both easier and more cohesive if we can restrict it to certain forms of superstition. Yet, as attractive as this proposition sounds, I am reluctant to deprive the topic of its diversity. So rather than arbitrarily rule out parts of the topic, I will achieve a degree of narrowing by placing primary emphasis on certain forms of behavior.

I begin by adopting a taxonomy of superstitious behavior. In an earlier work on this subject, psychologist Gustav Jahoda proposed four categories of superstition that provide a valuable framework for the present investigation:

Superstitions forming part of a cosmology or coherent world-view. Like Sir James Frazer, some behavioral scientists believe that all religion is superstitious, a misguided faith born of ignorance. Others hold that only "pagan" religion, with its magical rites and rituals, is superstitious. Although science and religion have traditionally been cast as antagonists, in reality they speak different languages. Religious faith exists without need of proof, while science is built upon proof. Psychologists and sociologists may study religious, philosophical, and ethical behavior, but they have little to say about the virtues of any particular religious tenet. Nevertheless, a number of spiritual and religious groups hold beliefs that fall within our definition of superstition. The royal healing touch survives today in the form of faith-healing ministers who, as "instruments of God," are said to alleviate all types of ailments and disability. The Mahareshi Mahesh Yogi, founder of Transendental Meditation, claims his followers can learn to levitate their bodies through meditation.[45] Because these beliefs fall within the realm of established science and are not supported by evidence, they can be classified as superstitious.[46]

Other socially shared superstitions. The great majority of superstitions come to us as part of our culture. People teach us rules, such as "black cats bring bad luck," that were once taught to them. Many of these rules are concerned with important human events: birth, marriage, illness, and death. A number of popular and scholarly books catalogue these common superstitions—for example, Anthon Cannon assembled a list of 13,207 superstitions and folk beliefs indigenous to the state of Utah.[47] With cultural superstitions, the primary challenge for psychology is to identify the factors that influence our acceptance and explain why these beliefs persist in the face of conflicting evidence.

"Occult" experiences of individuals. As we have seen, paranormal experiences, such as ESP and communication with the dead, are surprisingly common. If belief in these phenomena contradicts our scientific understanding of physics and psychology, then it, too, must be classified as superstition. In the case of ESP, we are particularly fortunate because the scientific community has given it considerable attention.

In the late nineteenth century, societies of "parapsychology" were established in Britain and the United States, and soon a number of parapsychological laboratories began investigating such phenomena as mental telepathy, precognition, and psychokinesis.[48] From 1935 to 1965, Duke University maintained a famous department of parapsychology, and in 1969 the Parapsychology Association was admitted to membership in the prestigious American Association for the Advancement of Science (AAAS). Yet despite its outward appearance as a reputable science, parapsychology has failed the crucial test. Years of research have produced no conclusive support for the existence of ESP; many of the studies have contained serious methodological flaws, or have produced results impossible to replicate. Therefore, ESP satisfies our definition of a superstition. Other experiences that fall into this category are ghosts, haunted houses, poltergeists, and premonitions.

Personal superstitions. The last category includes superstitions held only by an individual. This represents a large group of beliefs and actions that are neither learned from nor taught to others. Wade Boggs's pregame ritual is an example, as are the lucky shirts, hats, numbers, and colors common to athletes, gamblers, businesspeople, and others.

Although this classification scheme provides a simple lexicon of superstition, it is not without inconsistencies. For example, many superstitions, not just Jahoda's "socially shared" category, are at least partially shaped by social influence. The mere popularity of lucky hats and other magical clothing belie a social or cultural contribution to personal superstitions, and many reported occult experiences also share common elements. Superstitious beliefs of all kinds are undoubtedly encouraged by a social environment rich in believers. Nevertheless, these categories help to structure the discussion that follows.

Parameters of the Book

Every author imposes a personal view and makes choices. Here are some of the guidelines I have used in this book.

The individual over the group. As a discipline, psychology is primarily concerned with individual behavior, and as a result, this analysis of superstitious behavior examines the forces affecting the individual people who engage in it. Because human behavior cannot be understood apart from its social and cultural context, the effects of social environment and group membership will also be assessed, but only as they influence the behavior of individuals. Group-level analyses of superstition and magic are properly left to sociologists and anthropologists.

The common over the obscure. Although it is tempting to examine the most arcane and unusual examples of superstition (a temptation that I have, at times, found irresistible), most of what follows is concerned with the popular forms of irrationality encountered in daily life. One of the objectives of this book is to demonstrate the generality of psychological science and the extent of its application to everyday experience. Thus, I have focused on the dominant forms of superstition reported in the Gallup polls and other studies of popular belief.

Utilitarianism over mysticism. Finally, and most important, this book is written in a spirit of pragmatism. Our definition of superstition includes a number of relatively harmless, idle beliefs that typically have little influence on the believer's life. ESP is a good example. Although many people believe that extrasensory perception is possible, and in some cases report having experienced it, this belief rarely leads them to behave in any particular way. Few people attempt to harness the forces of ESP in their daily lives,[49] nor does the notion of ESP lead them to undertake or avoid any specific action. Therefore, although belief in ESP is clearly unjustified, it is a relatively benign form of irrationality that has few direct consequences.

But other superstitions are aimed at securing a particular end: winning a gamble, avoiding illness, or getting a hit. Superstitions of this type are not mere thoughts or beliefs; they are manifest as overt behavior. They are superstitious *acts*. In this case, a magical yet accessible cause is linked to a particular outcome. Chicken leads to hits. The science of psychology is concerned with all aspects of human behavior, the emotions and cognitions buried beneath the skin as well as more observable outward displays. The private and public realms are equally valued and equally viable subjects of investigation. But when science is applied to a specific human problem, this balance may not be appropriate. To the extent that superstitious behavior wastes time, effort, and money and prolongs ineffective responses to uncertainty, it is a more serious concern than mere superstitious belief. As a result, this book places greater emphasis on socially shared and personal superstitions that lead to action and somewhat lesser emphasis on most religious superstitions and occult beliefs.

This combination of a broad definition of superstition and an imposed value system is designed to retain the reality of the topic while providing a meaningful structure. In addition, by emphasizing the outcome-oriented superstitions, I hope to satisfy the dual objectives of providing a scientific account of a human curiosity and pointing the way to greater rationality. We begin by examining the characteristics of superstitious people.

2

The Superstitious Person

Group and Individual Differences in Magical Belief

Actors' superstitions are derived in great part from the feeling that you "need all the help you can get" to make it out there and get through a performance. It is comforting to think that there is something special about the place or time or set or costume, some omen or amulet one can fall back on. Actors are often wearing or carrying "something lucky" when they do their routine. Hollywood supports a number of highly paid astrologers who can coax good news out of the heavens for their clients. Something must cheer them on, from the galaxy if not from the gallery. Stars rely on the stars.

— Gary Wills, *Reagan's America*

In May 1988, Donald Regan, former White House Chief of Staff to President Ronald Reagan, released his memoirs to a flood of publicity. His insider's view of the presidency revealed that, over a seven-year period, First Lady Nancy Reagan had employed an astrologer to advise her on a wide range of topics, many of which bore directly on the affairs of state. According to Regan, "Virtually every major move and decision the Reagans made during my time as White House Chief of Staff was cleared in advance with a woman in San Francisco who drew up horoscopes to make certain that the planets were in a favorable alignment for the enterprise."[1] He claimed that Mrs. Reagan "insisted on being consulted on the timing of every Presidential appearance and action so that she could consult her Friend in San Francisco about the astrological factor."[2] Suggestions that certain days were "bad" for the President led to the cancellation of speeches and press conferences and, on occasion, the curtailment of all travel for days at a time. Regan never discussed the issue with the President, so he was uncertain whether Mr. Reagan knew the extent to which his administration had been controlled by the alignment of the stars.

In her own memoir, *My Turn*, Mrs. Reagan admitted that, after the attempt on the President's life in March 1981, she had regularly consulted astrologer Joan Quigley about her husband's schedule, but she maintained that "Joan's recommendations had nothing to do with policy or politics."[3] Quigley, on the other hand, claimed that she "was heavily involved in what happened in the relations between the superpowers, changing Ronald Reagan's 'Evil Empire' attitude, so that he went to Geneva prepared to meet a different kind of Russian leader."[4]

Although, as we have seen, belief in astrology is widespread, this issue was a substantial embarrassment for the Reagan administration, and Mrs. Reagan devoted a entire chapter of her book to explaining her actions. Understandably, she admitted to being afraid for her husband's life. Soon after he was inaugurated, the President narrowly escaped assassination, and in the months following the shooting, Pope John Paul II was wounded in St. Peter's Square and President Anwar Sadat was murdered in Cairo. In addition, there was the twenty-year curse: since 1840, every President elected or reelected in a year ending in zero had either died or been assassinated in office. Mr. Reagan was elected to his first term in 1980, and articles about the "twenty-year death cycle" had appeared during his campaign.[5] Mrs. Reagan had not been particularly concerned at the time, but, she wrote, "now that my own husband was president and an attempt had been made on his life, the historical pattern became terrifying to me."[6]

Mrs. Reagan was motivated by fear for her husband's safety, but why, given all the options available to her, was she moved to consult an astrologer? The answer lies in her background in acting:

> Another reason I was open to astrology was that I have spent most of my life in the company of show-business people, where superstitions and other nonscientific beliefs are widespread and commonly accepted. Maybe it's because the entertainment business is so unpredictable and impervious to logic, but starting with my mother, who was an actress, just about every performer I have known has been at least mildly superstitious. For example: It's bad luck to whistle in the dressing room. Never throw your hat on the bed. And never keep your shoes on a shelf that's higher than your head.[7]

Both Mr. and Mrs. Reagan were products of the entertainment subculture, which, like the worlds of sports and gambling, is a traditional stronghold of superstition. Mrs. Reagan undoubtedly felt she needed all the help she could get to ensure her husband's safety, and her background had led her to feel that astrology was a helpful response to the vagaries of life.

• • •

For any given individual, feelings about superstition may range from complete rejection to total endorsement, and the people who fall at opposite ends of this continuum may differ in other important ways. In this chapter we examine the evidence for individual and group differences in superstitious belief and attempt to create a profile of a typical believer. Moving from the wide to the narrow view, we begin by surveying superstitious social groups and the relationship of belief in superstition and the paranormal to broad demographic classifications, such as gender, age, and education. Finally, we examine the personality characteristics that are associated with these beliefs. First, a look at several superstitious subcultures.

Traditionally Superstitious Social and Occupational Groups

Common folk wisdom holds that a number of groups are, by nature or necessity, particularly superstitious. These people are said to practice superstitions that are either unique to, or characteristic of, their group. Mrs. Reagan's testimony supports a familiar view of actors. When a fellow performer cries, "Break a leg!" we understand it to be a good-luck incantation and not a malevolent wish. Wade Boggs is also an example, albeit a rather striking one, of a superstitious person in a traditionally superstitious occupation. As we will see, the reputation of superstitiousness extends to a variety of sports, both professional and nonprofessional. Other traditionally superstitious groups include gamblers, sailors, soldiers,[8] miners, financial investors, and, somewhat surprisingly, college students. Although there are many interesting anecdotal accounts of superstition among these groups, few systematic studies have been conducted. Of these, the best are investigations of scholastic athletes, college students, and craps players.

Superstition in Sport

Sport is an integral part of popular culture. A country's great sports help shape its heritage and sense of national identity. In the United States, some believe that baseball is the premier American sport. Many writers, including several of our finest novelists, have described the game with religious reverence. Others contend that football or basketball is the true American sport. But most would agree that sport is truly American.

The popularity of sport combined with the fact that its participants are a traditionally superstitious group make athletes, particularly professional athletes, the most famous of all superstitious people. Journalists have delighted in revealing the curious habits of the heroes of the playing field.[9] Buffalo Bills quarterback Jim Kelly forces himself to vomit before every game, a habit he has practiced since high school. San Antonio Spurs basketball star Chuck Persons eats two candy bars before every game: two KitKats, two Snickers, or one of each. San Francisco 49ers football coach George Seifert does not leave his office without patting a book and must be the last person to leave the locker room before a game. The Great (Wayne) Gretzky, star of the New York Rangers hockey team, always tucks the right side of his jersey behind his hip pads.

Uncertainty is an integral part of most sports. In basketball, the best professional players make only half their shots from the field. Quarterbacks in the National Football League complete, on average, only 58 percent of their passes.[10] Because the motivation to win or perform well is quite strong, it is not surprising that athletes resort to magic in an attempt to alter these percentages. Interestingly, superstitions within a particular sport are generally restricted to the least-certain activities. George Gmelch, an anthropologist and former professional baseball player, noted that the most capricious parts of the game are batting and pitching. Because winning depends on scoring more runs than the opposing team, a pitcher can perform very well and yet lose the game, or can give up several runs and win. A great pitch can be hit out of the park, and a bad one can become a crucial third strike. In batting, a 30-percent success rate makes one a "premier player," whereas 26 percent is only average.[11] In contrast, fielding is a more reliable enterprise. Infielders have approximately three seconds to prepare for a ball hit toward them, and outfielders have even more time. Few things can intervene to alter the ball's trajectory from bat to glove. As a result, when the ball is hit toward a fielder, the player successfully catches it or throws the batter out an average of 97 percent of the time. Gmelch observed that the superstitions of professional baseball players parallel those Malinowski observed in the Trobriand fisherman. Just as Trobrianders reserved their fishing magic for the uncertain open sea, baseball superstitions center around hitting and pitching. In the "safer waters" of the playing field, there is little need for magic.[12]

• • •

A group of studies of Canadian scholastic athletes represents the best systematic investigations of superstition in sport. Hans Buhrmann and Maxwell Zaugg found that among basketball players at the junior-high-school through university levels, success breeds superstition.[13] Starters, presumably the better players on a team, were more superstitious than non-starters, and teams with better win-loss records were more superstitious than their less fortunate competitors. In a second study, the same researchers identified the most popular superstitions among scholastic basketball players.[14] Some examples for male and female players are shown in Table 2.1. Although it presents only a few of the beliefs and behaviors observed in these Canadian athletes, Table 2.1 includes many of the superstitions common to the game of basketball. Free-throw rituals are particularly popular, as are various practices regarding dress. It is interesting to note that, consistent with the differing socialization of boys and girls, female basketball players are more likely to believe that dressing well is important to success; whereas males more often put their faith in dressing sloppily. When the sloppy dressers are combined with the neat dressers, we find that 86 percent of the boys and 90 percent of the girls make special sartorial efforts of one type or another.

In a comparison of several college sports, Jane Gregory and Brian Petrie found more superstition among participants in team sports, such as basketball, ice hockey, and volleyball, than among individual-sport athletes, such as swimmers and tennis players.[15] The authors attributed this result to the social transmission of superstitious beliefs among the members of sports teams. This notion is further supported by the popularity of group superstitions among team-sport players.

Although many of the magical beliefs held by athletes are purely indi-

Table 2.1   *Percentage of Male and Female Canadian Scholastic Basketball Players Reporting Various Superstitions*

Superstitious beliefs and behaviors	Males	Females
Slapping hand of scorer	93	95
Team cheer	87	89
Stacking hands	87	92
Scoring first point	84	85
Making last basket in warm-up	80	85
Standing in identical spot for free throw	78	74
Bouncing ball same way before free throw	76	71
Bouncing ball same number of times before free throw	67	65
Dressing well (feeling better prepared)	60	72
Shifting weight before free throw	38	39
Wearing a lucky item of clothing	31	39
Dressing sloppily (feeling better prepared)	26	18
Wearing a lucky charm on game days	22	29
Wearing socks inside-out for luck	10	5

Adapted from Buhrmann, Brown, and Zaugg (1982). Reprinted by permission of the publisher.

vidual (e.g., Wade Boggs's chicken), the world of sport is also famous for its group or team superstitions. In baseball, it is widely believed that, if a pitcher has held the opposing team hitless, it is bad luck to mention the "no-hitter" in the dugout during the game. Some say the best way to avoid "jinxing" the pitcher is to stay away from him altogether and keep quiet.[16] The Connecticut College women's basketball team has a group practice that is believed to bring good luck: when they join hands before the start of a game, the players break out of the huddle with a shout of "Together!" This cheer is never used at the beginning of the second half or at any other point in a game, and new players must be educated in its use when they join the team.[17]

Finally, Gregory and Petrie discovered a unique aspect of superstition in the game of hockey. Most superstitious beliefs in sport involve either personal superstitions aimed at improving individual performance or group superstitions directed toward team success. All players participate equally and no one is singled out—except in hockey. Success in ice hockey is highly dependent on the performance of a single player: the goalie. The hockey goalie's sole function is to minimize the opposing team's score by stopping or deflecting every shot the opposing team makes into the goal. It is a very difficult position to play, and a talented goalie is a highly valued member of the team. Not surprisingly, Gregory and Petrie found that a great number of hockey superstitions involved the goalie. For example, players often believe it is important to let the goalie go out on the ice first, and many players slap the goalie's pads for luck. Like the no-hitter in baseball, team members avoid mentioning a shutout to the goalie before the end of the game.

College Students and Exams

As someone who regularly teaches the psychology student's most feared course, psychological statistics (known widely as "sadistics"), I am keenly aware of the anxiety that examinations can bring. In the hours before an exam, particularly the first exam of the semester, I receive more calls from students than at any other time of the year. A diverse array of maladies of varying degrees of credibility emerge just in time to forestall the dreaded event. Personal, family, and cohort emergencies suddenly appear, and I am forced to listen to stories I would rather not hear. Both vomiting and crying are not unusual before, during, or after an exam, and in one case a student had an epileptic seizure.

College students are not famous for their superstitions. In fact, conventional wisdom suggests that the highly educated should be more skeptical than their less learned peers—an assumption we will examine more closely later in this chapter. Yet superstition is frequently associated with fear of failure, and when it comes to examinations, many college students are genuinely fearful. In a fascinating investigation of exam-related superstitions, two Canadian researchers found that college students are indeed a superstitious group.

As part of a larger study of college life, sociologists Daniel and Cheryl Albas gathered data over thirteen years from more than 300 students at the University of Manitoba.[18] Students filled out standardized questionnaires and recorded descriptions of relevant thoughts, sentiments, and behavior in examination logs. In addition, the investigators observed students in a number of locations, on and off campus, and conducted many formal and informal interviews. Based on this information, the Albases estimated that from 20 to 33 percent of their students used magic, primarily to bring on good luck rather than to stave off bad. They discovered that student's exam-related superstitions fell into two broad categories—the use of magical objects and the practice of special rituals. The Albases enumerated too many examples to present here, but a selection of beliefs and behaviors will help to give us a flavor of this subculture.

One of the most popular student superstitions involved clothing, and, with some exceptions, the predominant practice was "dressing down." Old sweatshirts were (and, I believe, still are) quite popular. One science student always wore an old scarf that he claimed "carries parts of my brain in it." Some students dressed up, however, and a young man who always wore a three-piece suit admitted, "It's not a very logical thing to wear to an exam because it's hot and restricting." Yet he maintained the belief that his suit improved his performance.[19]

Several students reported that they used special pens with which they had written previous successful exams. Such pens were thought to improve performance; having to take an exam without one's special pen would be cause for concern. An advertisement in a student newspaper read as follows:

> Help! I've lost my silver Cross pen. Deep psychological and sentimental value; never written an exam without it. Lost last Friday. If found contact Anna. . . .

Typically, textbooks cannot be used during an exam. At the University of Manitoba, students stacked books around the perimeter of the examination room or under their desks. Nevertheless, several students reported that being able to see their books during an exam improved their performance: "summaries come up through the covers."[20]

Some students used more common talismans, such as rabbit's feet, dice, and coins, as well as teddy bears and other cuddly toys. In this category the Albases reported one particularly unusual case. A young male student would not take an exam unless he had "found" a coin, which he interpreted as a sign of good luck. As a result, he would search for a coin on the day of an exam, often wasting precious study time "scrounging around bus stops" until he was successful—even at the risk of being late to the exam.

Of the individual-centered superstitious or magical acts aimed at bringing good luck, the overwhelming favorite was prayer. The Albases reported that even some nonreligious students prayed prior to exams. However, some observed secular rituals. For example, students reported knocking on the exam room door three times before entering, stepping over the threshold of the exam room with their right foot, or circling the exam building—regardless of the weather conditions. Another popular practice was listening to a "lucky song" or tape. One student said she played the song "Money Changes Everything" on the drive to school; another listened to Martin Luther King's "I have a dream" speech before every exam.[21]

It is clear that this kind of behavior is not unique to Manitoba. I have observed similar superstitions among my own students, and I am told that at Harvard University, where students are presumably very intelligent, many rub the foot of the statue of John Harvard before taking an exam.[22]

Gamblers

Most games of chance are just that. Their outcomes are random events, completely out of the player's control. The lottery player cannot will a "lucky number" to come up; the roulette player has no power over the spinning ball. Nevertheless, many gamblers act as though they were playing games of skill. In some games, such as blackjack and draw poker, the player draws on strategy in deciding when it is best to draw a card and when it is not. Furthermore, by understanding the odds, one can become a skillful bettor. (However, as we will see in the coming chapters, skillful bettor knows when not to make the bet.) But most gambling games do not involve skill.

Yet gambling is as old as human civilization itself. It was popular in ancient Egypt, Persia, China, India, Greece, and Rome. In England, dice-playing appeared during the Roman occupation, and by the eighteenth century gambling had been institutionalized in public gaming houses.[23] Historically, many gamblers have put faith in "luck" and the belief that chance events are, to some extent, under their control. In 1711, *The Spectator* published accounts of the "lucky numbers" used by British lottery players. One individual played the number 1711 because it was the current year; another played 134 because it was the minority vote on an important bill in the House of Commons.[24] Today similar beliefs are found in various "systems"—some published in popular books—for winning the lottery or betting on horse races, as well as in many personal and social superstitions of the gambling subculture.

There have been several studies of magical belief among modern gamblers, including investigations of bingo, poker, and roulette players,[25] but the most revealing of these is a study of craps players published by sociologist James Henslin in 1967.[26] (Craps is a wagering game played with dice.) Like Malinowski, Henslin used the method of participant observation, spending as much time as possible with a group of St. Louis cab drivers, both on and off duty. He soon discovered that the drivers frequently played craps in the early-morning hours between shifts. According to Henslin, the rules of the game are those shown in Table 2.2.

Craps is a game of pure chance. There is no skill involved in throwing dice. The movements of the clicking, tumbling cubes conform only to the laws of physics and probability, and as long as the dice are not weighted or rigged, every throw is a random event. Nevertheless, Henslin found that these taxi-drivers-turned-crapshooters employed a number of strategies that they believed increased their chances of winning.

Typically the shooter hopes to roll a particular number—a seven or eleven on the first roll, one's point on subsequent rolls. The most popular theory of dice-throwing holds that the number rolled is positively corre-

Table 2.2   The Rules of Craps

1.	Two dice are used.
2.	Bets are made on the outcome of a throw.
3.	If the shooter rolls a 7 or 11 on her first throw, she has rolled a "natural" and is automatically the winner.
4.	If the shooter receives a 2, 3, or 12 on her first throw, she has rolled "craps" and is automatically the loser.
5.	Whatever other combination shows up (a 4, 5, 6, 8, 9, or 10) is the shooter's "point."
6.	On second and subsequent throws of the dice, only combinations totalling either 7 or the shooter's "point" count. All other combinations are disregarded.
7.	If the shooter makes her "point" before a 7, she wins.
8.	If the shooter makes a 7 before her "point", she loses.
9.	Players can bet with or against the shooter.
10.	The shooter must give up the dice to another player when she fails to make her "point."

Source: Henslin (1967), pp. 316–317. Reprinted by permission of The University of Chicago Press.

lated with the velocity of the throw. A soft touch brings a low number; a hard throw brings a high one. Other methods of "controlling" the dice include taking one's time between rolls and "talking to the dice." This last strategy is often employed at the moment the dice are released, when one shouts out the desired number.

Another common method of controlling the dice is to snap one's fingers. Shooters often snap their fingers as the dice are thrown or as they bounce off the backboard. (Typically the dice are thrown on a flat surface, and the shooter is required to roll them in such a way that they bounce against a wall or some other backboard.) Henslin found that some of the drivers were extremely ritualistic in their finger-snapping and that, when a die would spin before falling to rest, a special form of the finger-snapping ritual often emerged:

> It sometimes happens that, after the dice are cast, one will spin like a top on one of its corners. When this happens, the shooter will frequently point with his index finger close to the die, wait until the die has slowed down, and, just as it begins to fall to rest from the spin, loudly snap his finger against his thumb in an effort to control the resultant point.[27]

Finally, Henslin's cab drivers espoused the belief that successful shooting required confidence. As a result, they frequently expressed great certainty about their ability to roll the points they wanted. For example, as they rolled the dice, players would often say, "There's a seven!" Once established, confidence had to be maintained, so players who were betting with the shooter often urged him not to "get shook." To retain control over the dice, the shooter had to "take it easy" and "take his time." Henslin pointed out that this view of confidence is very similar to one frequently promoted in competitive sports. Athletes are told not to "get shook," because a lack of confidence would interfere with their self-control and ability to concentrate. Of course, this theory might be valid for a skillful activity, such as basketball or baseball, but it has no relevance for games of chance.

Other beliefs surrounded the treatment of the dice. Dropping the dice was seen as a bad omen, but rubbing the dice was thought to improve one's luck. Often players would rub the dice against the playing surface, and in some cases they would rub them on another player. One shooter rubbed the dice under the chin of the player who was betting against him.

In addition to magical shooting techniques, players employed a number of betting methods to control the dice. It was commonly believed that the shooter could increase the chances of rolling his point if he raised his bet.

In one case, a player had rolled several times without hitting his point. After adding a few dollars to his bet, another player remarked, "He'll make it now. He put more money on it."

• • •

Henslin's craps players, like athletes and exam-takers, represent a subculture rich in magical thinking. Each of these groups confronts a situation in which a particular outcome is both uncertain and highly valued, and each appears to have made superstition an integral part of its activities.[28] In the next two chapters, we will examine a number of ways in which chance plays a role in the motivation, acquisition, and maintenance of superstition, but before going on, we should note two important themes in the superstitions of these groups.

The win-stay/lose-shift strategy. For gamblers and athletes, contests unfold over a period of time; before the game is over, success may come and go. Furthermore, the serious members of these groups play regularly, making it possible to discern larger cycles of fortune and misfortune. Although these fluctuations are usually mere random turns, they are often the impetus for magical belief. Some superstitions are aimed at maintaining successful play; others are summoned to end a slump. Superstitions of this type most often involve preserving the status quo when things are going well, and making various changes when they are not.

Faith in a "lucky" piece of clothing is thought to be the most common superstition among athletes, and it is clear that many of their beliefs, as well as similar ones involving personal hygiene, represent aspects of a "win-stay" strategy.[29] During a winning streak in the 1984-85 season, St. John's University basketball coach Lou Carnesecca wore the same crewneck sweater at every game. In an attempt to maintain the exact conditions present during a successful contest, athletes frequently refuse to wash their socks, underwear, or uniforms. In a practice reminiscent of the biblical Samson, Swedish tennis star Bjorn Borg would not shave once he had begun play in an important tournament. As a result, when he posed for pictures on the grass of Wimbledon's Centre Court with his winner's trophy held high, he wore a two-week-old beard.

On the other hand, when one's "luck runs bad," the status quo is counterproductive. Previously lucky items are often discarded, and new strategies are employed. When the St. John's basketball team ended its winning streak (at thirteen games) with a loss to Georgetown University, Lou Carnesecca's magic sweater disappeared, never to be seen again.

In 1978, anthropologist David Hayano published a study of the patrons of commercial poker clubs in Gardenia, California. He found that many regular poker players took certain actions to improve their luck.

Often losers would ask for a different deck of cards, take a different seat at the table (especially a seat vacated by a winner), or move to another table altogether.[30] Interestingly, a similar strategy is used by the management of some roulette clubs. If a particular croupier has lost a significant sum to the players at her table, the manager will often have a different croupier spin the wheel or, in some cases, the manager will spin the wheel. These actions are quite common despite the fact that roulette is, of course, a game of pure chance, and strategies of this kind can have no effect on the game.[31]

The influence of social structure on superstition. Students, athletes, and gamblers are social groups that involve varying degrees of group activity. Students do talk to each other about their schoolwork and sometimes study together, but typically, both the preparation for and the taking of exams are solitary enterprises. In contrast, craps is almost always a group activity. Sports can be either individual or team activities, but the most superstitious athletes are generally found in team sports, such as basketball, baseball, and hockey. These players work together as a unit, but their continued success depends on individual performance. Thus, team sports fall somewhere between student exams and craps, involving a mixture of group and individual activities.

The differing social structures of these groups parallel the kinds of superstitions they adopt. Student exam-takers most often hold personal superstitions that are unique and not shared with other people. The importance of dress is common to many students, but each student has his or her own distinctive magical garb. Lucky objects and pre-exam rituals are also nearly always peculiar to the believer. Craps players, on the other hand, learn most of their superstitions from other participants. Group activities produce socially shared superstitions. Magical betting and dice-throwing practices are the black cats and crossed fingers of the craps player's subculture.

The Demographics of Superstition

Athletes, college students, and gamblers provide interesting examples of superstition among narrowly defined social groups, but they are also relatively small segments of the population. What about the rest of us? Who are the most and least superstitious among us? We will approach this question in two ways. First, adopting a sociological approach, I will identify the larger demographic variables associated with superstitious belief. Later, adopting the methods of the psychology of individual differences, I examine the personality characteristics related to superstition.

Gender. A large number of studies have shown that women are more superstitious and have greater belief in paranormal phenomena than men. For example, Stuart and Lucille Blum, surveying the superstitious beliefs of 132 men and women from a variety of occupational groups in New York City, found that women were significantly more superstitious than men, and that walking under a ladder and knocking on wood were the most strongly endorsed superstitions. Gender differences in superstitiousness are also common among college students, as well as other groups; however, there are some exceptions.[32] Psychologists Jerome Tobacyk and Gary Milford found that college women had greater belief in precognition (the ability to predict the future) than college men, but men showed significantly greater belief in extraordinary life forms, such as Bigfoot and the Loch Ness monster.[33]

Age. Many studies of age differences have shown that older people are more skeptical than young people, but others have found the opposite relationship. The 1990 Gallup poll found that adults under thirty were more superstitious than older age groups, with 28 percent reporting that they were superstitious as compared to 18 percent overall. Belief in the paranormal was greatest in the 30-to-49 age group. In contrast, Buhrmann and Zaugg's research found that older scholastic basketball players were *more* superstitious than younger ones, but this result is somewhat misleading. All of the athletes in this study were quite young, ranging in age from 12 to 22—much younger than most of the Gallup respondents. As a result, the greater superstition of college-age players probably reflects more experience playing the game and a more complete immersion in its peculiar subculture.

An interesting example of the relationship between increased age and increased skepticism is found in a study of police officers and the full-moon effect. Many law-enforcement officials, emergency-room workers, and mental-health professionals believe that crimes, accidents, and psychological problems are more numerous during the full moon, the time of lunacy. The full-moon effect has stimulated considerable interest, but after examining all the relevant research, several investigators have failed to find evidence for a relationship between the phases of the moon and any measure of human behavior.[34] In a study of 51 male police officers, Robert Corrigan, Lee Pattison, and David Lester found that 63 percent of the officers believed in the full-moon effect and that younger, less experienced officers were more likely to believe than older officers.[35] Apparently, age and experience fighting crime leads to the moon's acquittal.[36]

A different conclusion was drawn by British folklorist Gillian Bennett. In her study of retired English women, 77 percent said that premonition

Table 2.3   Superstitious and Paranormal Beliefs among Different Age Groups

	Children	College Students	Adults
Some people can project their thoughts into others' minds	19	18	18
Some people can read others' thoughts	23	27	15
If I wish hard enough for something, I can make it happen	15	11	8
The moon or stars can affect people's thinking	5	13	19
I believe in flying saucers	60	48	60
Some people can see into the future	20	25	25
I have at least one good-luck charm	45	56	72
I believe in good and bad magic	25	13	11
I have at least one superstition	46	40	63

Source: Epstein (1993). Copyright by the American Psychological Association. Reprinted by permission of the publisher and author.

was possible, and 43 percent were certain of its reality.[37] Bennett suggested that these older women "salvage a great deal from their lifestyle, and, through their concept of the spiritual/supernatural world, endow their role with something of the holy." [38] Many of Bennett's women had lost their former roles as wives and mothers and the status that these roles provided. Their relationship with the supernatural helped them retain some of their former stature and sustain connections with loved ones separated by death or distance.[39] Bennett's findings suggest that, at least among these British women, increasing age may actually lead to greater belief in the supernatural.

The water is further muddied by a study conducted by psychologist Seymour Epstein.[40] Epstein surveyed three groups—children aged 9–12, college students aged 18–22, and adults aged 27–65—about various superstitions and paranormal beliefs. (The items and percentage of participants endorsing each are presented in Table 2.3.) Several of the beliefs in the Epstein study show little variation across the age groups. For example, thought projection and seeing into the future are consistently endorsed by approximately 20 percent of each group. However, some of these beliefs decrease with increasing age (e.g., good and bad magic), and others increase with age (e.g., having good luck charms and superstition). Taken in total, the relationship between age and superstitious or paranormal beliefs appears to be complicated; it is safest to say that, at this time, no general statement can be made about age and superstitious belief.

Education. Claiborne Pell, the recently retired senior U.S. Senator from Rhode Island, is an educated man. Former Chairman of the Foreign Relations Committee and the Subcommittee on Education, Arts and Humanities, he earned an A.B. *cum laude* from Princeton University and an M.A.

from Columbia University. A strong supporter of higher education, he created the Pell Grants program, which provides financial aid to needy college students, and was the principal sponsor of the 1965 law establishing the National Endowment for the Arts and the National Endowment for the Humanities.

But in addition to his involvement with traditional academic pursuits, Senator Pell is a supporter of "psychical research." In 1988, he received considerable attention in the press when it was discovered that he had hired "UFO enthusiast" C. B. Scott Jones, at an annual salary of $48,000, as a full-time aide to investigate various paranormal phenomena in the national interest. In addition, Pell attempted to create a federal commission to promote "human potential" research and invited Uri Geller to Washington to demonstrate his professed psychic powers for congressional representatives. In 1990, during the months before the Persian Gulf War, Pell's interest in the supernatural surfaced again when it emerged that Jones had written a letter to Secretary of Defense Richard Cheney expressing concern that the word "Simone" appeared when audiotapes of Cheney's speeches were played backwards. Jones, who holds a Ph.D. in International Studies from the American University, was investigating "reverse-speech therapy" and wrote Cheney out of concern that Simone might be "a code word that would not be in the national interest to be known."[41]

One might suspect that these events would be welcome ammunition for an opposition candidate, but in the hard-fought reelection campaign of 1990, the senator's interest in psychic research was barely mentioned. Fortunately for Pell, his challenger, former U.S. Representative Claudine Schneider, could not attack this point because she, too, is a believer in ESP and other psychic phenomena.

Finally, in November 1995, after Pell had announced his plan to retire from the Senate, the Central Intelligence Agency disclosed that for over twenty years it had supported a top-secret program, code-named Stargate, aimed at researching the value of psychic remote viewing (the ability to see objects and events that are miles away) for intelligence-gathering purposes. The CIA had spent a total of twenty million dollars on the Stargate program, but when an independent study by the American Institutes for Research evaluated the program, it found that evidence for the validity of remote viewing was lacking, and that even if remote viewing were clearly demonstrated, it would be of doubtful usefulness. When former CIA director Robert Gates was asked why the agency pursued the Stargate program, he cited competition with the Russians, who were engaged in similar research, and pressure from a few unnamed congressmen.[42]

Obviously, education does not make one immune to superstitious or paranormal beliefs. Indeed, most published studies of paranormal belief have used college students as subjects. Yet we might expect that higher education, particularly in the sciences, would lead to increased critical thinking and greater skepticism. The research on this point is somewhat mixed, but there is some evidence that formal education does lead to skepticism. In their study of people working in New York City, Stuart and Lucille Blum found a negative relationship between superstitious belief and years of education.[43] In 1982, Laura Otis and James Alcock published a study of several types of "extraordinary beliefs" among college students, professors, and members of the general public. In most instances, professors were found to be more skeptical than students; however, students showed the same level of supernatural belief as the general public.[44] Furthermore, there is evidence that certain academic fields are associated with greater skepticism than others. For example, Otis and Alcock found that, among their relatively skeptical professors, English professors were more likely to believe in ghosts, psychic phenomena, and fortunetelling. Similarly, a survey of over a thousand American faculty members on belief in ESP found social and natural scientists to be significantly more skeptical than representatives from the humanities, arts, and education. Among the social sciences, psychologists were the most skeptical.[45] Finally, a study of Harvard undergraduates found stronger belief in astrology, ESP, and UFOs among majors in the humanities and the social and biological sciences than among natural-science majors.[46]

My own educational history spans both ends of the humanities-sciences continuum and has brought me into contact with both skeptics and believers. As an academic psychologist, I now live among the skeptics, but in the late 1960s I was an English major, earning both a B.A. and an M.A. before leaving school for a stint in the workaday world. A graduate-school friend of mine from that early period had some rather bizarre magical beliefs that seemed to stem, at least in part, from his literary studies. He was a rather intense fellow who lived Hemingway and Faulkner rather than just reading them. As a modern-literature specialist, he studied Frazer's *Golden Bough* because it was a significant influence on T. S. Eliot and several other writers,[47] and he believed in sympathetic magic. My friend lived in graduate-student housing with his wife and their young son, and one night he told me that he kept all of their nail clippings in a special dish on his bookshelf. While studying late at night, he would chew them up and swallow them. I have oftened wondered whether this behavior represented an odd, eucharistic sort of eating disorder (he was a Catholic), but he said his intention was to prevent these materials from falling into the wrong hands. He believed that through contagious magic, some malevolent person could use the fingernail clippings to bring harm to his family. By disposing of them in this way, he was protecting his loved ones. I do not recall whether my friend had any special method for getting rid of hair clippings, but if he did, I hope it was not the same as his method for nail clippings.

Aside from this strange practice, my graduate-school friend was perfectly sane. He was one of the department's top students and a great father and husband—someone who was far more mature than I was then and someone whom I admired. As we will see, his belief in contagious magic was probably caused by a number of factors, but his relatively greater exposure to literature than to science may have played a role. Paranormal phenomena are almost never encountered in science classes, yet they are quite common in novels, poetry, and plays, even among the classics.

Although research suggests that education plays an antagonistic role in relation to superstition and the paranormal, the results are not clear-cut. Because the investigators could not randomly assign their participants to various educational groups, these studies may tell us less about the effects of higher education than they do about the people who choose to pursue different academic paths. Does study in the natural sciences—physics, chemistry, and geology, for example—lead to a more critical analysis of common superstitions, or do those who are skeptical choose to major in the natural sciences? Probably both hypotheses are true. As we will see in chapter 7, there is good evidence that certain educational experiences lead to greater skepticism; but people who are more skeptical may also, for whatever reason, be more likely to choose the natural sciences.

But several studies have reported conflicting results. For example, in a study of "traditional beliefs" among West African students, Gustav Jahoda found no effect of college education in general and no effect of science courses specifically.[48] Similarly, Charles Salter and Lewis Routledge studied ninety-eight University of Pennsylvania graduate students and found no differences in paranormal belief across major fields and no reduction in these beliefs with increased years of study.[49] Thus, although there is some evidence that certain educational experiences reduce supernatural belief, the relationship is far from ironclad. As we have seen, superstition is common on college campuses, and the New Age movement appears to be flourishing among college-educated people.[50] Surprising as it may seem, Senator Pell is probably not an unusual case.

Religion. As mentioned in chapter 1, there are some similarities between religious and superstitious belief. Although one is celestial and the other terrestrial, both involve an act of faith. The believer must place trust in forces beyond understanding. Moreover, some religious groups in the United States and abroad promote ideas, such as faith healing and levitation, that fall within our definition of superstition. Perhaps due to the apparent similarity of these belief systems, the relationship of superstition to traditional religious belief has proven quite difficult to articulate.

Again, the 1990 Gallup poll is our best source of data. With respect to paranormal phenomenon, such as telepathy and clairvoyance, religious and nonreligious respondents showed approximately equivalent levels of acceptance; however, there were differences in superstitious belief. Religious people reported fewer superstitions than nonreligious people, with Catholics slightly more superstitious than Protestants. Thus, according to the Gallup poll, religious beliefs are compatible with acceptance of the paranormal but less so with belief in superstition.[51] However, the picture is clouded by studies yielding conflicting results. For example, Burhmann and Zaug's study of scholastic basketball players found greater superstition among regular church attenders.[52] Similarly, a study of South Carolina college students found that "nonreligious subjects had fewer and less extensive paranormal beliefs than religious subjects."[53]

Thus, the relationship of religion to superstition and belief in the paranormal remains obscure. Part of the problem undoubtedly lies in the diversity of religious beliefs observed among the general public. For instance, even among Protestant sects alone, a great variety of belief systems are represented, from Presbyterianism to Unitarianism. Similarly, within a single faith, individual congregations can show very different practices. Catholic churches, for example, range from extremely formal "high-church" congregations to less formal, more progressive groups. To date, studies of the relationship of religion to beliefs in superstition and the paranormal have not fully addressed the diversity of contemporary religious views, and this lack of specificity is an important obstacle to more complete understanding of the connection between these belief systems.

Superstition and the Psychology of Individual Differences

The first time a *Homo sapien* attempted an explanation of another's actions, this primordial psychologist probably offered a dispositional interpretation: "she is good with the children because she is so patient." Other common explanations may have included control by gods or spirits or the effects of various foods, but we seem to have a basic tendency to attribute behavior, particularly the behavior of others, to lasting features of personal character. Biological explanations have also been consistently popular. In the second century A.D., the Greek philosopher and physician Galen proposed that an individual's personality results from the balance of four fluids, or "humors," within the body: blood, black bile, yellow bile, and phlegm. An excess of one of these humors produced a temperament that was either sanguine, melancholic, choleric, or phlegmatic.

Perhaps the most enduring and influential psychological theory in history held that physiology was the key to personality. The Greek philosopher and mathematician Pythagoras (sixth century B.C.) is thought to have originated the "science" of *physiognomy*, but the first major treatise on the subject was a two-volume work attributed to Aristotle, though probably written by a close colleague. The pseudo-Aristotelian *Physiognomonica* proposes, simply, that "dispositions follow bodily characteristics."[54] Physical appearance, particularly the construction of the face, was a window to the psyche within. Physiognomy was tremendously popular in the classical period, exerting a strong influence on the works of Homer, Virgil, Seneca, and others, and retained its popularity in the medieval period. Its influence can be seen in Geoffrey Chaucer's description of the Miller, a rather brutish character, in the General Prologue to *The Canterbury Tales*:[55]

The Millere was a stout carl° for the nones	*fellow*
Ful big he was of brawn° and eek of bones—	*muscle*
That preved° wel, for overal ther he cam	*proved*
At wrastling he wolde have alway the ram.°	*prize*
There was no dore that he nolde heve of harre,*	
Or breke it at a renning° with his heed.°	*running/head*
His beerd as any sowe or fox was reed,°	*red*
And therto brood, as though it were a spade;	
Upon the cop° right of his nose he hade	*ridge*
A werte,° and theron stood a tuft of heres,	*wart*
Rede as the bristles of a sowes eres;	
His nosethirles° blake were and wide.	*nostrils*
A swerd and a bokeler° bar° he by his side.	*shield/bore*
His mouth as greet was as a greet furnais.°[56]	*furnace*

*He would not heave off its hinges.

It is no surprise that, on the road to Canterbury, the Miller tells the bawdiest and most outrageous tale of all.

In nineteenth-century Europe the "science" of physiognomy experienced a renaissance. A Swiss physiognomer, Johann Lavater, had published the extremely popular *Essays on Physiognomy* in 1789. Appearing in many editions over the next 150 years, including abridged pocket versions, Lavater's volume was an eighteenth-century pop-psychology bestseller. It became "a basic resource in a gentleman's home, to be consulted when hiring staff, making friends and establishing business relations."[57] The French

Figure 2.1 Facial features of the sanguine, phlegmatic, melancholic, and choleric personality types. From Lavater's *Essays on Physiognomy*.

caricaturist Honoré Daumier was strongly influenced by Lavater, as was the novelist Honoré de Balzac. The illustrations from Lavater's *Essays* presented in Figure 2.1 show how some of Galen's psychology of the humors survived in Lavater's physiognomy.

As recently as 1942, American psychologist William Sheldon introduced "constitutional psychology," a theory that linked personality to body type. He identified three basic physiques, or "somatypes," each asso-

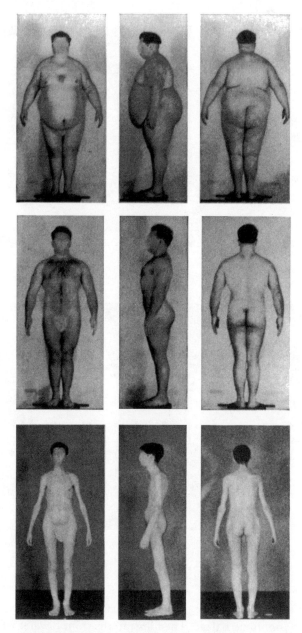

Figure 2.2 Extreme examples of Sheldon's body types: endomorph (top), mesomorph (center), and ectomorph (bottom). *Source:* Sheldon (1940), reprinted by permission of the William H. Sheldon Trust.

ciated with a distinct temperament. The endomorph (plump body type) was slow-moving and complacent, the mesomorph (muscular body type) was competitive and energetic, and the ectomorph (thin body type) was self-conscious and restrained.[58] Extreme examples of each body type are presented in Figure 2.2.[59]

Subsequent research in the 1950s seemed to validate Sheldon's theory. Studies showed that ectomorphs were relatively fussy children who were more likely to need psychiatric care as adults, and an investigation of delinquent and nondelinquent boys found that delinquents were more likely to be mesomorphs and less likely to be ectomorphs. Furthermore, these somatypes were associated with particular occupational choices. For example, commercial pilots were more likely to be mesomorphic than the general population, and within the same organization, research workers were more ectomorphic and less mesomorphic than factory workers. Today, however, Sheldon's constitutional psychology, like its predecessor physiognomy, has diminished in stature. It is generally accepted that temperament is related to body type, but most researchers have found much weaker correlations of body type to personality than those originally reported by Sheldon.[60]

Today, many psychologists still take a biological view of personality, asserting that the secrets of human nature can be found in our genetic inheritance. Indeed, recent research provides some evidence that a number of psychological characteristics are at least partially hereditary in nature, including shyness, activity level, introversion or extroversion, and general temperament.

A more popular view of disposition, however, and one more relevant to the psychology of superstition, is the trait approach. This theoretical approach assumes that our personalities are shaped by broad, consistent traits that may or may not be biological in origin. An individual's personality is conceived as relatively stable over time, and differences among individuals are attributed to differences in the extent to which they show various personality dimensions. Researchers who adopt this view use standardized tests and questionnaires to measure psychological traits, such as introversion/extroversion, intelligence, and neuroticism, in an effort to discover the relationship between these dimensions and everyday behavior. Often people who show different degrees of a particular trait also show contrasting patterns of behavior. A number of researchers have used this general strategy to come to an improved understanding of superstition and belief in the paranormal. In the following pages, we examine their findings.

Superstition and Personality

A wise researcher once argued that psychology had become the science of the behavior of college sophomores, alluding to the widespread practice, still common today, of drawing experimental subjects from introductory psychology classes.[61] For many academic researchers, college students are convenient and often quite cooperative research participants, but findings based on college samples must be interpreted with care. Often results cannot be generalized to other groups. Furthermore, most of what is known about personality and superstition has come from responses to questionnaires filled out by research participants. These self-reported data are vulnerable to a number of problems, including unreliable results, caused by misunderstood questions, and diminished validity, produced when participants, consciously or unconsciously, bias their responses. These caveats notwithstanding, researchers have identified some interesting relationships between a number of personality dimensions and superstitious belief.

The measurement of intelligence is at the center of the longest and most vitriolic controversy in the history of psychology. Advocates on the hereditary side of the nature/nurture debate argue that intelligence is an immutable inherited trait that all but completely controls an individual's eventual scholastic and career achievements. Environmental experiences can produce small fluctuations in performance, but approximately 80 percent of an individual's success or failure at a wide range of activities can be attributed to inherent intellectual ability.[62] Critics of this view have taken two primary tacks. Some argue that the concept of intelligence is faulty. Attempts to summarize an individual's varied talents and abilities with a single number—a score on an IQ test—are misguided. Thus, traditional methods of measuring intelligence produce meaningless results. Alternatively, those who suggest that environment is the dominant factor in IQ believe that the hereditary component of intelligence has been overestimated. Intelligence tests are of little value because scores are largely a function of social and educational experience, not innate ability.

The social implications of this controversy have been debated for a century. At one extreme, supporters of the eugenics movement have advocated controlling immigration and breeding for intelligence by preventing people with below-average IQs from having children. As recently as 1972, "feeble-minded and antisocial" men and women were legally sterilized by the State of Virginia.[63] Recent liberal trends have led to the devaluation of IQ tests. For example, the 1979 U.S. District Court ruling in *Larry P. v. Riles* held that standardized intelligence tests were culturally biased and discriminatory against African-American children, and that the use of these tests had led to the overrepresentation of minority children in classes for the educable mentally retarded. As a result, the California State Department of Education banned the use of intelligence tests in the assessment of African-American children for possible special education services. Since 1979, intelligence tests have been found nondiscriminatory in federal court cases in other states, but in California the policy stemming from *Larry P.* still holds.[64]

After years of debate and many revised conceptions of human intelligence, IQ measures remain a standard feature of most psychological assessments, and many personality researchers continue to explore the relationship between intelligence and behavior. In the case of superstition, common folk wisdom has held that superstitious people are less intelligent than nonsuperstitious people, and a number of studies have found this to be true. For example, a 1974 study of high-school seniors in Georgia found that students with above-average IQs were significantly less superstitious than students with average IQs. It should be noted, however, that, although statistically significant, in practical terms the difference between these groups was rather small.[65] Other studies have found belief in the paranormal to be associated with a lowered capacity for critical thinking and less-skilled logical reasoning.[66] Finally, in a study of 176 college freshman, Wayne Messer and Richard Griggs found that students who reported believing in paranormal phenomena, such as ESP, precognition during dreams, and out-of-body experiences, earned lower grades than their unbelieving classmates in an introductory psychology course. This result held even when course grades were adjusted for differences in students' Scholastic Aptitude Test scores.[67]

Although superstitious beliefs have been popular throughout history, particular notions do come in and out of fashion from time to time. As we have seen, the last two decades have witnessed increased belief in a variety of paranormal phenomena. Necessarily these variations in acceptability are reflected in the changing personality profiles of believers. In particular, although several studies have documented the negative relationship between intelligence and superstition, there is some evidence that, specifically for the belief in the paranormal, this relationship may be changing. The New Age movement has led to the increased popularity of these ideas among groups previously thought to be immune to superstition: those with higher intelligence, higher socioeconomic status, and higher educational levels.[68] As a result, the time-honored view of believers as less intelligent than nonbelievers may only hold for certain ideas or particular social groups.

Conservatism. Among the hundreds of books, book chapters, and research articles written on the psychology of superstition, only two report actual field observations of the overt superstitions of unsuspecting participants. One of these was conducted by New Zealander Roger Boshier. (We will save the other one for chapter 5.) To determine the relationship between conservatism and a common superstitious behavior, Boshier placed a sixteen-foot wooden extension ladder against a wall on High Street in the middle of Auckland.[69] Before beginning to collect data, researchers observed the behavior of midafternoon pedestrians and adjusted the placement of the ladder until half the passersby walked under the ladder and half walked around it. Those who avoided the ladder were classified as superstitious, while those who walked under it were labeled nonsuperstitious. Undoubtedly, some of the people who walked around the ladder did so for reasons other than superstition, and conversely, some of those who walked under may have done so reluctantly. Nevertheless, Boshier was convinced that his prop did a reasonable job of separating the superstitious pedestrians from the nonsuperstitious ones. In support of this view, he noted that during peak traffic periods, people lined up on either side of the ladder to avoid passing under it.

After walking past the ladder, people from both groups were stopped by research assistants and asked to fill out a questionnaire that included a test of conservatism. The test consisted of a list of issues and topics, of which the respondent indicated approval or disapproval. For example, some of the issues mentioned were "death penalty," "striptease shows," "hippies," "royalty," and "nudist camps." One hundred and eight people completed the questionnaire (50 superstitious and 58 nonsuperstitious), and 35 people refused, most of whom had walked around the ladder.

Boshier did find differences in conservatism, but only for certain age groups. Among the pedestrians under forty years old, the superstitious and nonsuperstitious groups showed similar levels of conservatism, but at higher age levels, participants tended to be more conservative in general, with superstitious participants being particularly conservative. Boshier did not speculate about the absence of a significant relationship among younger Aucklanders, but he did suggest that conservative individuals could be expected to be generally more cautious. In turn, this caution might lead one to avoid walking under ladders.

Another possible explanation for the relationship of superstition to conservatism comes from a theory of conservatism proposed by Glenn Wilson of the Institute of Psychiatry at the University of London. According to Wilson's theory, a pattern of attitudes called the "conservative syndrome" has its source in a *"generalized susceptibility to experiencing threat or anx-*

iety in the face of uncertainty."[70] This global fear is expressed as more specific aversions to a variety of threats, which, in turn, give rise to various conservative attitudes.

Uncertainty is, of course, a necessary prerequisite for the emergence of superstition, and as we have seen, early explanations of superstition implicated fear as a motivating emotion. Yet it is clear that not all superstitions are driven by fear. For example, the superstitions of gamblers are more reasonably interpreted as motivated by the hope of winning rather than by the fear of losing. The player who truly feared losing would be more likely to avoid gambling altogether. But some superstitions, such as the taboo against walking under ladders, are indeed motived by the desire to avoid calamitous endings. Thus, according to Wilson's theory, fear-based superstitions and a range of conservative attitudes have their common source in a generalized aversion to uncertainty.

Death threats and fears of death. Perhaps the most basic of all fears is the fear of death. Wilson's theory of conservatism identified this particular aversion as the foundation for religious dogmatism, but psychologist Jerome Tobacyk suggests that fear of death might also be a motivation for belief in the paranormal. He observed that a number of paranormal beliefs concern, either directly or indirectly, "personal survival of physical death."[71] To test his hypothesis, Tobacyk examined the relationship among traditional religious belief, paranormal belief, and two orientations toward death. *Death threat* was defined as the extent to which an individual's system of "personal constructs" is structured to anticipate death. If you need to substantially reorganize your core beliefs to accommodate the possibility of your own death, you would be rated high on the dimension of death threat.[72] *Death concern*, on the other hand, is "the degree to which one consciously confronts death and is disturbed by its implications."[73] This is a more immediate and emotional preoccupation with death that is not related to one's core beliefs. The person who has high death concern might be preoccupied with thoughts and worries about death; however, the high-death-threat person might not. Death threat is simply a discrepancy between one's central beliefs and the possibility of one's own death.

Tobacyk's results were remarkably clear. In two studies of college students he found that death threat was positively correlated with traditional religious beliefs but unrelated to paranormal belief. Conversely, the more emotional death concern was related to both paranormal and superstitious beliefs but unrelated to traditional religious belief. Tobacyk offered the following interpretation of the link between death threat and traditional religious beliefs:

> It appears that traditional religious beliefs, as a consequence of their accompa-
> nying institutionalized social support system concerning afterlife, enable indi-
> viduals to more readily construe death as a personal reality and therefore to not
> be as threatened by it.[74]

In contrast, greater conscious anxiety about death was found among those embracing paranormal beliefs. Thus, it appears that both religion and belief in the paranormal may provide a hedge against the fear of death, but they address different components of that fear.

Locus of control. Some people go through life believing that they are at the mercy of circumstance. Much of what happens, good or bad, happens *to* them, not *because of* them. Others are the captains of their fates, more often believing they can mold their own futures and assuming responsibility for both their successes and failures. This personality dimension, known as locus of control, has been the subject of much psychological research. For example, studies have shown that, on average, a more external locus of control is associated with greater anxiety and depression. More relevant to our present topic, research on compliance and conformity indicates that an internal locus of control leads one to be more questioning of authority and less submissive. Psychologist Herbert Lefcourt goes so far as to suggest that, had Adolf Eichmann and Lieutenant Richard Calley had greater belief in their personal agency, they would have avoided the historical atrocities with which they are forever linked:

> If these individuals had remained able to question the commands and legiti-
> macy of their superior officers, they might not have been the infamous "collab-
> orators" that they did in fact become; and if they had perceived themselves as
> responsible actors rather than as externally controlled pawns, they might have
> been more questioning and consequently more resistant to the dictates and per-
> suasions of others.[75]

This relationship between locus of control and resistance to suggestion has led many to view the superstitious individual as someone who has an external locus of control—someone who attributes life's events to unseen and mysterious uncontrollable forces. The skeptic, on the other hand, is likely to have an internal locus of control and be reluctant to accept extraordinary explanations for the happenings of life. Most studies have found this to be true for both superstition and belief in the paranormal. For example, in 1983 Jerome Tobacyk and Gary Milford published a study of paranormal belief among students at Louisiana Tech University. They measured the extent to which introductory psychology students believed in psi (the psychic ability to move objects and read minds), witchcraft, superstition, spiritualism (e.g., reincarnation and astral projection), extraordinary life forms, and precognition. Using a test designed to measure internal versus external locus of control, Tobacyk and Milford found stronger belief in these paranormal phenomena among students whose locus of control was relatively external.[76]

Interestingly, the relationship between locus of control and belief in the paranormal appears to hold for casual believers but not for that smaller segment of the population who are more personally involved. James McGarry and Benjamin Newberry conducted an unusual field study in which they approached people attending the 1977 ESP/Psychic Fair in Niagara Falls, New York. In addition, they mailed questionnaires to subscribers of an ESP newsletter and surveyed a group of college students. Drawing participants from all these sources, McGarry and Newberry established four levels of involvement in the paranormal: psychics (people who gave psychic readings); subscribers to the ESP newsletter who said they did not give psychic readings; people who attended the ESP/Psychic Fair but said they did not give psychic readings; and college students who said they did not give psychic readings. As expected, the investigators found that belief in paranormal phenomena was strongest among the psychics and weakest among the college students. The newsletter subscribers and fair-goers showed moderate levels of belief.

Contrary to other findings, however, McGarry and Newberry found that for the high- and moderate-involvement groups (psychics, newsletter subscribers, and fair attendees), belief in the paranormal was associated with an *internal* locus of control. Similar to other studies, believers among the college-student group were more likely to be people who thought their lives were controlled by external forces. By way of explanation, the authors suggested that, for those who are more personally involved, belief in the paranormal provides a sense of personal control: "[T]hese beliefs may render such a person's problems less difficult and more solvable, lessen the probability of unpredictable occurrences, and offer hope that political and governmental decisions can be influenced."[77]

Mental health and personality adjustment. The study by McGarry and Newberry seems to suggest that for those who have greater personal involvement, belief in the paranormal may actually be healthy. Although paranormal ideas are not rational in the sense of conforming to current scientific knowledge, they may, when deeply incorporated into one's world view or sense of identity, provide a sense of well-being. This finding— although it is merely a hint of a finding—is remarkable given that many other studies have found superstition and paranormal belief to be associated with poorer psychological functioning. In chapter 6, we will look more closely at the relationship between superstition and psychopathology.

Self-efficacy. When people experience a high degree of success in the activities they undertake, they begin to expect success in future enterprises. This expectation has been labeled self-efficacy, and some psychological theorists suggest that it is a good predictor of future action.[78] If we have high self-efficacy with respect to academic achievement and we have both the desire and the means, we are likely to begin academic studies and stick to them. If, however, we have the desire and the means but lack the self-efficacy (the expectation of success), we are less likely to enroll. Hypothesizing that superstitions are more common among those who have experienced less success and more failure, Jerome Tobacyk and Deborah Shrader examined the relationship between superstition and self-efficacy in a group of 180 university students. They found that greater belief in superstition was related to lower self-efficacy; however, the relationship held only for women, not for men.

Hypnotic suggestibility. A common view of superstitious people suggests they are merely gullible—they believe what they are told. As simple as this notion is, it is supported by evidence: believers are less adept at critical thinking and logical reasoning and often possess an external locus of control. However, hypnotic suggestibility—the degree of one's susceptibility to hypnosis—is thought to be distinct from general suggestibility or gullibility. Nevertheless, Mahlon Wagner and Fredrick Ratzeburg argued that hypnosis involves "imagery, imagination, and acceptance of phenomenal experiences suggested by an authority," and as a result, they hypothesized that hypnotic suggestibility would be associated with a positive attitude toward the paranormal. In a study of 208 upperclass college students, Wagner and Ratzeburg found just that. Participants who were higher in hypnotic suggestibility were more likely to have had a psychic experience and more apt to believe in parapsychology and the supernatural.[79]

Alienation. Unlike other systems of belief (religious, political, etc.), belief in superstition is rarely supported by organized social groups. Furthermore, these beliefs are often considered socially unacceptable. Jerome Tobacyk hypothesized that college students who showed stronger belief in the paranormal would also report greater feelings of alienation. What he found, however, was that alienation was associated only with belief in superstition, not with other paranormal beliefs. In reality, this result is not particularly surprising. The New Age movement and and the current popular fascination with the occult and religious spiritualism lend an impression of credibility to belief in the paranormal that does not apply to traditional superstitions. As a result, it seems reasonable that superstitious students should report feelings of alienation not shared by those who believe in the paranormal.

Superstition and Experiential Reasoning

University of Massachusetts psychologist Seymour Epstein (first mentioned above in the discussion of age and superstitious belief) has developed a theory of personality that he calls cognitive-experiential self theory, or CEST.[80] The basic premise of CEST is that people have two primary modes of thought: the experiential system, which is emotional and intuitive, and the rational system, which is logical and analytical. These two systems of reasoning are assumed to work simultaneously within the same individual, often influencing each other. (At its core, Epstein's theory represents a formal restatement of the classic conflict between head and heart.) In an increasing number of studies, Epstein and his colleagues have found considerable support for this dichotomous arrangement of human thought.

Of particular interest to us is Epstein's assumption that superstitious belief springs from the intuitive, experiential system. He suggests that many of the cognitive errors that we will encounter in chapter 4 and the paranormal beliefs that have become a common feature of contemporary culture are the result of the our more emotional, experiential side. Furthermore, in a number of studies, Epstein has assessed the relationship between superstition and several personality dimensions. Although it was not the primary goal of Epstein's research, his work makes a substantial contribution to our understanding of personality and superstition.

Aside from his examination of age and superstition discussed above, Epstein's most important study of superstitious thinking was an investigation of 250 college students published in 1991.[81] Using a variety of measures of personality, emotion, and superstitious thinking, Epstein discovered a number of additional features of superstitious people.[82] His findings are summarized in Table 2.4.[83]

The discovery that superstitious thinking was related to higher levels of neurotism indicated that those who endorse common superstitions are more likely to show features of emotional instability. The other personality dimensions associated with superstition are similarly negative (depression, anxiety, low self-esteem, and low ego strength—that is, difficulty responding constructively to stressful or challenging events); thus, a rather bleak

Table 2.4   *Personality Dimensions Associated with Superstitious Thinking*

Emotion or Trait Dimension	Superstitious Thinking
Negative Emotion	Higher
Introversion vs. Extroversion	(No Relationship)
Neurotism	Higher
Ego Strength	Lower
Depression	Higher
Anxiety	Higher
Anger	(No Relationship)
Self-esteem	Lower
Emotional Arousal	(No Relationship)

Source: Epstein, 1991. Adapted with permission of the author and the publisher.

image arises. But it is important to add that superstitious thinking was not related to introversion or extroversion, anger, or general emotional arousal.

In addition to these psychological dimensions, Epstein examined the relationship of superstitious thinking to several social factors, such as the quality of parental and peer interactions. He found no connection between superstitious belief and features of the maternal relationship, but he did find that those who showed greater superstition were more likely to have fathers who were overprotective (versus fostering independence) and more likely to be rejected by their peers. Thus, taken together, Epstein's research paints a picture of the superstitious person as more passive, more isolated, more anxious, and in poorer mental health than someone who is not superstitious.

Epstein understands superstition as a system of belief to which people resort when they feel helpless in dealing with critical life events.[84] Superstitious thinking arises when people are taxed by psychological dysfunction and are raised under conditions that foster feelings of hopelessness. Conversely, more reasoned thinking is associated with better psychological functioning and greater independence.

Profile of a Superstitious Person

By way of summation, we should now be able to construct a profile of an ideally superstitious person. Table 2.5 provides a brief synopsis of this chapter by listing the variables that research has shown are related to superstition or to belief in the paranormal.

Before we discuss this profile further, a cautionary word. The person we have created in Table 2.5 is an impossibility. This Frankenstein-like creature could never walk and live among us. Its features have been scavenged from distant sources and unnaturally stitched together here with little regard for blood or tissue type. For example, our superstitious friend could be described as a conservative young adult, yet we know that Boshier's superstitious pedestrians were more conservative only when they were over forty years old. This kind of inconsistency is unavoidable because, as we have seen, superstition is a very broad topic. Researchers have concentrated on different aspects of belief and behavior, and as a consequence, different, and sometimes contradictory, findings result.

An additional problem stems from the fact that most of the studies used to construct our profile examined only one variable at a time.[85] It is quite

Table 2.5   Profile of the Superstitious Person.

Variable	Category or Level Associated with Superstitious Belief
Social or Occupational Subgroup	
	Actor, Athlete, Gambler, Miner, Sailor, College Exam Taker
Demographics	
Gender	Female
Age	Not conclusive
Education	Less Educated
Academic Field	Arts, Humanities, Education
Religion	Nonreligious
Family and Peer Relationships	
Fathers	Overprotective
Peers	Rejecting
Personality	
Intelligence	Lower
Conservatism	Higher[a]
Fear of Death	Higher
Locus of Control	External
Self-efficacy	Lower
Hypnotic Suggestibility	Higher
Alienation	Higher
Neurotism	Higher
Ego Strength	Lower
Depression	Higher
Anxiety	Higher
Self-esteem	Lower

[a] Differences emerged only for participants who were over 40 years old.

possible that individually, these characteristics are associated with higher levels of superstition, but combined in the same person, as they are in Table 2.5, they would produce a *non*superstitious person. For example, based on separate investigations, we have made our superstitious person both less educated and more alienated. In fact, together these variables might produce an exceptionally skeptical individual. This happens when two variables do not combine additively; in other words, they interact. Instead of building upon each other in a $2 + 2 = 4$ fashion, they combine unpredictably: $2 + 2 = 0$. Imagine, for example, a naive physician who, in treating a feverish patient, has two medicines from which to choose. Each is moderately effective but will not completely eliminate the symptoms. In an attempt to maximize the effectiveness of the treatment, the doctor prescribes both medicines, only to find that her patient's fever continues unabated. Instead of producing a summing of the effects of two independent treatments, the medicines react in an unexpected way and, apparently, neutralize each other. The same may be true of the variables associated with superstition. We will not know how these characteristics interact with each other until studies are conducted that examine two or more variables in the same group of participants.

Although our profile of a supremely superstitious person is not without blemishes, it leads to a number of conclusions. First, without exception, the features of this personality are not very desirable. Our believer is less intelligent, more conservative, more fearful of death, more susceptible to hypnosis, and more alienated than his or her nonsuperstitious peers. Some of these characteristics are consistent with the common stereotype of a dull, anxious, and gullible believer in lucky charms and talismans, but there are a few surprises. The stereotype gives us no hint that the superstitious individual should be nonreligious. Given that a number of common religious beliefs fall within our definition of superstition, we might reasonably predict the opposite result.

A second surprising aspect of our creature is her gender: the Bride of Frankenstein, not Frankenstein himself. The stereotype of the superstitious person is silent on this subject. Indeed, a number of the traditionally superstitious subcultures are dominated by men (e.g., athletes, gamblers, miners, and sailors), which might lead us to believe that men are more superstitious than women. Yet research tells us the reverse is true. Psychologists and sociologists have devoted considerable attention to the study of gender differences.[86] It is a controversial and politically charged topic, but a number of reliable differences have been found. In particular, research on gender and locus of control may provide a clue. In childhood and early adolescence, boys and girls do not differ in locus of control, but in college, women begin to show a greater external locus of control than men. Since most studies of superstition have used this age group and, as we have seen, an external locus of control makes one more susceptible to superstitious and paranormal beliefs, it is understandable that our creature is a woman. Although this is a reasonable interpretation, it is not the only possibility, and its validity can only be established by further research.

Caveat

The study of group and individual differences has been a good introduction to the study of superstition. As lay psychologists, people often view human behavior as the outward symptoms of lasting traits and dispositions, and within the field of scientific psychology, the trait approach has a long history. In the case of superstition, we have learned some common features of believers, but this is hardly the entire story. Although the differences found in this body of research are consistent enough to suggest they are not the result of chance fluctuations in the data, these differences are still quite small. The personality characteristics that emerge at the group level are of little help in predicting whether a particular individual will be superstitious. For example, we have learned that believers are less intelligent, on average, than nonbelievers. Yet everyday experience, as well as the studies of college students and professors cited earlier, shows that magical thinking is quite common among the intelligent and well-educated. Clearly there is more to the psychology of superstition than an understanding of personality traits.

One limitation of the trait approach stems from the weakness of its primary assumption. The consistent and influential behavioral tendencies that sociologists and trait psychologists hope to identify are often less consistent and less influential than hypothesized. Each individual moves within an environmental context that can exert considerable influence. As the context changes, the influence of a particular personality dimension may swell or shrink. One may have a fatalistic, external locus of control in a number of domains, such as personal relationships and athletic accomplishments, but when one is placed in another setting (e.g., a successful work environment), a more internal view may predominate.

Another limitation of the trait approach stems from another aspect of the role of the environment. Although dispositions contribute to our personalities, we are not wooden. Important experiences change us and shape our behavior. Both Wade Boggs and Nancy Reagan point to events in their past that formed the beginnings of their superstitious beliefs. The profile that we have created provides a rough outline of a typical superstitious person, but to fill in the details for any individual case, we must learn how superstitious behavior is acquired. In chapter 3, we examine how various experiences build superstitious acts and gestures.

3
Superstition and Coincidence

For Locke, man is a rational animal and his thinking is governed mainly by reason, for which there are logical laws. Association is a phenomenon that explains certain behavior against reason.
—Edwin R. Guthrie and George P. Horton, *Cats in a Puzzle Box*

Bjorn Borg, the five-time Wimbledon champion, comes from a superstitious family. He and his relatives are known for a variety of personal superstitions, several of which center around spitting. As she sat in the competitors' box during the 1979 Wimbledon final, Borg's mother, Margarethe, ate candy for good luck. When Bjorn reached triple match point against Roscoe Tanner, she spat out the piece she had been chewing—perhaps in preparation for a victory cheer. Before she knew it, Tanner had rallied to deuce. Sensing she had made a mistake, Margarethe retrieved the candy from the dirty floor and replaced it in her mouth. Soon her son had won the championship for the fourth time. Earlier that same year, Borg's father, Rune, and his grandfather, Martin Andersson, were fishing and listening to the French Open final on the radio. Bjorn was playing Victor Pecci of Paraguay. Borg's grandfather spat in the water, and just at that instant, Borg won a point. Andersson continued to spit throughout the match, going home with a sore throat. Borg won in four sets.[1]

• • •

Some people may have temperaments or traits that increase their likelihood of being superstitious, but superstitious behavior, like most behavior, is acquired through the course of a person's life. We are not born knocking on wood; we learn to do so. We are not innate believers in astrology; we become believers. There are many psychological paths to superstition, but one of the most important of these is through direct experience with the world. We learn to be superstitious because, as Bjorn Borg's mother and grandfather can attest, our superstitions appear to work. Something good or bad happens coincident with our having done something specific. As a result we are more likely to engage in similar behavior in the future, or, if the outcome was negative, to avoid it. This method of acquiring superstitious behavior depends on events coming together in time, something psychologists call *contiguity*.

The Psychology of Contiguity

That human beings are sensitive to coincidence is both an often overlooked psychological truth and a monumental understatement. When important events happen together, they can change our behavior, alter our thought processes, and lift or dash our spirits. The psychology of coincidence is a topic large enough to justify a book of its own. For our purposes, coincidence has much to do with the development of a variety of superstitious beliefs and behaviors.

The primary dictionary definition of *contiguous* describes a spatial relationship, "touching or in close proximity,"[2] rather than a temporal one, but psychologists have most often used this term to describe a similar relationship in time. Nevertheless, both spatial and temporal contiguity have profound effects on human perception and learning. Much of our behavior is a response to patterns in our environment. As *Homo sapiens* we are sensitive to a myriad of very complicated patterns, but perhaps the most basic and pervasive pattern of all is produced by two objects aligned in space or two events paired in time. Our primary concern is with the role of contiguity in the acquisition of new—superstitious—behavior, but a short detour into perception will dramatize the importance of this principle for human psychology.

Contiguity and Perception

In the early decades of this century, a group of German psychologists were studying perception, our psychological experience of various sensory stimuli. They were known as the Gestalt School (not to be confused with the Gestalt therapy of Fritz Perls), and the most prominent among them were Max Wertheimer, Wolfgang Köhler, and Kurt Koffka. These researchers noted that we experience various stimuli, particularly visual stimuli, not as a group of constituent elements, but as a more complete and unified totality: the whole is *different from*—not *greater* than—the sum of its parts.[3] Working in Germany and, after the rise of Hitler, in the United States, they discovered a number of rules of grouping and unifying stimuli, some of which rely on the contiguity of objects or events.

Gestalt psychology began in 1910 on a train ride from Vienna to Germany's Rhineland. It is ironic that, years later, Köhler would study insightful problem-solving—the sudden flash of inspiration that leads to a solution—because his future colleague, Max Wertheimer, had just such an experience as he embarked on a vacation in the Rhineland. On the train, Wertheimer was struck with an idea for an experiment in apparent motion, the illusion of continuous movement when still pictures are flashed briefly in succession. He never made it to the Rhine. At the next stop, he left the train, rented a hotel room, and purchased a toy stroboscope.

Today, the word stroboscope, or "strobe," refers to a flashing light that breaks up the blur of rapid motion into visible pieces. A mechanic's timing light freezes the spinning of the engine's fly wheel; stroboscopic photographs reveal the symmetry of splashing drops of water. Wertheimer's toy produced the opposite effect. In the late nineteenth and early twentieth centuries, before the popularization of these phenomena in motion pictures, the stroboscope was, in the words of the *Oxford English Dictionary*, "a scientific toy which produc[ed] the illusion of motion by a series of pictures viewed through the openings of a revolving disc."[4] Rather than abolishing movement, it produced movement through the staccato presentation of a sequence of frames. The stroboscope of Wertheimer's day was more akin to the old cylindrical zoetrope or the flip books still sold today. Alone in his hotel room, Wertheimer convinced himself of the usefulness of his research idea, and after securing more sophisticated equipment, he began an extensive investigation of apparent motion, or what he called the *phiphenomenon*.

Figure 3.1 helps to illustrate the phi phenomenon in what is called a "two-flash" display. If frames A and B are flashed by a slide projector in quick succession, with a brief period of empty white frame between each

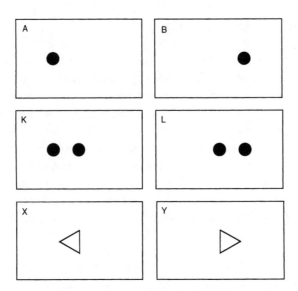

Figure 3.1   Examples of stimuli used to demonstrate apparent motion.

flash, the observer sees the dot move from left to right. The effect requires very careful timing of the interval between the flashes. In fact, there are two perceptual thresholds to straddle. If the interval between the flashes is too brief, the dots appear to flash on and off simultaneously, and no motion is seen. If the time between flashes is too long, the observer sees the dots as they are: two distinct objects turning on and off in succession. No motion. Between these two, often in the range of a tenth to a quarter of a second between flashes, movement of a single dot is seen when, in fact, separate dots are flashing on and off.

The lower frames of Figure 3.1 produce different apparent motion effects. Frames K and L contain two dots, one of which appears in the center of each rectangle. If the interval between the frames is very brief, but sufficient to produce motion, the left-hand dot of frame K appears to jump to the right-hand position in L. The center dot remains in place. If the interval is increased slightly, the pair of dots in K appears to move as a unit to the right. Finally, frames X and Y produce the illusion of movement in three dimensions. Alternating these triangles produces the illusion of a pennant spinning around a vertical shaft. In all of these cases, the effect depends upon careful timing. If the interval between the presentation of each frame is too brief, the flashing appears to be simultaneous. As the time separating the end of one stimulus and the beginning of the next increases, the perception of smooth movement disappears and the stimuli appear to flash on and off in succession. Thus, the perception of apparent motion requires that events occur in close temporal proximity (a tenth to a third of a second apart), but not with complete contiguity. In most cases, if one stimulus comes on just as the other goes off, we see them as a single event. The illusion of a single moving object is the bridge between seeing one stationary flash and two stationary flashes.

Approximate temporal contiguity is not the only requirement for these illusions to work. Research has shown that the perception of apparent motion can be affected by the length of time each stimulus is presented and the distance between the stimuli (angle of optical displacement). Objects, such as the dots in A and B, can appear to jump across wide distances in successive frames, but eventually the illusion begins to fail as the angle of separation becomes too great.[5]

Everyday problems with apparent motion and temporal contiguity are quite familiar. Most of us have been in a movie theater when something starts to go wrong in the projection room. The falling groan of the sound-track catches our attention first, but soon the slowing film reduces the action on the screen to jerky, robotic movements. The magical fluidity of film is destroyed by the breakdown of temporal contiguity. (I remember being thrilled, as a child, by the ultimate end of this process as the film came to a stop and the last frame suddenly melted and turned brown in the heat of the projection bulb.)

Wertheimer's early studies of time and movement led to more extensive developments in the study of space. The Gestalt psychologists gained wide attention for demonstrations of our basic tendency to organize collections of individual pieces into unified wholes. This principle allows us to see the separate flashing dots and triangles of Figure 3.1 as intact, moving units and the fragmented images of Figure 3.2 as meaningful objects. The group's investigations led to the identification of the Gestalt Principles of

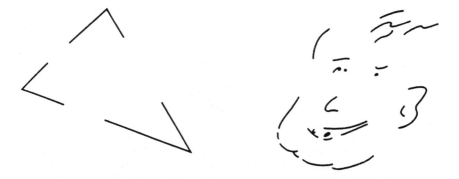

Figure 3.2 Degraded figures that illustrate how fragmented stimuli are organized into meaningful objects.

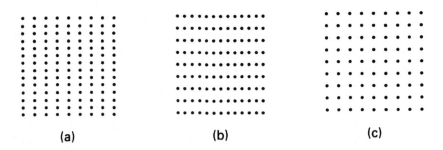

Figure 3.3   The perceptual effect of proximity. The left-hand and center arrays are seen as columns and rows, respectively. Equal spacing in the right hand figure produces an ambiguous display. *Source:* Bruce and Green (1990), reprinted by permission of Erlbaum (UK) Taylor & Francis, Hove, UK.

Perceptual Organization, a set of visual features that allow us to group the pieces of a picture. One of these principles is *proximity*, a close relative of spatial contiguity.[6] For example, Figure 3.3 shows how subtle differences in proximity can create important changes in perceptual organization. In the left-hand display the dots are slightly closer in a vertical direction and the array is seen as a series of columns. Closer spacing horizontally in the central example produces the perception of rows. Finally, the equal spacing of the right-hand display produces an ambiguous grouping. It is the principle of proximity that allows you to group the printed letters of this sentence into words. Figure 3.4 demonstrates some of the problems that result from the breakdown of proximity. The discontinuity of the top row makes it difficult to read as a meaningful word. In contrast, proximity makes the scrambled grouping of the second row just as difficult to read. Finally, our

G   E   S   T   A   L   T

PRI   NCIP   LEOFPRO   XIMITY

WAVED

Figure 3.4   The effects of proximity on the perception of words. There are other Gestalt principles at work in this last example. *Good continuation* is our tendency to see straight lines rather than turns. Thus we see a continuous horizontal line across the tops of the E and D in WAVED. This principle also contributes to our seeing the dots in Figure 3.3 as lines, rather than merely as groups of dots.

language has different levels of organization. Unlike Chinese or Japanese characters, which stand for whole words, each English word is made up of important subunits: letters. To read a particular word, its letters must be individually recognizable; and as the last line of Figure 3.4 demonstrates, complete contiguity makes recognition difficult. Our tendency to group the pieces into a larger whole is an obstacle to teasing the letters apart. Thus, the relationship of proximity to the grouping of objects in space parallels that of the timing of flashing dots to the perception of apparent motion. When things are completely contiguous, a new physical unit is created and no psychological grouping can occur. On the other hand, when proximity is lacking, as in the top row of Figure 3.4, the elements resist grouping. However, if the individual pieces are distinct yet close, we form larger units by imposing a perceptual grouping (e.g., letters into words). Again, the important effect is created by approximate, but not absolute, contiguity.

Contiguity and Learning

Our perception of the objects and events around us is profoundly affected by timing and spacing. Furthermore, just as our senses—not mescaline—are the doors of perception, so is perception the gateway to thought. The content of our thinking begins with the psychological experience of things around us. As we will see in chapter 4, the direct effects of contiguity on human cognition can lead to irrational thinking and superstitious beliefs, but at the moment, our concern is with superstitious behavior—in particular, behavior that is acquired through direct experience with the environment: learned behavior.[7]

• • •

Just as Gestalt psychology had an unusual beginning on a train to the Rhineland, the scientific study of learning began in William James's basement. The older brother of novelist Henry, William James was one of the founders of the field and the first great figure in American psychology. As a young physiology professor at Harvard University, he established the first psychological laboratory in the country in 1875, the same year Wilhelm Wundt opened the first European laboratory, and following its publication in 1890, James's *Principles of Psychology* became a standard text for generations of students. Despite his eminent status, James has been called an unsystematic psychologist. He believed that empiricism was important to the study of psychology, and he spent as much as two hours a day in the laboratory. Nevertheless, James held a low opinion of psychological research. As a pragmatist, he felt that the fruits of research were small in comparison to the work required to obtain them. (At certain points in my own research career, I have agreed with him.) He preferred to study behavior by "psychologizing"—reflecting on ordinary experiences—rather than by conducting experiments. As a result, his role in the history of psychology was that of an important forerunner, teacher, and popularizer rather than a scientific contributor. But downstairs something else was happening.[8]

In 1895, Edward L. Thorndike entered graduate school at Harvard University. As an undergraduate at Wesleyan University he had had only limited exposure to psychology, but soon after graduation, he read James's *Principles* in preparation for an academic competition. Thorndike won the competition and was so impressed with James's text that he admonished his undergraduate psychology professor for not using it at Wesleyan. Thorndike applied to Harvard and registered for a psychology course taught by James.[9]

In the following year, Thorndike began to study the "instinctive and intelligent behavior of chickens," work that, despite its barnyard beginnings, would produce some of the most important findings in the history of psychology. But in the 1890s, when laboratory psychology was still in its infancy, animal research was not as commonplace as it is today. Thus, one of Thorndike's most difficult challenges was finding a permanent home for his subjects. There was no space at Harvard, so he kept the birds in his apartment in Cambridge until his landlady evicted them. Having failed to find Thorndike space on campus, James generously offered to house the animals in the basement of his home. Years later Thorndike wrote, "the nuisance to Mrs. James was, I hope, somewhat mitigated by the entertainment to the two youngest children."[10] Thorndike finally found laboratory space at Columbia University, where he completed his doctoral degree. So, after a summer of boarding his animals at his parents' home, Thorndike traveled to New York carrying two of his "most educated chickens" in a basket.

Although his research on the "mental life of animals" began with chickens, Thorndike's most famous subjects were cats. His experiments in James's basement led to the development of the puzzle box, an open-framed crate fashioned with a trap door that the inhabitant could open by stepping on a panel or pushing a lever. At the beginning of the experiment, Thorndike placed a hungry cat in the puzzle box and a bowl of milk outside. As anyone who has tried to transport a cat in a box knows, cats hate to be confined. Thorndike found that on the first trial, the cat would thrash around randomly until eventually it stumbled upon the solution. When returned to the box in subsequent trials, the animal showed less and less unproductive behavior until eventually, the well-educated feline calmly and efficiently escaped the box and obtained its reward.

The progress of his cats' education demonstrated what Thorndike called the *Law of Effect*: behavior that produces positive results is strengthened, and that which produces negative results is weakened. This is the basic principle of operant or instrumental conditioning: learning through consequences. It is a simple yet very powerful idea, and as demonstrated by Thorndike and those who followed him, it underscores the importance of contiguity.

At about the same time Thorndike was putting cats in boxes, a Russian physiologist was studying a different kind of conditioning in dogs. Having completed an illustrous career in the field of digestion, for which he earned a Nobel prize in 1904, Ivan Pavlov accidentally discovered "psychic reflexes." While studying salivation, he found that dogs who had been tested several times began to salivate at the mere sight of food. Indeed, some animals began to salivate at the sight or sound of the approaching experimenter. In his later, very famous experiments, Pavlov rang a bell and then gave the dog a taste of meat. After several trials, the dogs began to salivate at the sound of the bell, whether it was followed by meat or not. He had discovered the conditioned reflex.

Pavlovian, or classical, conditioning is distinguished from operant conditioning in two ways. First, it is a passive process. Pavlov did all the work—he rang the bells and presented the meat; he determined the pace and nature of the conditioning regime. The dog merely salivated on cue. Thus, Pavlov was more in control of the process of learning than the dog was. In contrast, the subject must be an active participant for operant conditioning to occur. If Thorndike's cats had not been so hell-bent on getting out of the box, frantically clawing and rolling about, no learning would have occurred. They needed to press the panel to see the door open and to obtain their reward. Second, classical conditioning has its greatest effect on the autonomic nervous system—the nerves that control the involuntary activities of circulation, respiration, perspiration, digestion, glandular secretions, and salivation.[11] Pavlov had discovered conditioned reflexes. He showed that a reflex action, such as salivation, which is typically elicited by a very specific stimulus (food), could, after adequate training, be elicited by bells, lights, tones, or a variety of other stimuli. Operant conditioning, on the other hand, is not limited to a few basic bodily functions. It affects the full range of what we think of as voluntary actions. Obviously, behavior that is conditioned cannot actually be "voluntary" in the usual sense, but learning from the consequences of our actions is perhaps our most powerful and pervasive way of adapting to the environment.

Once again, contiguity is very important, specifically temporal contiguity. In Pavlovian conditioning, the bell must be followed closely by food to have salivation conditioned to it. In operant conditioning, learning occurs most quickly when the response is followed immediately by its consequence. If pressing the panel of the puzzle box opened the escape hatch only after a five-second delay, the solution would take much longer to learn. Like the perception of motion, both require careful timing, but only operant conditioning leads to the learning of superstitious behavior. Indeed, the study of superstition is an important chapter in the psychology of learning. It begins in the puzzle box.

• • •

Over a hundred years before Thorndike, Pavlov, and Wertheimer, the British empiricists John Locke, Bishop George Berkeley, David Hume, and David Hartley tried to uncover the principles of learning and understand how we come to associate ideas. Seventeenth-century French philosopher René Descartes had held the rationalist view that human beings were equipped with an innate capacity for reason and that all knowledge came from rationalism and logic. In contrast, the empiricists, like many psychologists who would follow them, argued that ideas are learned through direct experience. The Scottish-born Hume proposed three principles of association: that like ideas are associated, which he called *similarity*; that thinking about a cause leads us to think about its effect, which he called *causality*; and that things proximate in time or space are linked to each other, which he called *contiguity*.[12] Thus, the role of contiguity in learning had been articulated long before Thorndike built his first puzzle box. Nevertheless, it was this associationist principle that led a University of Washington psychologist to return to the puzzle box in 1936.[13]

Thorndike introduced the puzzle box, but Edwin R. Guthrie perfected it. To systematically examine the effect of contiguity on learning, Guthrie fitted a puzzle box with a camera to record the moment of escape. A pole mounted in the center of the box opened the hatch when pushed in any direction and, at the same moment, tripped the camera's shutter. Thus the animal's final pole-pushing response was automatically recorded. In their classic book, *Cats in a Puzzle Box*, Guthrie and coworker George P. Horton presented the results of their research with this apparatus. What emerged was a dramatic testimony to the power of contiguity. As each cat learned to escape from the puzzle box, it adopted a characteristic method of pushing the pole. One leaned against it; another lay prone and rolled into it; still another pushed it with his paw. Whatever movement had first produced escape tended to be repeated on subsequent trials, and because many different feline movements could potentially tip the pole and open the hatch, the animals adopted very different methods. Indeed, the posture of each animal at the moment of escape was so distinctive that, when the researchers accidentally confused the photographs of two cats, the mistake was quickly detected.

The Operant Conditioning of Superstitious Behavior

While Guthrie and Horton were photographing cats in Seattle, a young Harvard researcher was busy clarifying the principles of operant conditioning.[14] As the story goes, Burrhus Frederic Skinner, a graduate student in psychology, was studying learning in rats when he began to tire of his work. He had been using a straight-alley maze. In this arrangement, a hungry rat was placed at one end of a long runway and a small morsel of food was placed at the other. Skinner released the animal at one end of the alley and recorded its behavior as it ran from one end to the other. Following each trial, Skinner had to lift the animal out of the apparatus, reload the goal box with food, and replace the rat at the beginning of the alley. After many trials, laboratory work of this kind can become very tedious, and Skinner, a lifelong tinkerer and inventor, found a better way. He built an apparatus that allowed the animal's training to proceed without intervention from the experimenter. In its final version, Skinner's apparatus was a simple chamber fitted with a lever. When the rat pressed the lever, a microswitch closed, and a food pellet was automatically dispensed in a nearby opening in the chamber wall. Later a similar apparatus was developed for pigeons. The bird responded by pecking a disk on the wall of the chamber, and when a reward was earned, the pigeon was allowed to eat grain through a hole in the chamber. Today there are thousands of similar devices in laboratories and classrooms all over the world. Although Skinner never liked the name, these devices are most commonly known as "Skinner boxes." Modern computer-control equipment has been added, but the basic box is essentially the same as it was in the early 1930s. This simple chamber is still a fertile research tool and an important teaching aide.

After inventing the operant chamber, B. F. Skinner went on to complete a long and distinguished career in psychology. He discovered the basic principles of operant conditioning and demonstrated the power and scope of this type of learning in human affairs. He and his descendants developed behavior therapies that provide effective treatments for such diverse problems as autism, childhood hyperactivity, obesity, and smoking. Other applications of Skinner's work have led to valuable advances in industrial and organizational management, automobile safety, education, and many other fields. Although he is most famous for his ideas about behaviorism and society, as outlined in the utopian novel *Walden Two* and the controversial bestseller *Beyond Freedom and Dignity*, Skinner's scientific contribution remains arguably the most important in the history of psychology. His contemporaries in the research community often disagreed with him, but they overwhelmingly acknowledged the significance of his work. When the American Psychological Association gave Skinner its first Citation for Outstanding Lifetime Contribution to Psychology just two weeks before his death in 1990, hundreds of psychologists, many of whom did not subscribe to his theories, filled the lecture hall beyond capacity to hear the legendary scientist's remarks. Made frail by both age and the leukemia that soon took his life, the diminutive white-haired scientist walked with a cane, leaning on the arm of a younger psychologist, and as he slowly entered the room, the audience rose to its feet and applauded for several minutes.

The "Superstition" Experiment

In the early decades of his career—the 1930s, 1940s, and 1950s—B. F. Skinner wrote many scientific articles, but the most famous of all[15] was "'Superstition' in the pigeon," published in 1948. This has become a classic of the psychological literature, but it is also one of the most unusual articles ever published. Most scientists present the results of their experiments in quantitative form. A glance at any psychological journal will reveal page after page of tables and graphs. Indeed, quantification is the hallmark of all modern science. Yet Skinner's most famous experimental report was a narrative. He outlined the methods he used to conduct the study and then merely described the behavior of his pigeons in the chamber, almost as a naturalist might describe the behavior of animals in the wild. Nevertheless, this experiment is a dramatic demonstration of the power of coincidence in operant conditioning and the role of temporal contiguity in the development of superstitious behavior.

The procedure was quite simple. Skinner placed a hungry pigeon in a chamber where the feeder was controlled automatically by a timer, completely independent of the pigeon's actions. Every fifteen seconds, food would appear. Although the most efficient strategy might be to perch in front of the feeder and wait patiently for it to turn on, Skinner's pigeons were very active. After a few minutes in the chamber, each bird developed a distinctive ritual. One walked in circles, making two or three revolutions between reinforcements; another rapidly thrust its head into one of the upper corners of the apparatus. Still others bobbed their heads up and down, as if trying to keep an invisible soccer ball aloft. These peculiar behaviors were created by simple temporal contiguity. According to Skinner, the accidental pairing of some random act of the pigeon with the presentation of food was enough to reinforce these idiosyncratic behaviors. Soon the birds were dancing around the chamber as if their movements caused the operation of the feeder. The cats in Guthrie and Horton's photographs had a similar appearance. They adopted distinctive methods of pushing the pole, as if their specific action were required to escape from the puzzle box when, of course, any push would do. In the superstition experiment, however, the birds' behavior had no effect on the presentation of reinforcement. This was a case of conditioning by coincidence.

The superstition experiment soon became a popular classroom demonstration, and Skinner used to execute it with the flair of a stage performer. As part of a standard lecture, he would bring a Plexiglas chamber into the classroom, place a pigeon inside, and start the timer. The class would watch for a few moments, observing the relative passivity of the bird at the beginning of the hour; then Skinner would cover the chamber with a cardboard box and continue his lecture. The buzz of the electrical feeder mechanism could be heard every fifteen seconds, but the pigeon was hidden from view. Near the end of the lecture, Skinner would remove the box to reveal the once-stationary bird now feverishly pecking at the floor of the box or engaging in some other seemingly senseless behavior. The demonstration was—and still is—a consistent crowd-pleaser.

Can People Acquire Superstitious Behavior Through Operant Conditioning?

Skinner's pigeons did show behavior reminiscent of human personal superstitions. The repeated spitting of Bjorn Borg's angling grandfather seems very similar. So does Wade Boggs's penchant for chicken. Of course, Boggs is a member of a social group that is more superstitious than the general population, but his adoption of a unique nutritional regime looks like conditioning in the form of the accidental correlation of barbecue and RBIs.[16] Nevertheless, some were skeptical of Skinner's interpretation. One group argued that the pigeons were exhibiting instinctive behavior, not the effects of conditioning. According to this view, while waiting between reinforcements, the birds filled the time with not learned behavior, but behavior that is part of the evolutionary heritage of the species, behavior that comes naturally to all pigeons. Skinner had mistaken instinct for conditioned eccentricities.[17] Others could not accept that simple conditioning could be responsible for the complexities of human superstition. Later research with humans helped to clarify the situation.

For many years, the status of Skinner's view of operant superstition remained in an unusual position. On the one hand, he and others accepted the results as genuine and extended them to interpret complex human behavior, including the origination of tribal rituals, the development of pathological obsessions, compulsions, and phobias, and the acceptance of many medical and nonmedical "cures."[18] Meanwhile, a small group of researchers, supported by sound experimental evidence, questioned whether Skinner's study demonstrated conditioning at all. Others were not convinced that what was true for pigeons could be true for people. Although a replication of Skinner's study with human participants would have settled a number of arguments, such a study was not conducted for many years. Finally a few investigators began to approach the topic, some using children as subjects and others using adults. Of those studies attempting to condition superstitious behavior in children, the best was published in 1987 by Gregory Wagner and Edward Morris of the University of Kansas.

Wagner and Morris went into a preschool to conduct their research with three- to six-year-olds. They observed individual children in a small room fitted with a two-way mirror. On one wall of the room, the experimenters placed a plastic box for holding marbles and a child-sized mechanical clown named Bobo. At the beginning of the experiment, each child was allowed to choose a small toy that he or she wanted to win. When the child entered the observation room, he or she was introduced to Bobo and told that, from time to time, the clown would dispense a marble, which the child should place in the plastic holding box. If enough marbles were collected, the child would earn the toy. In the end, all of the children would receive their chosen toy, though of course they did not know this. As in Skinner's original experiment, Bobo was programmed to dispense marbles (from his mouth!) on a fixed schedule, regardless of the child's behavior. For some children the timing was one marble every fifteen seconds, and for another group it was every thirty seconds. Children were observed through the two-way mirror for one eight-minute session per day for six days.[19]

Wagner and Morris's results were very similar to those obtained by Skinner thirty years before. Seventy-five percent of the children developed a distinctive superstitious response. Some children stood in front of Bobo and grimaced at him; others touched his face or nose; still others wiggled or swung their hips. One girl smiled at Bobo, and another kissed his nose. In each case, the children exhibited these behaviors repeatedly across several sessions. Like Skinner's pigeons, each child developed a distinctive response, as if his or her actions had produced the marbles. Unfortunately, we do not know if Wagner and Morris asked their preschoolers how Bobo gave them the marbles, since this is not in their report. It would have been interesting to know how the children described their superstitions.

Skinner's experiment was repeated with adults in a clever experiment conducted by Koichi Ono of Komazawa University in Tokyo, Japan.[20] Again the experimenter used a small room, but instead of Bobo the clown, the room contained the experimental booth shown in Figure 3.5. Japanese university students volunteered to be the participants who would sit in front of a table fitted with three response levers. The partition at the back of the booth contained a signal light and a device that kept track of points. Each student participated individually during a single forty-minute session. Ono told the students that they were not required to do anything in particular but that they should try to earn as many points as possible. Points appeared on the counter on different schedules for different participants, sometimes at regular intervals and sometimes at varying intervals, but always completely independently of anything the students did. Electrical equipment in another room recorded any movement of the levers, and each student was observed through a two-way mirror.

Once again a number of superstitious behaviors soon emerged. Some persisted throughout most of the session; others were transitory, appearing for short periods and then disappearing, often to be replaced by new superstitious behaviors. As might be expected, most of these behaviors involved patterns of lever pulls. For example, one student made four rapid pulls on a single lever then held the lever for several seconds. The student used this pattern repeatedly for over thirty minutes, alternating among the three levers. Other students used different patterns of lever-pulling. Of course,

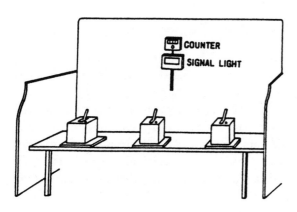

Figure 3.5 The booth used in Ono's (1987) human superstition experiment. Copyright (1987) by the Society for the Experimental Analysis of Behavior, Inc. Reprinted with permission.

the students' responses had absolutely no effect on the delivery of points, but in each case, a careful analysis of the data revealed that each superstitious pattern of lever-pulling began with a coincidence: a point being given at the end of a sequence of responses. Similar to Skinner's findings with pigeons, the contiguity of response and reinforcement sculpted stereotyped superstitions out of random behavior.

Not all of Ono's university students developed superstitious behavior, but most did. Of those who did, the great majority of superstitions involved lever-pulling, but some exhibited different kinds of responses. One student behaved in such an unusual manner that Ono described her actions in the following brief narrative. Remember, all the points mentioned were delivered automatically, by a timer that ran completely independently of the particpant's behavior.

> About 5 minutes into the session, a point delivery occurred after she had stopped pulling the lever temporarily and had put her right hand on the lever frame. This behavior was followed by a point delivery, after which she climbed on the table and put her right hand to the counter. Just as she did so, another point was delivered. Thereafter she began to touch many things in turn, such as the signal light, the screen, a nail on the screen, and the wall. About 10 minutes later, a point was delivered just as she jumped to the floor, and touching was replaced by jumping. After five jumps, a point was delivered when she jumped and touched the ceiling with her slipper in her hand. Jumping to touch the ceiling continued repeatedly and was followed by points until she stopped about 25 minutes into the session, perhaps because of fatigue.[21]

Fatigue, indeed! It is difficult to imagine a more dramatic example of the power of temporal contiguity in the learning of superstitious behavior. Clearly, Ono's study suggests that adults can be just as susceptible to conditioned superstitions as pigeons and preschoolers.

Conditioned Superstition or "Playing It Safe"?

When he published his original article, Skinner placed the word *superstition* in quotation marks because he saw pigeons' behavior as an analogy of human behavior. Like many psychologists, he wished to avoid anthropomorphizing his subjects by imbuing them with human thoughts and beliefs. Others, however, have been less cautious, suggesting that the animals in conditioning experiments are engaged in a process of inductive reasoning.[22] According to this cognitive interpretation, the pigeons in the superstition experiment made a reasoning error in believing that their bobbing and spinning caused the feeder to operate. Without doubt, reasoning

errors have much to do with human superstition, but we will save that discussion for the next chapter. However, there is a third view. Peter Killeen of
Arizona State University suggests that, when the outcomes are important
(e.g., food to a hungry pigeon), we are all hoping to find possible solutions
to the problems we face.[23] If, when the true nature of the problem is
unclear, we find something (like turning a circle) that may produce the
desired result, we have a strong bias to repeat it. This is particularly true if
the response costs us little yet the reward we seek is great. In a sense,
Killeen is suggesting that the superstitious pigeons are hedging their bets.
The birds continue to make their idiosyncratic movements *just in case*
these actions really *do* make the feeder operate.

This view is a terrestrial restatement of what is known as Pascal's
wager. Seventeenth-century French philosopher and mathematician Blaise
Pascal argued that even if there is only a slim chance that heaven and hell
really exist, one should live a Christian life to protect against the risk of
damnation. He argued that those who begin to practice out of reasoned
self-interest will eventually become true believers, thereby guaranteeing
their eligibility for salvation. If, however, there is no afterlife, the loss is relatively minor: the mild inconvenience of having needlessly lived a Christian life is outweighed by the possibility of avoiding eternal damnation.
This immodest proposal continues to be the subject of some debate.
William James is credited with the obvious rejoinder: if God is a god who
values the genuineness of one's conversion, Pascal's strategy may not
work.[24]

This hedging-their-bets interpretation of Skinner's whirling pigeons is
remarkably similar to a common feature of human behavior. When asked
about their superstitions, many people deny that they really believe. They
justify the use of charms or superstitious rituals by saying, "I don't want to
take any chances." Recall Wade Boggs's testimony, "I don't like surprises."
Human behavior is rarely the result of a single psychological principle, but
according to Killeen's analysis, a tendency to act superstitiously emerges
when the reward is very important and the cost of superstition is minimal.

This theory, like the reasoning-error interpretation, sounds as if the
individual adopts a conscious strategy. But we need not credit Skinner's
pigeons with the power of intellect for the theory to hold. The psychological processes of learning through operant and classical conditioning are
thought to be fundamental. They are common to virtually all species, and
in humans, conditioning can occur without conscious awareness. Indeed, a
popular prank among psychology students is a game that might be called
"Condition the Professor." Understanding that lecturers are reinforced by
students who nod and smile in the audience, a class agrees to make these

signs of assent only when the professor has made some arbitrary movement. In one case, a class responded only when the professor moved to his
left. The students received their ultimate reward when, halfway through
the lecture, the professor stumbled off the edge of the podium. (Although I
have never been a victim of this game, it is probably only a matter of time.)

If these conditioning processes are basic to all species, the playing-it-
safe theory might be based on natural selection. For a species to survive, it
must inherit physical attributes that are suited to its natural habitat. Where
flesh and fur alone are insufficient, the organism can adapt behaviorally.
This makes the ability to learn through reinforcement extremely important
to survival. It is often said that *Homo sapiens* are poorly prepared to live
in many climates and environments; our bodies are vulnerable to heat,
cold, and physical attack. But we are blessed with an unparalleled ability
to learn, both from direct experience and through language and instruction. An evolutionary interpretation of conditioned superstition suggests
that it is a basic behavioral adaptation. When the stakes are high, we are
particularly susceptible to conditioning. There is a strong tendency to
repeat any response that is coincident with reinforcement. In the long run,
this tendency serves the species well: if turning in a circle really does operate the feeder, the bird eats and survives another day; if not, little is lost.

The Pigeon with the Lucky Hat

Skinner's original experiment demonstrated the most famous type of
conditioned superstition, but it is not the only one. Indeed, three forms of
conditioned superstitions have been identified.[25] Pigeons that bob and spin
are the victims of *simple superstitions. Concurrent superstitions* result
when the rewards received for one action encourage other, unrelated
behavior. (We will discuss concurrent superstitions later in this chapter.)
The last is *sensory superstition.*[26] This form of conditioned superstition is
a common aspect of our everyday experience. It involves giving special
importance to some feature of our surroundings—say, a lucky hat.

I was introduced to lucky clothing when I was ten years old, away at
overnight camp for the first time. My camp counselor had a lucky baseball
hat, which he wore almost twenty-four hours a day. I remember that it was
a plain felt hat, green without any team insignia, and I was particularly
impressed that he wore it even while swimming. This kind of superstition
gives special status not to an idiosyncratic action, but to a particular object
or a feature of the setting. As we have seen, personal superstitions of this
type are extremely popular. Many of the exam-taking college students we

met in the last chapter employed special pens, sweatshirts, or jewelry. Others listened to a particular song or ate a special meal prior to exams. In the world of sports, superstitions involving clothing or equipment are quite common. These magical things can also emerge through operant conditioning, but in this case, superstitions arise out of the context of conditioning.

Up to now, we have concentrated on the back end of the conditioning process—the contiguity of a response with reinforcement—but an important piece of operant conditioning happens earlier. Figure 3.6 shows how a pigeon's key-pecking can be controlled by the color of the light projected through a translucent key. (Pigeons have very good color vision, and many of the response keys used to train them can be lighted different colors or even have simple images projected on them.) If pecking the key when it is green leads to the presentation of grain and pecking it when it is red has no effect, the bird soon learns to peck only when the key is lighted green. The key light is a *discriminative stimulus*. The power of this stimulus is such that, if a pigeon is pecking as the light changes from green to red, it will suddenly turn on its heel and look away, as if delivering a social snub. The bird will peck the key hundreds of times an hour when the light is green,

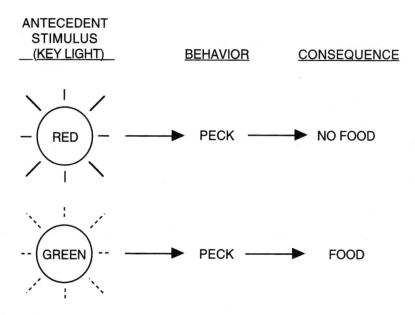

Figure 3.6 The ABC contingency. Antecedent stimulus (A), behavior (B), and consequence (C). Training in this context will lead to pecking only when the keylight is green.

and not at all when the light is red. In a sense, the well-trained pigeon exhibits two distinct forms of behavior. Green-key behavior is rapid, constant pecking, interrupted only by going to the feeder when food is presented; typical red-key behavior is more variable and may include walking around the chamber, preening, or flapping the wings.

Antecedent stimuli lead to all kinds of behavior, and their influence is omnipresent. Children quickly learn to ask for privileges from the parent who has rewarded such requests in the past. But someone else's behavior can also act as a discriminative stimulus. Older children often learn which parental mood is conducive to requests for money or other privileges. Domestic animals, like cats and dogs, can tell the time of day by the angle of sunlight and the activity in the house. When the usual feeding time arrives, they become more active and seek out the person who usually provides their meal. Many forms of what we think of as trial-and-error learning also involve behavior that is developed in response to a stimulus. After sufficient experience working with a particular conductor, orchestra musicians learn the precise motion of the baton that signals the moment to play. Before the musicians become accustomed to the conductor's style, however, they will occasionally play at the wrong time.

I once observed a dramatic demonstration of this last example. In high school, I played cornet in the school band, and one year I participated in a summer orchestra program. A large group of musicians from neighboring high schools was directed by a very talented conductor and music teacher. At one point in a long rehearsal, he asked whether we could tell, from the movement of his baton, exactly when to play. We had been practicing the beginning of a slow section in which the entire group needed to come in on the first note. We assured him that we could do it, but he was doubtful. To test our abilities, he devised a simple experiment. He raised the baton high over his head and told us to play when we thought the time was right. Then, very slowly—perhaps taking a whole minute—he lowered his arm in a vertical arc. We all watched intently, instruments poised, for what seemed like forever, and miraculously, as the stick approached waist height, we hit the note approximately together. He was very impressed, and so were we. Obviously, hours of practice had brought us under tight stimulus control. We had learned the specific angle of the baton—waist height—that signaled when an entrance would be rewarded by the simultaneous entrance of others and the praise of our leader.

In most cases, an antecedent stimulus is a reliable guide when reinforcement is available. The conductor's baton is a true indicator of when the musicians' play will lead to the desired outcome. But some contexts are less clear, particularly when they are new. What appears to be a salient and meaningful aspect of the environment may, in fact, be irrelevant. Skinner demonstrated this type of superstition in an experiment he conducted with William Morse.[27] Once again, a very simple procedure produced clear evidence of conditioned superstition in pigeons.

The Sensory Superstition Experiment

Morse and Skinner placed a hungry pigeon in a chamber and provided a lean schedule of reinforcement. At intervals varying between one and fifty-nine minutes, a peck on the response key would operate the feeder, allowing a few seconds of access to grain. Under this schedule, pigeons pecked throughout the session at a slow and somewhat variable pace. During most of the experiment, the key was lighted orange, but at widely spaced intervals, it was switched to blue for four minutes. The blue light was functionally irrelevant. In this case, the schedule went on just as it had when the orange light was on, and the change of color signaled no change in the experimental procedures. Nevertheless, after some time had passed, the bird began to treat the blue light as if it had special meaning. When it came on, pecking increased dramatically—even though the schedule had not changed. A positive superstition had emerged. Over time, however, the importance of the blue light would sometimes shift. After pecking faster when the key was blue, a bird might eventually peck at a slower rate when the blue light was on than when the orange light was on. A positive superstition had become a negative one—as if the light had changed from being lucky to being unlucky.

Just as the coincidental relationship between an action—spitting—and a desired event—scoring a point—can lead to superstitious behavior, the accidental relationship between a feature of the environment and reinforcement can create what Morse and Skinner called sensory superstitions. In a more recent study of sensory superstition, several different colors were used, and the results showed that even when the amount of reinforcement was carefully controlled and held equal in each key color, sensory superstitions still emerged, with individual pigeons showing distinctive patterns of response to the various hues. One pigeon pecked very rapidly during the green light; another made very few pecks. Although this type of superstition is not completely understood, it appears to begin with the pigeon's initial, idiosyncratic response to the change in stimulus—pecking faster or pecking slower—and is later maintained by reinforcement.[28]

Similar results have been obtained in laboratory studies of humans.

You will recall that in Ono's study of conditioned superstition, a signal light was mounted on the partition of the experimental booth (see Figure 3.5). While each student worked at the levers, the light appeared red, green, or orange. The colors were presented for equal time periods in a random sequence, and like the blue light in Morse and Skinner's experiment, they had nothing to do with the prevailing schedule of reinforcement. An equal number of points were received during each color. Six of the twenty students produced patterns of lever presses that indicated sensory superstitions. The most striking was a woman who pulled a different lever for each color of the signal light. When it was red, she pulled rapidly and exclusively on the left lever; when it was green, she pulled the middle lever; and when it was orange, she pulled the right. Like the other examples of superstition in Ono's study, this one could be traced to coincidental events early in the session. At the beginning of the experiment, a few points were delivered while the red light was on and the woman was pulling the left lever. Then more points appeared on the counter while the orange light was on and she was pulling the middle lever. Soon the full three-color pattern emerged and continued throughout most of the session. Of course, neither the lever-pulling nor the lights had anything to do with the points received.

Sensory Superstitions and Lucky Pens

We can draw an analogy here to everyday human superstition. Morse and Skinner's pigeons pecked faster in the blue light, as if they believed they would receive more food when it came on. Given that hits bring pleasure to the baseball player and successful matches bring pleasure to the tennis player, athletes who use lucky items of clothing are exhibiting a kind of sensory superstition. They seek out a particular context for play because they have been rewarded under these circumstances in the past. In recent studies of exam-related superstitions among Connecticut College students, Adair Kendrick and Craig Wilkinson found that many students who used lucky clothes, pens, or other accessories believed their magic items had a direct effect on their test-taking performance.[29]

Just as the blue light lost its power for some pigeons, however, lucky items often become unlucky. Lou Carnesecca wore his sweater for thirteen games straight, but after losing the fourteenth to Georgetown University (during the game, Georgetown coach John Thompson wore a T-shirt designed to look like Carnesecca's sweater), he retired it forever.[30] Some students have told me that they now consider their once lucky clothes especially unlucky: "I used to wear it all the time, but I would never wear it now." As we will soon see, other psychological processes are involved in this kind of superstitious behavior, but personal superstitions involving magical items are, in large part, learned through operant conditioning.

Superstitious Rituals and Operant Conditioning

But how do we get from kissing Bobo's nose to Wade Boggs's five-hour pre-game ritual? Much of the behavior we think of as superstitious occurs as part of long invariant sequences of behavior. For example, a goalie on the Connecticut College hockey team prepares for each game by executing an elaborate ritual that has many of the features of a rainmaker's incantation. He begins, in his dorm room, by listening to a special song before going to the rink; in the locker room, he puts on his uniform in a specific, idiosyncratic sequence; and once on the ice, he repeatedly taps each stanchion of the goal in a rigid pattern. Obviously, contiguity can have little to do with superstitious behavior that occurs hours before the desired reward is received. Nevertheless, the uniquely personal nature of these rituals suggests that a conditioning process of some kind is at work. In fact, there are several ways in which operant conditioning can lead to the development of longer sequences of superstitious behavior.

A Human Penchant for Ritual

As a species, we have an unparalleled ability to adapt and learn. Evolution has given us the capacity to perceive and respond to extremely intricate aspects of our surroundings, and we have acquired formidable powers of memory. Of course, the power and pervasiveness of our language further distances us from other animals. As a result, conditioning processes in humans are never as simple as they are in pigeons and rats. A lever-press or a key-peck may be a reasonable measure of rat or bird learning, but people have a way of complicating things. Even when the context is as controlled and barren as a Skinner box, human research participants soon build longer sequences of responses out of simple ones. When the responses in question are superstitious, the result is a conditioned ritual. Although research has yet to provide a complete understanding of how superstitious rituals are established, it appears that several psychological processes may be involved. The simplest of these is exemplified by concurrent superstitions.

This type of superstition involves the linking of two responses, one of which has nothing to do with reinforcement and another that actually produces reinforcement. I often listen to cassette tapes on my drive to work, and one winter I began to experience occasional problems getting the player to work; I would insert the tape and nothing would happen. Silence. Searching for a solution, I removed the tape from the player, tapped it against the steering wheel, and reinserted it in the player. Music! The next time the player stalled, I repeated this sequence of responses, but I soon discovered that the tapping had no effect. When the tape player finally expired completely, the true nature of the problem was revealed. My tape-tapping is an example of a concurrent superstition. As my cassette player approached its demise, it passed through a stage where inserting a tape was only intermittently reinforced by the sound of music. Inserting the tape was still an essential response, but the relationship between tapping and reinforcement was merely coincidental.

In the laboratory, pigeons and rats often develop concurrent superstitions, but the most interesting study of this topic involved introductory psychology students at Harvard University.[31] During the summer and fall of 1961, Charles Catania and David Cutts recruited forty-two male and female volunteers to participate in an experiment. Again the arrangement was very simple and lasted only one session. Each student sat at a table in a small room. On the table, was a box that contained two push buttons and a point counter. Students were asked to press only one button at a time, and as in Ono's study, they were not told how points were delivered. In this case, however, one button actually produced points, and the other never did. The presses on the right button were reinforced on a variable interval schedule averaging about thirty seconds between reinforcements. The left button did nothing.

Despite the simple nature of the task, almost every student superstitiously pressed the inoperative button throughout the entire session. Furthermore, when asked how they earned points, students reported that it was important to press both buttons. One case illustrated how compelling concurrent superstitions could be. In selecting their volunteers, Catania and Cutts tried to weed out any students who had studied reinforcement, but midway through his session, one man bolted from the room and announced that he knew how the apparatus worked because he had studied operant conditioning before. To his credit, the young man thought he should disqualify himself from the experiment. Before sending him away, the researchers asked him how he earned points, and he replied, "I press twice on the left button and once on the right."[32] Although it may have confused him, the student was asked to return to the experimental room and complete the session.

These examples of concurrent superstition show how two responses—

one of which is superstitious—can be linked together to form a short sequence. Catania and Cutts used a simple procedure that closely approximated the narrowly controlled context of the operant chamber, yet their Harvard students thought the problem was much more complicated than it really was. The result was the conditioning of brief superstitious sequences that are the beginnings of longer rituals. More elaborate superstitions can be produced by making the task slightly more complicated.

While studying problem-solving, I discovered that under the right circumstances, bright young college students could be induced to construct very complicated and thoroughly superstitious solutions to a simple problem.[33] Connecticut College students participated in the study as part of the requirements of an introductory psychology course. The task was to earn as many points as possible in a primitive video game. During a single session, individual students sat alone in a small room working at a computer. Again, they were not told how the game worked, but they were asked to earn as many points as possible. The game involved repeated trials with the matrix and circle presented in Figure 3.7. At the beginning of each trial, the circle always appeared in the upper left-hand box of the matrix. The computer program was designed so that only the "Z" key and the "/" key worked. A press on the "Z" (left) key moved the circle down one square, and a press on the "/" (right) key moved the circle to the right one square. Points could only be earned by moving the circle from the upper left to the lower right by some combination of four left and four right presses. If, a fifth press was made on either key, the matrix disappeared for a few seconds, and no points were given.

In one experiment, only a few of the paths through the matrix produced points.[34] For example, in one case, a sequence of left and right movements produced a point on every trial as long as it began with two left presses (moving the circle down two rows). Thus, the remaining moves toward the goal had to pass through the lower half of the matrix. This version of the game is depicted in the lower matrices of Figure 3.7. Naturally, students found this task somewhat more difficult, but most managed to earn a point on almost every trial. Furthermore, as long as points were given consistently, nothing unusual happened. Some students experimented with several paths through the matrix; others played it safe and stuck to one that worked. At the end of the session, when they were asked how the game worked, most described it reasonably well. Some underestimated how many solutions there were, but none misunderstood the basic nature of the task.

But something interesting happened when a degree of uncertainty was added to the game. In some experiments, points could only be earned on

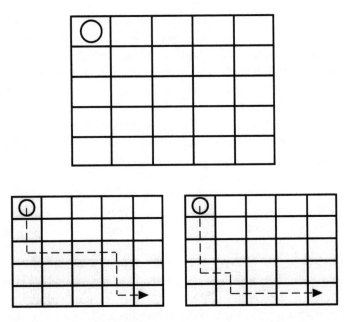

Figure 3.7   Matrix video game used in studies of superstition and problem solving. The upper rectangle shows the computer screen as it appears at the beginning of a trial. Presses on one key of the keyboard move the circle down; presses on another key move the circle to the right. Points are earned by moving the circle to the lower right-hand corner of the matrix. The bottom rectangles show examples of paths that produce points when the reinforcement is limited to sequences beginning with at least two downward movements of the circle. Under this condition, points are only given when the circle remains in the shaded area.

50 percent of the trips through the matrix. The point schedule was random and had nothing to do with the route chosen. Under these conditions, our student game-players suddenly began to see their task in a different light. Naturally, the problem was more difficult, and descriptions of the game were often more tentative. However, many of the students now proposed elaborate theories about how the game worked. Some said particular boxes had to be entered: "some key boxes must be hit and they alternate from time to time making it almost unpredictable." Others said certain boxes had to be avoided.[35] One student said that the keys of the computer had to be pressed very slowly.[36] Of course, none of these things were true, and when the students were told how the game really worked, they often expressed surprise that their theories had been wrong.

To examine these curious results more directly, Ruth Heltzer and I designed a simpler experiment. In this case, all paths through the matrix were equally viable as long as they ended in the lower right box. Rather than ask the students to earn as many points as possible, we simply asked them to figure out how the game worked. Students were divided into two groups, both of which received points on only 50 percent of the trials.[37] One group received points every other time they entered the lower right box, and the other received points on a random 50 percent of these trials. Again, the results were quite striking. Almost everyone who experienced a consistent pattern of points (on alternate trials) described the game accurately, but as in the previous studies, those who received random points offered bizarre descriptions of the game. A common theory held that points were earned by performing a specific sequence of paths through the matrix on successive trials. For example, one young man was convinced that points were awarded when the player completed a series of four different paths through the matrix. He confessed that, in the time allowed, he had only discovered three of the four.

These experiments provide yet another example of the effects of accidental reinforcement. When the game behaved inconsistently, the coincidence of a point being received at the end of a particular path created superstitious beliefs about the nature of the game. However, these studies make two additional points about superstitions that involve longer sequences of behavior. First, when the basic context of learning involves a series of actions, accidental reinforcement affects the whole series, not just the final moves. In contrast to rats and pigeons, humans in search of reinforcement respond to very complicated features of the environment and can quite easily engage in intricate patterns of behavior. For the students playing this game, the response that was reinforced was not a single movement of the circle or a single press of the key; it was the entire path from upper left to lower right. Furthermore, a number of students constructed faulty solutions that linked several different sequences together into longer series.

These results bring us closer to an understanding of superstitious rituals. In our everyday lives we are confronted with many tasks that are, by definition, sequential: cooking a meal, washing the car, or assembling furniture, for example. Experience tells us that each step in the process must be done in order and that our failure to execute any one of the steps adequately will result in an unsatisfactory outcome. Thus, in many situations, it is natural for us to expect our actions to be part of a causal chain. Unfortunately for the students playing our game, the sequence chosen had no causal relationship to the points.

The second point demonstrated by these experiments is the self-sustaining nature of longer sequential superstitions. Many of the students who subscribed to unusual theories about the workings of the game attributed the absence of points to some mistake they had made. For example, one woman wrote:

> I either went down & across or across and then down. The times in which I didn't score any points, I counted it as that I was supposed to have gone the other way.[38]

Her description of the game suggested that on each trial there had been a correct solution; a point could have been made on every trip through the matrix. According to this view, when she failed to receive a point, it was because she had chosen the wrong path. Recall that the young man who thought points were earned for a series of four different paths attributed his failure to not having discovered the third sequence in the series. Similarly, the woman who said the keys had to be pressed very slowly believed that when she failed to receive points, it was because she had pressed the keys incorrectly. In each case, our video-game players believed that not earning points said more about their style of play than it did about the game. Superstitious theories survived despite contradictory results.

The resilience of these superstitious ideas is not difficult to understand when we consider our everyday experience with sequential tasks. In most cases, there is only one way to succeed but many ways to fail. For example, to bake an angel food cake—a challenging enterprise for most of us—one must execute each step very carefully. A failure can be caused by the omission or mismeasurement of an ingredient, the incorrect oven temperature, or an inadvertent bump of the oven door. Our experience with such tasks leads us to expect that correctly executed sequences will be successful every single time. When something goes wrong, we assume we are to blame. Other enterprises are, by nature, uncertain. The college student who does everything possible to prepare for an exam may still get a lower grade than he or she had hoped for. The baseball player who practices diligently and carefully prepares for each game can still only expect to get a hit about 30 percent of the time. In these cases, random successes make the conditioning of superstitions more likely, but the self-blame associated with failures often persists.

In the next chapter we consider the interplay of cognition and superstition—how our modes of thought build and sustain superstitious ideas. The resilience of the superstitions observed in our video-game–playing college students in the face of conflicting results can be understood by looking at cognitive processes: a well-developed pattern of thought kept them from revising their view of the game. But what we observed in a simple experimental context is remarkably similar to a phenomenon associated with the magical rituals of traditional cultures. When a shaman fails to produce rain at the end of a rain-making ritual or to cure an ailing parishioner, the local believers tend not to question the validity of the magic; instead, the faithful suspect that there was an error in the ritual or that the shaman is a pretender.[39] Video games are far removed from ritual cures, but they share this important similarity.

Rituals as Time-Fillers and Place-Holders

Modern life has made us remarkably impatient. Things happen in an instant, and we have come to expect them that way. We are frustrated when a computer takes an extra five seconds to crunch our numbers, even though it would take hours to complete the calculations without the computer. We pound the steering wheel when we have to wait for a red light. In seconds we can talk to people anywhere in the world, but if the connection takes minutes rather than seconds, we may hang up. Even when we have not been spoiled by modern technology, we often find ourselves waiting for an important something to happen that, to our chagrin, cannot happen for some time. The shopper stuck in a long line feels caught between the impulse to flee and the desire for the item she is buying. These are unstable situations that are sometimes resolved by waiting, sometimes by giving up. When such wait-flee conflict situations are repeatedly encountered, rituals may develop to fill the time.

You will recall that some writers criticized Skinner's original superstition experiment, saying that what Skinner saw was not accidentally reinforced behavior but instinctive responses that served to fill the time between reinforcers. According to this view, some superstitious behavior may emerge early in training, but it is eventually replaced by behavior that merely helps the animal wait. As we have seen, however, there is much evidence that superstitious conditioning is genuine and occurs in both humans and animals. Rather than discredit Skinner's notion of superstition, the waiting behavior observed by his critics actually provides a key to understanding how some forms of ritualistic behavior develop.

When a rat is placed in an operant chamber on a schedule of intermittent food reinforcement, it often develops what is called *adjunctive* behavior or *schedule-induced* behavior. These are behaviors that occur during the waiting periods, when food is not available, and in some cases they are more frequent and intense than the target behavior of pressing a lever for food. For example, if a drinking tube is present in the chamber, the rat will drink excessively during the period between reinforcements. This drinking is not due to thirst, in the usual sense of the word, because it occurs even when the rat is given unlimited water before the beginning of the session. When a water bottle is not available, the animal finds some other behavior to fill the time, such as scratching at the corners of the chamber or spinning along in a running wheel.[40] Pigeons and other animals exhibit similar forms of adjunctive behavior.

A number of laboratory studies have shown how adjunctive behavior can be produced in human participants. For example, a group of researchers at La Trobe University in Australia studied schedule-induced behavior in university students by having them play a simple video-poker game for small amounts of money.[41] Individual students sat in a small room that contained many more objects than is typical in most experiments: a computer, several small tables, a refrigerator, two empty packing cases, Coca-Cola, "Cheezels," and drinking water, among other things. This rather cluttered environment had two purposes: it provided items that could be eaten or drunk to facilitate adjunctive behavior, and the tables and packing cases restricted movement to areas of the room that could be easily observed by the experimenters.

In one condition of the experiment, the students developed a number of behaviors. Every 60 seconds, a press on the computer's space bar made an array of cards (a hand) appear on the screen accompanied by the amount of money won. Presses before the 60 seconds had elapsed did nothing. Under these conditions, all of the students showed some form of adjunctive behavior, such as pacing, body-rocking, finger- or foot-tapping, grooming, or hand-wringing. In addition, they displayed some bizarre behaviors that may have been superstitiously reinforced. One student pressed the space bar with a bare foot; another tore scrap paper into hundreds of pieces and arranged them in symmetrical patterns. In two other conditions of the experiment, when the interval between presses was reduced to 5 seconds and when the students merely listened to a taped discussion and did not play the game, these adjunctive behaviors became rare.

The most satisfying theory of these adjunctive behaviors is that they are evolutionary versions of the shopper's flee-wait dilemma. Imagine a frog searching for food in the wild. If its current environment is rich with insects, there is no conflict; the frog stays where it is and feeds at its own pace. Similarly, if the area has become barren, the frog leaves to forage elsewhere. An unstable situation arises when the insect population is somewhat thinner than desirable. The frog, like the shopper, experiences a conflict between the urge to stay and collect those insects that are hovering about and the urge to move to another feeding area. A similar conflict arises if there is little food in the area yet the local terrain makes it difficult to travel. The evolutionary theory of adjunctive behavior proposes that, at these moments, the animal engages in repetitive behavior that maintains the status quo. Adjunctive behavior fills the time between feedings and keeps the animal in the current environment when there is a strong motivation to flee. The theory also suggests that this behavior is instinctive, having emerged because it helped the species survive natural selection.

Whether correct or not (and there is some controversy on this point), the evolutionary theory captures an important feature of rituals: coping with conflict. In humans, adjunctive behavior, such as pacing, smoking, and drumming one's fingers, often appears when we are placed in a difficult situation from which there is no immediate escape and when there is time to engage in these behaviors. The professional basketball player is in a stressful enterprise throughout the game, yet ritualistic behavior only appears before the game begins or when play has stopped. During the game, action is fast and completely controlled by the demands of play; there is no time to fill with adjunctive behavior. Pregame rituals are common, but the most obvious rituals appear at the free-throw line. When a player is fouled, he or she is often awarded one or two free shots at the goal. The game clock stops while this operation is completed, and the player is free to take as much time as necessary. It is a very public moment. For this brief, nervous interlude, the attention of every player and every spectator is focused on the shooter at the foul line. When a college or professional game is televised, the camera routinely shows a closeup view of the athlete preparing for the shot, shooting, and reacting to the result. Despite the fishbowl nature of this aspect of the game, free-throw rituals are common. Many players dribble the ball a prescribed number of times before shooting. Former Boston Celtics guard Dennis Johnson bounced the ball one time for each year he had played professionally. New York Knicks center Patrick Ewing carefully rotates the ball in his shooting hand until his fingertips rest along one of the seams.

In contemporary daily life, one of the most common places to observe adjunctive behavior is at the local automatic-teller machine. Looking remarkably similar to a pigeon pecking for food in an operant-conditioning chamber, the experienced bank-machine user punches the keys with a rapid melody of electronic beeps. The most common transaction is a cash withdrawal, often in preparation for a purchase minutes later. Everything goes smoothly until there is a brief interruption while the computer checks the account and the monitor pleads, "PLEASE WAIT WHILE YOUR TRANSACTION IS BEING PROCESSED." This break in the action typically lasts no more than five seconds, but it is enough for some time-filling behavior. Common examples of automatic teller adjunctive responses include humming, straightening the hair, and looking around. My personal ritual is drumming the edge of the bank machine's metal counter with my fingers.

When Is a Ritual Just a Routine, and When Is a Ritual Superstitious?

Almost every serious athlete has a routine that he or she follows prior to a competition. The high jumper prepares to jump by performing a regular series of actions before running toward the bar. The diver approaches the board exactly the same way each time. Many musicians and entertainers have similar pre-performance routines. For example, Russian pianist Shura Cherkassky, known for the spontaneity of his play, always steps onto the stage with his right foot first. In many cases, these personal rituals serve a number of valuable purposes and are not at all superstitious. For the high jumper, the routine is an attempt to focus on the actions and circumstances that are associated with success. All of the pieces of the pre-jump ritual become part of the context of the jump, and when a good performance is achieved, the whole sequence is strengthened. As a result, the experienced jumper uses a regular pre-jump routine in an effort to recreate the circumstances of past performances and minimize variations that might threaten the outcome. Psychological research supports the importance of this strategy, and coaches often encourage athletes to develop a standard routine.

Many modern athletes also prepare themselves mentally for each performance. The diver concentrates on what she is about to do and, in some cases, tries to visualize a perfect dive, mentally rehearsing each body movement. These thoughts are themselves part of a useful pre-performance routine, and the physical aspects of the athlete's ritual—pacing, rolling the head and neck, or shaking out the arms and shoulders—help to block out other thoughts and focus attention on the dive. Finally, the routine provides emotional comfort. As we have noted, rituals of this type occur in stressful circumstances, and both the mental and physical aspects of the pre-performance ritual become a kind of mantra that undoubtedly helps to block anxiety and lower the athlete's heart and respiration rates.

Thus, rituals often serve a useful and rational purpose. So when are they superstitious? A routine becomes superstitious when a particular action is given special, magical significance. Because there are a number of benefits to pregame or pre-performance rituals, it is often difficult to draw the line between superstition and useful preparation, but some cases seem fairly clear. Shura Cherkassky's manner of stepping on stage at the beginning of his concerts should probably be considered a superstition because, unlike the high jumper's preparation, it can have no direct effect on his piano playing. Similarly, when Bill Parcells was the coach of the New York Giants football team, he had a pregame ritual that included stopping at two different coffee shops on the way to the stadium. He would arrive in the locker room with two cups of coffee, one purchased at each shop.

Superstitions are often encouraged by the social influence of people around us. However, we know that a series of actions is often perceived as a unit, and the coincidental relationship between the peculiar shape of the routine and reinforcement can lead to conditioned superstition. The college students playing the matrix video game gave special significance to their idiosyncratic paths through the maze because they had been accidentally reinforced. Routines of this type are most common when the outcome is uncertain. To the detached observer, the success of the athlete appears somewhat random. Sometimes the diver will achieve a beautifully executed dive, and sometimes the movements are awkward and out of balance. In both cases, the diver and the preparations are the same, but the results are very different. As the matrix-video-game studies suggest, the randomness of the outcome is an important force in the development of superstitious rituals. Thus, the initial motivation for a routine may be the time-filling and stabilizing effects of adjunctive behavior (as well as the cognitive and emotional benefits described), but the eventual articulation of a superstitious ritual grows out of accidental reinforcement—or social influence combined with accidental reinforcement.

• • •

Operant conditioning is not just for rats and pigeons. It is a powerful influence in our lives, helping us learn and adapt to our surroundings. Most of the time conditioning serves us well, but sometimes it goes awry. Random, coincidental events lead us to engage in bizarre and unproductive behavior. These operant superstitions can be fleeting or persistent, but for humans, they rarely occur in a vacuum. Although we can, under some circumstances, be conditioned without being aware of it, those who engage in common superstitions typically think about what they are doing. Operant conditioning and cognitive processes sometimes operate in parallel spheres, barely influencing each other, but more often they interact. For example, what a person thinks or is told about a problem may enhance or interfere with his or her ability to solve it through direct experience. Conversely, conditioning processes often alter our thinking about a situation. When rewards are available for an act we believe is wrong, we sometimes rationalize our actions rather than give up the reward.

Coincidence and accidental conditioning explain many superstitious behaviors; however, superstitions also appear as magical beliefs and misguided judgments. Language and thought are the greatest achievements of our species, but just as operant conditioning can lead us astray, our thinking is sometimes faulty. Quirks of cognition color our perception of the world and lead us to irrational belief and superstitious behavior. Moreover, the superstitions that grow out of accidental conditioning are often maintained not by reinforcement, but by the peculiarities of human thought. In chapter 4 we turn to the ghosts that rise from the machinery of our intellect.

4
Superstitious Thinking

I know too well the weakness and uncertainty of human reason to wonder at its different results.

—Thomas Jefferson

At Belmont Park on October 27, 1990, Bayakoa, a six-year-old mare who had won the same race the year before, ran to victory in the Breeders' Cup, 6 3/4 lengths ahead of her closest competitor. But for those who watched in the stands and in the national television audience, this commanding performance was overshadowed by the horror of the race.

During the fall 1990 season, a shadow seemed to have fallen over the track. Just in the last two weeks, four horses had sustained career-ending injuries, and earlier that day in the Sprint, Mr. Nickerson, a four-year-old colt, had suffered an apparent heart attack in the far turn. As he fell he took the trailing Shaker Knit with him, and the slower horse suffered a spinal cord injury. In the Juvenile race, one owner withdrew his entry due to a shin injury, saying, "I don't want to take a chance with this valuable a horse on a track where so many things are happening."

With a million-dollar purse at stake, the Distaff Breeders' Cup, a 1 1/8 mile race for fillies and mares, soon developed into a duel between Bayakoa, threatening to repeat her win, and the filly Go For Wand, a strong candidate for Horse of the Year. They ran nose to nose through the stretch when suddenly, less than one hundred yards from the finish, Go For Wand's right front foreleg collapsed, breaking at the ankle. As the crowd of fifty-thousand gasped, the filly went down directly in front of the grandstand, throwing her jockey into the air and rolling to rest under the rail. Suddenly she was up again, staggering horribly across the track on a bent and broken ankle before falling for the last time in front of the outside fence.

Sitting in her box seat, Go For Wand's owner, Jane du Pont Lunger, felt her excitement over the possibility of a great victory dissolve into tragedy. As difficult as this moment would be for anyone, Lunger felt an additional pang of responsibility. Since Saratoga, she had always worn a lucky pair of mud-splattered shoes whenever Go For Wand ran, but today, for the first time in four of Go For Wand's races, she had neglected to wear them.[1]

Superstition and Human Thought

The psychology of human thought is a subcategory of cognitive psychology. Attention, memory, and perception are basic processes that cognitive psychologists study as a way of understanding the foundations of thought, but when we speak of thinking we mean logical reasoning, problem-solving, deciding, and believing. Many of these psychological processes also involve language, perhaps the most obvious manifestation of intelligence.

These abilities are so central to the human experience that we think of them as essential aspects of our humanness. This was also the classical view. Aristotle believed that animals possessed a *psyche* with the power to sense, remember, and imagine, but that thinking was reserved for the human psyche.[2] The modern view is less divisive. Some still believe that there are uniquely human abilities; for example, linguist Noam Chomsky maintains that *Homo sapiens* alone have the ability to learn the syntax and grammar of language. Yet most psychologists believe that human and, for instance, chimpanzee cognition differ in degree rather than kind. We are smarter than chimps but not, in any essential way, distinct from them. A Darwinian view of cognition prevails.

Jefferson was right. Although human thought is prodigious, it is not without weaknesses and uncertainties. In a number of situations, we are

prone to irrational rather than rational behavior. We make erroneous conclusions, show biased judgment, and ignore important information. Since
the 1950s, cognitive psychologists have discovered many of these common
cognitive failings, several of which contribute to superstitious behavior and
belief. In particular, superstitious thinking springs from misunderstandings
of probability and random processes, errors of logical reasoning, and cognitive shortcuts that sacrifice accuracy. Since the single common feature of
all superstitions is their emergence under conditions of uncertainty, it is
appropriate that we begin with superstition and probability.

The Mathematics of Cognition

Three of the most basic concepts of mathematics are expressed by the
relations *greater than* (>), *less than* (<), and *equal to* (=).[3] More fundamental even than counting, these ideas mark the beginnings of quantification in
the description of relative magnitude: more, less, the same. Now closely
associated with mathematics, these concepts predate its classical beginnings and are useful far beyond the manipulation of variables and con-
stants. Much of our day-to-day thinking is quantitative, whether we are
aware of it or not. We are forever making choices, deciding what to do or
not do, and making judgments of value. In most cases, these thoughts and
actions do not involve explicit quantities, but they do involve comparisons
of relative magnitude. Coke > Pepsi. Clinton = Dole.

When life is uncertain, we apply an informal calculus of probability. We
make judgments about the likelihood of rain, the soundness of our investments, the honesty of a politician's statements, and the adequacy of our
children's education. Some of these assessments involve formal analyses of
quantitative information (e.g., stock portfolios and bank statements), but
most are informal judgments. A journalist, for example, tries to determine
whether her editor will like a particular story idea. Her judgment is not
stated numerically, but it is probabilistic—intuitively fashioned out of past
experiences with the editor. If, based on the information available, the
reporter calculates the probability of a favorable reception to be lower than
some psychologically comfortable criterion, she may pursue other topics.

We also assess the desirablity of certain outcomes or activities in a
quantitative way. If, for example, the reporter is particularly interested in
the story, she may present it to her editor despite a high likelihood of rejection. Similarly, gamblers play the lottery against daunting odds because the
potential rewards are great. Were the value of the reward reduced, neither
the reporter nor the gambler would proceed.

In fact, much of our everyday thinking can be understood as quantitative judgments and decisions made by a consumer in a behavioral economy. Of course, we do make such judgements when we are actually in the marketplace. We weigh the enjoyment of a Moo Shu pork dinner against the value of the money it would cost. We compare the greater comfort of a luxury car with the additional money we would have to pay for it. In many cases, our decisions and actions are controlled by these assessments. Other judgments have a similar economic flavor, although they may not involve numbers or money. For example, I periodically consider the pleasures of a neat desk and office in relation to the effort involved in straightening and organizing my work area. Too often, the effort looms larger than the joy of neatness, and my office remains a den of chaos and inefficiency.

In many instances, all of this thinking is quite rational. Our judgments are rule-based and objective, and the decisions we make are supremely sensible. But sometimes reasoning fails us. When quantitative thinking is involved, the most common errors fall into two broad categories. The first is innumeracy: misunderstandings of mathematics and, in particular, the principles of probability.[4] The errors of the second type occur when the context of the problem clouds or biases our thinking. We begin with the calculation of everyday probabilities, odds, and chances.

The Basic Ratio

When math teachers approach the topic of probability, their lectures often acquire a vaguely sinful flavor as they turn to problems involving playing cards, dice, and horse races. Yet these examples are fitting. They are, after all, games of chance, and despite their uncertain nature, each has clearly defined features and rules of play that qualify them for the quintessentially rational description that mathematics provides. Most of our everyday problems are less well defined, but frequently we can make reasonable estimations of the probabilities involved.

Probabilities are expressed as fractions (1/4) or real numbers (.25) that range between the two certainties of zero and one. A probability of zero means the event in question cannot happen, is certain not to occur; whereas a probability of one means the event will happen, must occur. In honor of the superstitious craps players of chapter 2, let us consider one of the the simplest of all examples: a single die. It is a perfect cube with six sides, each marked with the appropriate number of dots. Given a fair die and an honest, random toss, the probability of rolling a one (or any other specific number) is one out of six, 1/6, or .17. Given six fair rolls, our best prediction would be that only one of these would reveal a single dot. In actual practice, it is quite likely that our six rolls would produce no ones or, alternatively, two or even three ones. But after a large number of rolls, we would expect approximately 1/6 or 17 percent to come up ones.

In the case of a single event, such as rolling a one, the numerical expression of a probability is produced by this simple ratio:

$$\frac{\text{Number of desired events}}{\text{Number of possible events}}$$

If, rather than only a one, we were interested in rolling any odd number (1, 3, or 5), the numerator of our fraction would change, yielding a probability of 3/6 or 1/2. For a standard deck of fifty-two playing cards (minus jokers), the probability of randomly drawing the queen of hearts is 1/52. The probability of merely drawing a heart of any type is 13/52, or 1/4; of drawing a queen of any color, 4/52, or 1/13.

Up to this point, we have been working with probabilities or, colloquially, chances. Another kind of ratio is implied by the term *odds*. In this case, the ratio is not expressed as a fraction or a decimal; instead, it is a ratio derived from the probability of failure versus the probability of success. For example, in horse racing, the track will post the odds of a particular horse winning in terms of odds against versus odds in favor. Therefore, an extreme long shot might be given odds of 99 to 1. These odds are another way of saying that the house believes the probability that the horse will lose is 99/100 and the probability that it will win is 1/100. A faster horse might be given odds of 5 to 2, meaning that it is believed to have 5/7 probability of losing and a 2/7 probability of winning. Because these probabilities cover all possible outcomes (winning and losing), they always add up to 1.0, but when stated as odds, the denominators are removed. Thus, probabilities of 2/3 versus 1/3 become odds of 2 to 1.

That's all there is to it. Calculating the probabilities of combined events, such as the chances of correctly picking the first and second finishers in a horse race, is a slightly more complicated process, but for single events, it is a matter of a simple ratio. Yet people have enormous difficulties working with probabilities. Of course, all things mathematical are a headache for some people, but even when thinking about probability requires no numbers, people often make important mistakes. Some of this misguided thinking results merely in clouded judgment and uninformed opinion, but at other times, it forms the basis for superstitious behavior or belief in the paranormal. Our list of common problems with probabilities begins with the simplest mistake of all.

Connecting Unconnected Things: The Gambler's Fallacy

An important misconception of the workings of chance comes from the belief that something wholly mechanical and random is somehow affected by the things surrounding it. In most cases, it is not. Consider the roulette wheel. It is a mechanical device designed to select one number from a set of thirty-eight.[5] If it is constructed fairly, each spin of the wheel is a unique random event, unconnected to other forces. The wheel has no mind, no soul, no sense of fairness. Its face is blank. Yet, we often treat it otherwise. As we have seen, the managers of some roulette parlors—who might be expected to understand the workings of their trade—will change the croupier at a table that has run a string of bad luck. The wheel does not know who is spinning it, and we cannot give the wheel the power to sense its croupier without entering the twilight zone of paranormal forces. Yet both the staff and the players of roulette parlors frequently impute the wheel with a mind of its own.

The roulette player who falls victim to the gambler's fallacy believes that past spins have a bearing on future ones. Many players will bet on red after spinning a series of consecutive black numbers, saying that a red number is "due." This is a common mistake. Each spin of the wheel is an independent event and has no effect on subsequent spins. Even if twenty-five blacks were rolled in a row, the probability of a red on the next spin would be unchanged. The gambler's fallacy is also common among sports-casters, especially baseball announcers. If a player has gone hitless for several trips to the plate, he is said to be "due for a hit." The commentator's error is sometimes compounded by invoking a specious science of chance: "By the law of probability alone, we would expect him to get a hit one of these times." Of course, there is no such law. The principle of independence tells us that a string of failures does not make a hitter more or less likely to succeed the next time he steps up to the plate. Hitting in baseball is a skilled activity, and many things can affect a hitter's performance—illness, fatigue, practice, and, perhaps most important, the pitcher's skill. But the pattern of recent hits and outs has no effect on the probability that the next time at bat will be successful.

The gambler's fallacy is an expression of the common notion that things even out. Many people believe the universe is founded on a Karma-like homeostasis that answers every yin with a yang. They subscribe to a balance-sheet view of the cosmos in which no good deed goes unrewarded and no cruelty goes unpunished. In the blindly scientific world of proba-bilities, things *do* even out—but only in the long run. After many tosses of a coin, approximately 50 percent will come up heads and 50 percent tails, as we might expect. But this long-run balance is due to the fairness and independence of each toss, not to some moral principle that offsets a string of heads with a string of tails.

Another violation of independence is committed in the opposite direction when an athlete or a wager is thought to be "hot." To help lottery players choose their bets, many state lottery commissions publish lists of recent winning numbers. Some numbers will have paid off more than once, and some numbers will never have won. After examining these reports, some players bet on previous winners believing that they were "hot," and others bet on losing numbers believing that they were "due." But the dancing ping-pong balls in the lottery drum do not appreciate history. They have no memory, and their behavior is not affected by previous drawings.

Struggling with Randomness

As nature abhors a vacuum, so does human nature abhor randomness. We prefer order over chaos, harmony over cacophony, and religion over the prospect of an arbitrary world. Indeed, for many years it was believed that humans were incapable of behaving randomly. For example, when the participants in one study were asked to mimic a random sequence of coin flips by writing the resulting heads and tails on a piece of paper, they failed miserably. Their imaginary coins were much more orderly than real ones.[6] Similar studies, using a variety of tests, have consistently shown failures of human randomness—even when the particular humans involved were graduate students in statistics![7] As a result, some psychologists concluded that the tendency to infuse order is a basic human trait.

For a time, all indications were that random behavior was impossible for humans and nonhumans alike. There was some disagreement about the explanation for this deficit, but the basic conclusion that randomness could not be mimicked was widely accepted. As a result, an exceptional scientific opportunity presented itself. Since the principle drawn from the evidence was a negative proposition (i.e., randomness is impossible), it required only a single success to be overturned. Any investigator who could convincingly demonstrate that random behavior was possible could refute several decades of research. Enter Allen Neuringer of Reed College.

First, in a series of studies with pigeons, Neuringer and collaborator Suzanne Page showed that previous animal studies had been flawed.[8] After correcting earlier mistakes, they found that pigeons could indeed learn to peck randomly. Since the publication of Page and Neuringer's study, several other researchers have duplicated its results with both pigeons and rats. Having destroyed one myth, Neuringer went on to challenge another.

Believing that random behavior was a highly skilled response that must be acquired through reinforcement and practice, he set out to teach college students to produce random sequences. He sat Reed undergraduates in front of a computer and asked them to type sequences of ones and twos on the keyboard, but unlike other investigators, Neuringer gave his students feedback on their performance. After each trial, the computer screen printed a report of how random the last sequence had been. At the beginning of their training, all the students produced nonrandom sequences, but after several hours of practice, they all learned to make long series of ones and twos that, according to a number of very stringent tests, were random. Another myth shattered.

Neuringer's demonstrations notwithstanding, it is clear that we have difficulty with randomness. Furthermore, this difficulty affects our thinking about probability. For example, most people who are asked to evaluate the two series of six coin flips presented below say the second one is much more likely to occur.

$$\text{H H H H H H}$$
$$\text{H T T H T H}$$

In fact, both series have the same probability. The principle of independence tells us that each individual coin toss has an equal probability of 1/2 for a head and 1/2 for a tail, and to calculate the probability of several independent events coming together—their intersection—we merely multiply the individual probabilities. Thus, the probability of both sequences is determined by this simple equation:

$$\frac{1}{2} \times \frac{1}{2} \times \frac{1}{2} \times \frac{1}{2} \times \frac{1}{2} \times \frac{1}{2} = \left(\frac{1}{2}\right)^6 = \frac{1}{64}$$

Indeed, any other sequence of six coin flips has the same probability: 1/64. Similarly, any sequence of seven flips has a probability of:

$$\left(\frac{1}{2}\right)^7 \text{ or } \frac{1}{128}$$

Nevertheless, for two reasons, the first series, six straight heads, seems inconsistent with our concept of randomness. First, it is unbalanced. Knowing that heads and tails are equally likely, we expect any series of tosses to have approximately the same number of each. The second group of coin tosses meets this expectation, but the first seems highly skewed and, as a result, improbable. Of course, in the long run, the heads and tails will even out, but on the way to this point, there will be many sequences that are heavily populated with one or the other.

This is an example of what cognitive psychologists call the representativeness heuristic. Knowing that one hundred coin tosses are supposed to produce about fifty heads and fifty tails, we expect smaller strings to be representative of the larger group. Unfortunately, things are not that simple. With predictable regularity, short sequences will deviate substantially from a fifty/fifty split.[9]

A second common difficulty with randomness emerges when a random sequence appears systematic. For example, the sequences H H T T H H and H T H T H T seem to violate our expectation that random events are irregular and unpredictable. Randomness is mindless, erratic noise. It is not supposed to appear regular or methodical. Yet, as we have seen, each of these orderly sequences has the same 1/64 probability as any other six-toss series. At various points, any random process, like flipping coins, rolling dice, or having babies (in high school, I knew a family with seven girls and no boys: probability $\approx$ 1/128) can appear biased or systematic without being either.

These misunderstandings of randomness affect our thinking about daily life. In the world of sports, there is much talk of slumps and winning streaks. When a baseball player has hit safely in ten or more games, radio and TV announcers are likely to mention his hitting streak each time he comes to bat. Similarly, the manager whose team is "mired" in a slump will often change the batting order, hoping to get a win. Yet these fluctuations in performance are a natural feature of any random enterprise. In basketball, it is commonly believed that players get "hot." Suddenly every shot goes in, and the player is flooded with an intoxicating feeling of invincibility: it is impossible to miss. When one player has the "hot hand," it is standard practice to give him the ball as often as possible in an attempt to make points quickly. Former Detroit Pistons guard Vinnie Johnson was called "The Microwave" because he had a reputation as a streaky player who could suddenly get "hot" and sink a succession of shots to give his team an insurmountable lead. To examine the validity of this phenomenon, psychologist Thomas Gilovich and his colleagues studied the shooting of the Philadelphia 76ers basketball team during the 1980–81 season.[10] The 76ers were the only team in the National Basketball Association that kept a record of the sequence of each player's hits and misses. After examining several players' records for the entire season, Gilovich found that each player's shooting was consistent with a simple random process. None of the "hot" streaks was anything out of the ordinary. Not surprisingly, Gilovich's analysis of the "hot hand" has met with a cool reception among basketball professionals.

It is not difficult to see how misunderstandings of randomness can lead to superstition. If a basketball player changes socks and suddenly gets "hot," he may attribute his success to the change of clothes rather than to normal fluctuations in his performance. Indeed, British psychologist Susan Blackmore found that, as a group, believers in ESP have a poorer understanding of random processes, such as coin-flipping, than nonbelievers do.[11] Believers make more pronounced underestimates of the likelihood of strings of heads or tails than nonbelievers. As a result, they are more likely to attribute such occurrences to paranormal phenomena.

People often report that a magical object or action is initially lucky, then loses its effect. Formerly lucky things can sometimes become actively unlucky and taboo. A student once told me that her brother believed his performance on exams could be sabotaged by someone wishing him good luck, so his family was under strict orders to avoid doing so on the day of a test. When we understand that normal, random processes can involve surprisingly long streaks of both fortunate and unfortunate "luck," it is more difficult to attribute the ups and downs of life to the fluctuating powers of some object or ritual.

Coincidence

As we have seen, human beings are extremely sensitive to coincidence. We are fascinated and bewildered by events that come together despite seemingly impossible odds. Their very improbability leads us to search for their deeper significance. A number of famous authors have written extensively on the topic,[12] and both Swiss psychiatrist Carl Jung and Austrian biologist Paul Klammerer kept logs of coincidences they had experienced or heard of—over a twenty-year period in Klammerer's case.[13] Many people subscribe to a form of religious determinism that attributes all earthly events to God's direct influence and leaves no room for unplanned happenings or random processes, and several modern writers, including Sigmund Freud, Carl Jung, Arthur Koestler, and D. H. Lawrence, have expressed the view that mere coincidence does not exist.

As Freud's student and intellectual heir, Jung believed in a wide variety of paranormal phenomena, including ESP and ghosts. The psychological theory he developed was based on the mystical concept of a *collective unconscious*, a reservoir of latent memories inherited from our ancestors, both human and nonhuman, that contains basic ideas and concepts called *archetypes*.[14] Because it rests on these supernatural and unscientific foundations, Jung's theory has been much more widely embraced by artists, poets, and members of the New Age movement than by contemporary psychologists.

Nevertheless, Jung's concept of *synchronicity* represents the most famous theory of coincidence. Jung endorsed the notion of *unus mundus*, or "one world," which asserts that all reality, both physical and psychical, spiritual and worldly, is part of a single, related whole. Synchronous events, which he defined as coincidences that have subjective meaning to the observer and cannot be explained by physical cause and effect, were, in his view, the result of unconscious processes. He reported the following example:

> A young woman I was treating had, at a critical moment, a dream in which she was given a golden scarab. While she was telling me this dream I sat with my back to the closed window. Suddenly I heard a noise behind me, like a gentle tapping. I turned round and saw a flying insect knocking against the window-pane from outside. I opened the window and caught the creature in the air as it flew in. It was the nearest analogy to a golden scarab that one finds in our latitudes, a scarabaeid beetle, the common rose-chafer (*Cetonia aurata*), which contrary to its usual habits had evidently felt an urge to get into a dark room at this particular moment.[15]

Jung's theory suggests that his patient produced this example of synchronicity through the influence of unconscious archetypes which, though psychological entities, are capable of ghostly influences on the physical world. Her unconscious drew the beetle to the window and into the room.

Although it is easy for us to see how Jung and others could have attributed special significance to coincidental events, modern science does not. Mathematicians and psychologists who study coincidence have demystified it. A number of common logical errors and mathematical misunderstandings make some events seem more improbable than they really are, and our response to an improbable event is affected by a number of psychological factors. Nevertheless, belief in superstition and the paranormal is often strengthened by happenings that seem too unlikely to be mere chance. As we search for alternative hypotheses, superstitions often leap up to fill the void. Thus, a thorough discussion of superstition must examine the psychology of coincidence.

Chain Letters and the Law of Truly Large Numbers. When the likelihood of an event is described as "one chance in a million," we tend to think the odds are impossible. Yet given a million opportunities, the million-to-one shot will often happen. The noted statistician Sir Ronald Fisher stated what has come to be known as the Law of Truly Large Numbers[16] when he wrote, "The 'one chance in a million' will undoubtedly occur, with no less and no more than its appropriate frequency, however surprised we may be that it should occur to *us*."[17] Large numbers make unlikely events almost certain. Despite extremely long odds, someone will eventually win the lottery because millions of people play. A recent personal example helps illustrate the importance of large numbers to the maintenance of superstition.

While I was writing this book, I received a chain letter.[18] The old pyramid money-making schemes ("mail a dollar to the person at the top of the list") are now illegal in the United States, but superstitious chain letters, offering good luck, are allowed. Perhaps because the sender, like many people, was embarrassed by his or her belief in superstition, the typed envelope revealed no return address. Inside, a single sheet of paper described the basic rules of the chain and examples of good fortune that blessed those who kept it going. I was asked to make twenty copies of the letter and send them out to "friends and associates" within ninety-six hours. In return for this small labor and my $6.40 in postage, I could expect to receive "good luck" in four days. The bulk of the letter described a number of individuals who, after continuing the chain, had won millions in the lottery or experienced wonderful happenings. As a further inducement, the letter described various calamities that had befallen those who had failed to continue the chain, including lost fortunes, jobs, and lives. Finally, in a statement that seemed to be written specifically for me, the letter claimed that the chain worked "even if you [were] not superstitious." This was Pascal's Wager redux: one need not be a true believer; merely going through the motions will suffice.

At first glance, the recipient might be impressed with the events described in the letter; alternatively, one might question its veracity. And there is much to question. But even if we accept every word at face value, an understanding of the large numbers involved in such a scheme makes the events described in the letter less surprising—even commonplace. Let us begin by making a few conservative assumptions. First, if we give each participant the full four days to respond and if we give the Postal Service four full days to deliver the letters to those next in the chain, we are left with an eight-day cycle for passing on the letter. Often the cycle would be much shorter, but the eight-day figure is both reasonable and conservative. By dividing 365 days per year by eight days, we find that forty-five cycles would occur each year. Now, if we very cautiously estimate that only two of twenty recipients would actually continue the chain, the number of participants in a year of circulation is equal to 2^{45} or 35,184,372,088,832 (this is thirty-five million millions). Obviously, this number far exceeds the population of the planet (which is approximately 5.3 billion). If we consider the number of people who—like me—tempt fate by breaking the chain, the total number of recipients grows to an even more staggering figure. For every two faithful participants, there are eighteen who drop the ball, a ratio of 1 to 9. Thus, the number of nonparticipating recipients is equal to 2^{45} x 9 or 316,659,348,799,490 (316 million millions), and the total number of recipients—participants and nonparticipants—is 351,843,720,888,320 (351 million millions).

If one does not consider the enormous number of people who receive chain letters, the benefits of participating seem remarkable; however, these letters form not a chain, but an ever-expanding web. Millions of people participate, and with such large numbers of recipients, the lucky and unlucky events described in the letter are not remarkable. Our estimates ignore such factors as people who receive multiple copies of the letter and letters that are lost in the mail, both of which undoubtedly occur; furthermore, the assumption of two participants for every twenty recipients, although apparently conservative, is probably an overestimate. Nevertheless, it is obvious that these letters create an exploding galaxy of mail. Moreover, the letter I received was said to have been in circulation since 1953! With so many people receiving the letter, it is surprising that even more amazing events are not described (e.g., "Ronald Reagan mailed the letter and within four days he was elected President of the United States!").[19]

Yet obviously few people consider these large numbers as they ponder their decision to copy a chain letter. In addition, like many superstitions, the distribution of chain letters appears to cut across demographic barriers. In 1990 and 1991, a well-publicized chain letter circulated among many famous television and print journalists. Like the one I received, this letter promised good luck for those who continued the chain and bad luck for those who did not. Although they knew they were being superstitious, most of these intelligent, hard-bitten news people copied the letter and sent it on to several friends. Those continuing the chain included then deputy publisher (now publisher) of the *New York Times*, Arthur Sulzberger, Jr., *Washington Post* executive editor Benjamin C. Bradlee, Random House vice president Dona Chernoff, and ABC news correspondent Pierre Salinger. The chain-letter affair made most of these journalists uncomfortable, and a variety of justifications were offered. For example, clinging to the logic of Pascal's Wager, Gene Forman of the *Philadelphia Inquirer* wrote: "You understand that I am not doing this because I'm superstitious. I just want to avoid bad luck."[20]

Understanding coincidence. One of the pioneers of the growing, yet still small, field of the psychology of coincidence is Ruma Falk of Hebrew University in Jerusalem. She illustrated one common difficulty in the understanding of everyday coincidences by describing a personal experience.

While in New York City, standing at the street corner nearest where she was staying, Falk had a chance encounter with an old friend from Jerusalem. As might be expected, the two friends asked each other, "What are the chances of this happening?" The real answer depends upon what "this" we are talking about. If "this" is the chance encounter of these specific people in New York on a particular day, the probability is extremely small, and the friends' amazement is justified. But as Falk points out, everyday analysis of coincidence tends to be overly narrow. We focus on the specific event rather than the larger category of potential coincidences from which it is drawn. She described the problem more accurately by asking, What was the probability that—during the course of the year she was living in New York City—she would encounter "at any time, in any part of the city, anyone from my large circle of friends and acquaintances?"[21] The appearance of any one of her friends would have produced an equivalent coincidence, and any time or place in the city would have been equally surprising. Although several unknowns make it impossible to actually calculate this probability, it is clear that the chances are far more reasonable in Falk's restatement of the problem than in the typical, narrowly focused view.

This misunderstanding of chance-encounter coincidences is caused by a confusion of the *intersection* and *union* of events. In real life, each coincidence appears as a specific case—Falk and one of her friends. Therefore, we tend to think of the coincidence as a unique intersection: these particular friends, at this specific and very distant place, at this particular time. The probability of events coming together (intersecting) is calculated by multiplying the individual probabilities—an operation that tends to give intersections lower probabilities than either of the events alone. For example, in Falk's case, if we (somewhat arbitrarily) estimated the probability of her being on the particular corner during a particular minute at 1/10,000 and the probability of her friend being on that corner as 1/1,000,000, the probability of their being there together (by coincidence) would be the product of these numbers, or 1/10,000,000,000. In reality, the coincidence could have been produced by any number of similar encounters. Thus, the probability is the *union* (or sum) of the individual probabilities. Adding positive fractions, such as the probabilities of individual events, builds the numerator and increases its value, for example:

$$\frac{1}{4} + \frac{1}{4} = \frac{2}{4} = \frac{1}{2}$$

Given many opportunities for a chance encounter of this type, the probability increases substantially. Because we are struck by the specifics of our personal coincidence, however, we tend to underestimate its likelihood.[22]

This kind of error is further compounded when considering near matches. Often a coincidence is not a pure occurrence. You may have a chance meeting with a friend one day, then run into her on another day at a place somewhat near the first meeting point. You may meet someone who was not a friend of yours but who went to your high school. Although we are still surprised when they occur, these lesser coincidences are much more likely than we think. In these cases, the definition of a coincidence expands to include many more possibilities, and the union of these potential near matches can produce odds that are no longer so dismal.[23]

When it comes to superstition and coincidence, it is easy to see how a similarly constricted view of events can strengthen magical beliefs. In the case of the Go For Wand tragedy at the Breeders' Cup, Jane du Pont Lunger's mud-spattered shoes appear to have been specifically associated with her horse's race performances. As a result, only an accident that resulted in the death of the jockey would have importance equivalent to or greater than the actual events of that day. Given the apparent low probability of accidents like these, Lunger's forgotten lucky shoes appear to have created a disastrous day at the track. Although few outcomes can rival a career-ending injury, it is clear that merely losing the race would have confirmed the superstition. Go For Wand had enjoyed a great season and was considered an excellent candidate for Horse-of-the-Year honors. A poor showing would not have garnered as much attention as the accident that befell her, but this far more likely event would also have confirmed Ms. Lunger's superstition. As we will see, several other features of this coincidence enhance its psychological impact and substantiate the power of the forgotten shoes.

When math and statistics professors teach probability, one of their favorite examples of the vagaries of everyday odds is something called the "Birthday Problem." Typically, the instructor will ask the class, "What do you think are the chances that two people in this room have the same birthday?" Even in a fairly large class, most students will say the odds are quite low, and they are surprised to hear that the probability of a match is greater than .50 for a class as small as twenty-three students. My statistics courses are required for psychology majors and, as a result, can be as large as ninety students. Typically, a quick poll of the class identifies a match, and it is not uncommon to find two or three pairs of students born on the same date. The source of this underestimation of probability is the same as that in the chance-encounter situation. We tend to confuse intersection and union by thinking about matching one specific birthday rather than any pair of dates.[24]

Our difficulties with probabilities can lead us to underestimate or over-estimate the likelihood of everyday events. When we think about the Birth-day Problem we underestimate, but when we think about winning the lot-tery, for example, we tend to overestimate our chances. These mistakes can stem from innumeracy, from a lack of relevant information, or from both. Often we just do not have all the facts we need. To demonstrate this point, I sometimes ask my statistics students the following question: "If you die from a firearm injury in the United States, what is the probability that it will be at your own hand?" The answer is approximately .48. Suicide forms the largest category of firearm deaths in the United States. Homicides (including legal interventions) constitute approximately 47 percent, and the remainder is distributed between accidents and undetermined causes.[25] In this country, suicide is a social taboo that is rarely discussed, whereas homi-cide is widely reported in the media and, like all crime, vigorously debated by politicians, law enforcement officials, and social scientists. Because we rarely hear about suicide, we are not aware of the scope of the problem (31,102 deaths in 1993).[26] There is nothing suspicious about this uneven presentation of information. Typically, the news media do not publicize sui-cides out of respect for the victims' families and fear of encouraging imita-tion.[27] But this lack of balanced reporting skews our thinking about firearms policy and the relative importance of suicide-prevention pro-grams.[28]

The Breeder's Cup tragedy represents another case in which an unlikely event becomes more likely when we know the facts. At first glance, the death of Go For Wand seems improbable, but a closer examination sug-gests that the chances were better than we might guess. When thorough-breds run in intensely competitive races, their fragile limbs are subjected to great pressure and their hearts pound violently. In the wake of the 1990 Breeder's Cup tragedy, Mark Simon of the *Thoroughbred Times* undertook a statistical analysis of the incidence of "breakdowns" in horse racing.[29] Because the deaths of three horses on a single day seemed unlikely, many had suggested that Belmont Park was "jinxed" or in some way unsafe. Simon discovered that, during the fall 1990 season at Belmont, the proba-bility of a horse not finishing a race due to physical distress was .0039. Many of these DNFs were due to breakdowns, but because there is no standard lexicon for the classification of equestrian injuries, it is impossi-ble to say how many of these injuries ended careers.[30]

The 1990 fall season was an unusually bad one at Belmont Park. In the fall of 1989, the probability of a horse not finishing due to physical distress was only .0012, and in the spring seasons of 1989 and 1990 the probabil-ities were .0021 and .0024 respectively. However, in 1990 the North

American average for all tracks was .0040. Therefore, the number of DNFs during the fall season at Belmont was about average for all tracks, and earlier seasons had been exceptionally safe. It seems unlikely that so many tragic accidents should occur in such a brief period of time, but as we have seen, random processes will—more often than we think—produce strings of chance occurrences. Thus, there was no Belmont jinx.

Finally, it should be noted that DNFs due to physical distress are not as unlikely as we might think. Although we could conservatively estimate the denominator to be 1000 or even 10,000, the 1990 average of .0040 for all North American tracks is only 1/250. Thus, at a particular track, we could expect one breakdown for every 250th horse that comes to the gate. This is still a low probability, but not as low as many everyday uncertainties that give us great concern. For example, the probability of being infected with HIV, the virus that causes AIDS, from a blood transfusion ranges from 1 in 40,000 in urban areas to 1 in 150,000 in rural America. The probability that you will be a victim of violence in the suburbs is 1 in 2,000.[31] In relation to risks like these, Go For Wand's odds of one in 250 are not as long as they might seem.[32]

The Psychological Power of Coincidence

Problems with the mathematics of probability are the most important reasons for giving undue significance to coincidental events, but several psychological factors also influence our appreciation of a chance occurrence. The context of the event can heighten our surprise, which may, in turn, strengthen our belief in superstition. Although the role of context in our response to coincidence is a topic that is still ripe for further research, several influences have been discovered.

The second part of Ronald Fisher's Law of Truly Large Numbers suggested that our appreciation of rare events is affected by point of view, "however surprised we may be that it should occur to *us*."[33] Years later, Ruma Falk addressed this question in her research at the Hebrew University, demonstrating that we are indeed egocentric about coincidences. In one experiment, high-school and university students wrote a brief description of a coincidence that they had experienced. These descriptions were circulated among the participants and rated for their degree of surprisingness. As a group, the students rated their own coincidences significantly more surprising than those of the other participants. In another experiment, 215 Hebrew University students were asked to report their birthdays and a "name-sum"—a personal number calculated by adding together numbers associated with the letters of one's name.[34] This information was tallied, and the names of individuals whose birthdays or name-sums matched someone else's were written on the blackboard. As expected, most students did not have matches, but those who did rated these matches significantly more surprising than those who did not. Everyone was informed of the coincidences in exactly the same way, but personal involvement made them more meaningful. When a coincidence is experienced in the context of superstitious action or belief, as it was for Ms. Lunger at the racetrack, this self-versus-other bias builds greater faith in one's own superstitions than in those practiced by others.

You do not have to be a psychologist to know that people engage in selective remembering. The lonely, lovesick individual tends to ruminate on the joys of a past relationship and forget the difficult times. Alternatively, the person trapped in an unwanted relationship remembers only the fights and none of the fun. The magical quality of coincidences similarly biases our memory. As we live from day to day, we tend to remember events that can be meaningfully connected and forget those that, while of a similar nature, do not add to our sense of coincidence. For example, when you are surprised to meet a person who has the same unusual last name as your first-grade teacher, there is a tendency to forget all the other people whose nonmatching names you have heard throughout the intervening years before finally encountering this person.[35] This biased remembering makes coincidences seem to occur more often than they should by chance alone.[36]

Variability: Superstition and the Ups and Downs of Life

Just as randomness causes difficulties, so does the more general problem of variability. Coin flips and shots in basketball are discrete, dichotomous events: they can produce one of only two possible outcomes—head or tail, hit or miss. A sequence of several coin flips or shots produces a series of discrete events that, as we have seen, can often conflict with our conventional understanding of randomness. Yet many important processes are not discrete but continuous. For example, the price of a company's stock on the New York Stock Exchange varies freely and can, theoretically, assume an infinite range of values. Similarly, our subjective experience of health or illness is a continuous, moment-by-moment process that can be extremely variable. This kind of inherent variability can strengthen superstitious beliefs when a change produced by normal fluctuation is attributed to something else. Consider the following scenario:

> One winter day you are stricken with a bad cold. First you get a sore throat and runny nose. By day two, you have a hacking cough, a headache, and a body

ache, and you can barely drag yourself through the day. Dissatisfied with the side effects of most drugstore cold medicines, you decide to try something different. A friend has recommended a homeopathic remedy that she found extremely effective with a recent, particularly troublesome cold. She gives you a bottle of belladonna tablets and tells you to take one four times a day. You begin this therapy on day three, and by day four, your cold is almost completely gone. The treatment seems to have produced a rapid cure, without a hint of side effects. From that day forward, you become a convert to homeopathic medicine and, like your helpful friend, sing its praises to others in need.

This kind of personal experience is very common and often forms the basis for belief in homeopathy and a wide variety of unsubstantiated medical therapies. And why not? Seeing is believing. But what have you seen? Before answering these questions, a few words about homeopathy.

Homeopathic medicine was invented by the eighteenth-century German physician Samuel Hahnemann and has remained popular to the present day, both in the United States and Europe. It is based on the magical principle of homeopathy (similarity) described by Frazer (see chapter 1) which, in this version, holds that "like may be cured by like."[37] Specifically, homeopaths believe a disease can be eliminated by taking dilutions of substances that, in larger amounts, create the same symptoms as the ailment. Hahnemann tested a number of natural substances on healthy people, and the product of his research was a catalog of substances that bring on various symptoms. These are used in diluted form to treat a wide variety of diseases. belladonna is a popular homeopathic medicine made from the poisonous deadly nightshade plant.[38] It is sold in a highly diluted form, but taken at full strength, it can produce coma and death.

Despite its enduring popularity, homeopathy is not endorsed by the modern medical establishment for two reasons. First, the mechanism by which each remedy is purported to affect its cure is suspect. A basic principle of homeopathic medicine holds that the greater the dilution of the substance, the stronger its effect. As a result, the remedies used are often so highly diluted that it is doubtful whether any of the original substance remains. In the case of belladonna, this may be for the best; but if the substance is no longer present, how can it have an effect? Second, and more important, scientific investigations of homeopathic medicine have failed to support its usefulness.[39] So why do people believe in it? There are several reasons, but our scenario suggests two cognitive explanations: placebo effects and the misinterpretation of variability. We will discuss placebo effects later in the chapter.

We generally take medicine only when we are sick. Illness is already upon us, and we have a strong desire for restored health. Unbeknownst to most people, this situation is biased in favor of success. Simply because we are at a low point, an improvement is more likely than a further worsening of our condition—whether or not we treat the illness.[40] In the case of the typical common cold, the virus runs its course naturally, and we soon regain our good health. This cycle can be completed in a relatively few days, as in the case of our homeopathic scenario, or it can go on for two weeks. If the improvement comes soon after the beginning of treatment, we are likely to attribute it to the medicine, but we arrive at this conclusion unscientifically. We can never know what would have happened had we not treated the illness. To correct this problem, medical experiments compare a group of people who received the treatment (the treatment or experimental group) to a group who did not (the control group). Only when there is an adequate comparison group can we tell whether the observed changes differ substantially from the normal variation of the illness. Unfortunately, as individuals struggling to find solutions to our medical problems, we rarely have the luxury of a control group.

In the case of a chronic or terminal disease, the misinterpretation of variability has more serious consequences. People who are stricken with incurable illnesses often fall prey to unsubstantiated medical treatments. Throughout history, unsavory entrepreneurs have sought wealth through quackery; some purveyors of medical miracles even seem to believe they have something to offer. Faith healers and psychic surgeons remain popular despite the lack of evidence for their effectiveness,[41] and the AIDS epidemic has given rise to a new crop of ineffective nutritional and drug therapies.[42] Unsuspecting victims have spent large sums and suffered needless therapy in the hope of a cure, and some people who are seriously ill have chosen these unproven methods over accepted medical treatments—with tragic results. The Food and Drug Administration regulates many therapies, and consumer groups help warn the public about others, but a multitude of useless remedies are still uncritically promoted in the media and sold to millions of trusting customers. Moreover, many who have used these treatments are convinced that they work. Again, there are several explanations for this belief, but the misinterpretation of normal changes in condition is often a contributing factor—especially when these therapies are applied to diseases that are known to have a variable course, such as multiple sclerosis, AIDS, arthritis, and some forms of cancer.

Figure 4.1 diagrams the course of a hypothetical terminal disease.[43] The overall trend is downward, but as in the case of many illnesses, the path is punctuated by periods of relative health followed by relapse. We are most likely to seek treatment—both legitimate and illegitimate—at low points in the disease process (A); and when the erratic course of the illness leads to

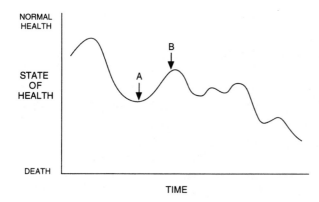

Figure 4.1   The variable course of a hypothetical terminal disease. If an ineffective medical treatment is applied at point A, the improvement at B may be attributed to it. *Source:* Hines (1988), Figure 18. Reprinted by permission of the publisher.

a period of improvement (B), we may attribute our relative health to an undeserving therapy. Similar fluctuations in condition are typical of several chronic, nonterminal illnesses, such as arthritis and multiple sclerosis, and research has found that sufferers of these diseases are particularly vulnerable to faith and psychic healers.[44]

When Shortcuts Fail Us: Heuristics, Biases, and the Maintenance of Superstition

For the last three decades, a large group of cognitive psychologists has doggedly pursued the illogical aspects of human thought. Having shaken off the standard propaganda about the "wonders of the human brain," they spend their time demonstrating how feebleminded we really are. Their studies of judgment and decision-making show that, although we are a very capable species, our ability to process information is limited.[45] These limitations fall into two broad categories. *Heuristics* are common rules and strategies that we use to simplify our thinking, and in many cases, they serve us well. Without engaging in a detailed analysis of every problem that arises, we can often employ a heuristic shortcut that will lead to a useful solution. In our discussion of randomness and coin-flipping, we encountered the representativeness heuristic, which says simply that a person or object will be representative of the group from which he, she, or it is drawn. If a man is described as "very shy and withdrawn, invariably helpful, but with little interest in people or the world of reality," we are more likely to believe that he is a librarian than a salesman because his personal traits are more consistent with the profile of a librarian; he seems representative of that group. In the case of random coin flips, a string of six heads in a row seems unlikely because it appears uncharacteristic of a process that should result in 50 percent heads and 50 percent tails. In many cases, heuristics lead to good decisions. Our everyday experience often generates rules to live by. For example, years of grocery shopping may lead to the following observation: "When I buy completely ripe bananas, they often turn brown and soft before they are eaten." This heuristic might well be very reliable and prove quite useful in purchasing provisions. As in the case of the librarian-versus-salesman judgment, however, the representativeness heuristic is little more than a stereotype that can do more harm than good.

The second category of shortcut is less a collection of adaptive strategies than a set of limitations that have been thrust upon us: *biases*. The complexity of many common problems makes it impossible—even for the talented *Homo sapien*—to gather and evaluate all relevant pieces of information. Sometimes important aspects of the situation are separated in time, making it difficult to detect their relationship. For example, the cause of a current illness may be a food eaten fifteen days earlier. In other cases, there is too much data for us to process. Under these circumstances we often show a bias, attending only to some aspects of the problem and ignoring others. This approach simplifies the process of judgment and decision-making, but, like heuristic reasoning, it can often lead to error.[46]

The topic of reasoning errors has become one of the most popular in the field of cognitive psychology.[47] Research in heuristics and biases has led to a new understanding of our decision-making in business, medicine, and government. As we will soon see, these cognitive errors also play a role in the maintenance of superstitious beliefs.

Illusory Correlations

When Wade Boggs eats chicken, Nancy Reagan consults an astrologer, or Jane du Pont Lunger wears her mud-spattered shoes, they do so in part because things turn out better than when they do not—or so they think. Each has detected a relationship—a correlation—between these actions and things they care about: hits, the safety of President Reagan, or winning horse races. Unfortunately, the everyday perception of correlation is prone to bias. We often fail to consider all relevant information, and, particularly when we are motivated to find a relationship, we focus our attention on events that seem to confirm that a relationship exists.

Although the following method of thinking is foreign to most of us, the clearest way to detect a correlation between two separate events (e.g., the presence or absence of muddy shoes and the presence or absence of a first-place finish) is by examining a 2 x 2 table. Imagine a group of sixty students, half of whom used a new study guide prior to taking a quiz and half of whom did not. The author of the study guide is interested in determining the relationship between using the guide and passing the quiz.[48] Figure 4.2 shows three possible results of this simple experiment. Table (a) shows a strong positive relationship between using the study guide and passing the test. The degree of relationship between two variables is often described by a correlation coefficient that ranges in value from -1.0 to +1.0. The correlation in Table (a) is a positive and very strong +.83. It would equal 1.0 if the lower left and upper right cells both contained zeros.[49] In other words, there would be a perfect positive relationship between using the study guide and passing the test if everyone who used the guide passed the test and everyone who did not use the guide failed. Table (b) provides less encouraging news. There is absolutely no relationship between using the guide and passing the test: correlation = 0. In this case, the results suggest that the quiz was fairly difficult (less than half the class passed); however, the pass/fail ratios are the same for students who used and did not use the guide. (8/16 = 12/24 = 1/2.) As a result, the study guide was not a factor in quiz performance. Finally, Table (c) shows a particularly damning outcome. There is a negative correlation between using the guide and passing the quiz.[50] Apparently, instead of improving performance, the study guide misled and confused most of those who used it. *Not* using the guide led to better performance.

In our everyday attempts to detect correlation, things are not as neatly arranged as they are in Figure 4.2. Our successes and failures occur over time, and it is not easy to assemble them into 2 x 2 tables. Furthermore,

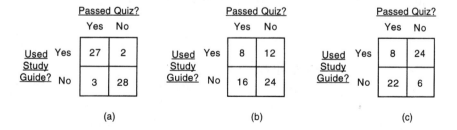

Figure 4.2   Three sets of hypothetical results from a field test of a study guide. Each 2 x 2 table divides the sixty students into those who used and did not use the study guide and those who passed or did not pass the quiz. For example, in Table (a) twenty-seven students used the study guide and passed the quiz.

without some instruction in the basics of correlation, many people fail to realize that we must look at all four cells of the table to determine whether a relationship is present. Without examining the pass/fail ratios in both rows of Table (c), it would be impossible to say whether the two variables were related.

Cognitive psychologists have found that, in a number of situations, we are susceptible to *illusory correlation,* a bias that leads us to believe things are related when they are not. This bias appears in two forms, depending on its cause.[51] The first, attentional bias, is the result of paying too much attention to the upper left-hand box of the 2 x 2 table and not enough to the other three. For example, in one experiment a group of nurses was asked to look at one hundred cards, each of which contained excerpts from a patient's record.[52] The nurses were asked whether there was a relationship between a particular symptom and a particular disease. When the data from the cards are summarized in a table, as they are in Figure 4.3, it is clear that the symptom and the disease are not correlated; people with the symptom are equally likely to get the disease or not get it. Conversely, about half the people who do not have the symptom will still go on to get the disease. Nevertheless, 85 percent of the nurses said there was a relationship between the two. Additional testing showed that the crucial factor was the number of Yes/Yes cases. If the number in this cell was relatively large, people said the two events were related—regardless of the numbers in the other cells. Thus, by paying attention only when things occur together, we tend to see a correlation when none is there.

This example shows that even when we have no particular stake in the outcome, attentional biases can convince us that things are related when they are not, but a second form of illusory correlation is produced by the motivational effects of prior belief. Often we are not impartial in our assessment of the situation. For various reasons, we may already believe that a relationship exists between two variables, and this prior belief can

Got Disease?

		Yes	No
Patient Had Symptom?	Yes	37	33
	No	17	13

Figure 4.3 The relationship between a particular symptom and the development of a disease. Based on 100 hypothetical patients used in a study of the perception of correlation (Smedslund, 1963).

bias our judgment. The influence of prior belief was dramatically demonstrated in a series of studies by clinical psychologists who use projective tests, such as the Draw-a-Person test and the Rorschach ink-blot test. Most scientific research has shown these assessment instruments to have limited (Rorschach) or no (Draw-a-Person) validity, yet they remain popular among clinicians. To gain an understanding of this phenomenon, researchers Loren and Jean Chapman asked clinicians to examine a group of tests and assess whether there was a relationship between a certain patient response and a psychological condition. Psychologists tended to find a relationship between test response and diagnosis only if they believed such a relationship existed—even though, objectively, the two were completely unrelated. Therefore, one explanation for the continued popularity of projective tests is illusory correlation: clinical psychologists believe test results are related to patient diagnosis, and they see what they believe.[53]

● ● ●

Illusory correlation plays an important role in the maintenance of many superstitions.[54] Believers hope to gain an edge over uncertainty and are often quite motivated to find something that "works." Unfortunately, in most cases, undue attention is paid to times when the superstition was exercised *and* a happy outcome ensued. Other cases are ignored. For example, let us return to the spattered shoes. Jane Lunger's shoes first became muddy at Saratoga in 1990, a race Go For Wand won. She wore the shoes for the next three races, and her horse was the fastest in the field. Finally, at the Breeder's Cup, the shoes were forgotten, and Go For Wand broke down. These results are presented in Table (a) in Figure 4.4. The numbers reflect a perfect correlation of +1.0, but some important information is missing. When a superstition is first introduced, there is a tendency to wipe the slate clean and evaluate its performance only on the basis of subsequent events. But what about the other times the filly raced? The addition of races prior to Saratoga completes the picture and makes it possible to assess the power of Ms. Lunger's shoes.

Go For Wand's complete record is presented in Table (b) of Figure 4.4. She was a remarkably talented horse, losing only twice in twelve starts. (Coincidentally, the tragic 1990 Breeder's Cup was her thirteenth professional race!) Furthermore, both of her previous losses were second-place finishes. But, when we examine the horse's full racing career, with and without the muddy shoes, the importance of Ms. Lunger's footwear is diminished. Most of the time Go For Wand was a winner, and her owner's shoes appear to have nothing to do with it.[55] In addition, we can reduce any sense of responsibility Ms. Lunger may feel by noting that, prior to

	Won Race?	
	Yes	No
Wore Muddy Shoes? Yes	4	0
Wore Muddy Shoes? No	0	1

(a)

	Won Race?	
	Yes	No
Wore Muddy Shoes? Yes	4	0
Wore Muddy Shoes? No	6	3

(b)

Figure 4.4 The relationship between Ms. Lunger's wearing her lucky mud spattered shoes and Go For Wand's race performance. In Table (a) only the races associated with the superstition are presented: the 1990 season, from Saratoga to the Breeder's Cup. In Table (b), the horse's full racing career is presented.

Saratoga, Go For Wand raced safely in eight races—without the help of Ms. Lunger's muddy shoes.

Wade Boggs's faith in chicken is based on an even more dramatic reliance on limited information. Whatever experience he may have with non-chicken pregame meals is now completely overshadowed by years of eating nothing but chicken. By faithfully exercising his superstition he has systematically eliminated one half of the 2 x 2 table. To demonstrate this point, Mr. Boggs's results for the 1988 season (the last year he won the American League batting title) are presented in Figure 4.5. Based on his own testimony, we can assume that Mr. Boggs ate chicken before every one of his 155 games; therefore, all of his trips to the plate—both successes and failures—are recorded in the upper row of the table. It is impossible to know whether or not his choice of meal helped because we have nothing to compare it to. We know that chicken is correlated with Mr. Boggs, but we do not know whether or not chicken is correlated with hits.

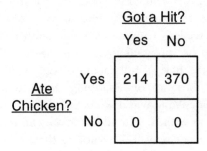

	Got a Hit?	
	Yes	No
Ate Chicken? Yes	214	370
Ate Chicken? No	0	0

Figure 4.5 The relationship between Wade Boggs's pregame chicken consumption and his batting performance.

Ms. Lunger's and Mr. Boggs's superstitions pose problems that are somewhat unique. Certain parts of the 2 x 2 table are difficult or impossible to evaluate. Mrs. Lunger's superstition did not develop until late in Go For Wand's career, and it would not be obvious to everyone that it should be evaluated in relation to the filly's pre-Saratoga performance. Mr. Boggs exercises his superstition with such religious regularity that it is impossible to assess its validity. Everyday experiences with superstition are often less skewed. The use of a lucky object will sometimes be successful and sometimes not. On other occasions, fortunate things happen without the aid of superstition. When, under these varied circumstances, belief persists, selective attention or prior belief in the virtue of the superstition is often the explanation. By placing great value on successful cases and ignoring the other three quadrants of the 2 x 2 table, the believer falls prey to illusory correlation.

Keeping the Faith

The effect of prior belief on the perception of correlation leads us to a related issue: the resilience of superstitious ideas in the face of conflicting information. The American philosopher Charles Peirce is famous for having outlined four paths to understanding, the least recommended of which was "the method of tenacity"—clinging to a familiar idea simply because it is familiar and comfortable.[56] This is a very unscientific approach, yet a human one. The ideal scientist should be ready to reject the most dearly held maxim at a moment's notice, provided it is convincingly refuted. Nevertheless, in the real and less-than-ideal world, most of us—scientist and nonscientist alike—give up familiar ideas with great reluctance.

From time to time, either at the insistence of others or to satisfy ourselves, we may reassess our beliefs. We ask questions and devise tests of assumptions. However, when we are committed to a particular view, we find it difficult to be objective. Our personal investment influences both the questions we ask and the conclusions we make. Often the problem stems from difficulties with inductive reasoning, the process of drawing general conclusions from a specific case—a notoriously fallible procedure, but a necessary aspect of science and experimentation. Consider this personal example.

One autumn day, I took my then three-year-old son to the park. It was the first really cold day of the season, and he was wearing a pair of red mittens. I was wearing grey woolen gloves. As I pushed him on the swing, I asked, "What is the difference between mittens and gloves?" His answer was very confident: "Gloves don't have trains on them." He had made an inductive error. I had asked him to draw a conclusion, to extract a general rule regarding gloves and mittens. His job would have been simpler had the items in question differed in only one way, but this was not the case. Our handwear was of contrasting colors, sizes, and shapes (fingers versus no fingers), and, most important, the backs of his mittens were embroidered with a train engine on each hand. Trains have always played an important role in my son's life; therefore, the lack of trains on my gloves was, by far, the most salient distinction to his young mind.

Though more sophisticated, adult scientific reasoning often involves induction. A test is devised, and based on its results, conclusions are drawn. Errors, like that commited by my son, are common when all the alternative conclusions have not been considered (fingers versus no fingers), and they are particularly likely when the scientist is committed to one answer. In this case, the investigator is apt to construct the test so as to validate his or her beliefs. This last example is known as confirmation bias, and it can be an obstacle to effective reasoning for scientist and nonscientist alike.

The influence of prior belief in astrology on reasoning about the validity of horoscopes was demonstrated in a study by psychologists Peter Glick and Mark Snyder.[57] Glick and Snyder found twelve people who believed in astrology and fourteen who were very skeptical of astrology and asked them to interview a person whose horoscope had been prepared by a professional astrologer. The horoscope suggested that the individual in question was very extroverted. When asked to test this hypothesis, both believers and skeptics asked a large number of questions aimed at confirming the conclusion about extroversion (e.g., "Do you like to go to parties?") and few questions aimed at denial. Furthermore, the target person was, in fact, a confederate—a person in the employ of the experimenter. This confederate was instructed to answer in the affirmative to both introverted and extroverted questions. Thus, the information each skeptic or believer obtained depended entirely on what questions were asked. Since both groups asked predominantly confirming questions in approximately equal numbers, both groups received the same information.

So how did the two groups respond to this confirming information? As might be expected, believers received information that was consistent with their view of astrology and they tended to say the horoscope closely matched the target person's personality. This was true whether the individual questioner asked a small or a large number of confirming questions. This result shows that prior belief tends to bias the observer in favor of astrology, regardless of the information obtained. In contrast, skeptics received information that was generally confirming of the extroverted hypothesis but inconsistent with their skeptical view of astrology. In contrast to the believers, skeptics who asked more confirming questions—and therefore received more confirming information—said the horoscope was more accurate. Skeptics who chose to ask more disconfirming, introverted questions—and therefore received more disconfirming information—said the horoscope was less accurate. Thus, both skeptics and believers showed a confirmation bias in their choice of questions, even when, in the case of the skeptics, they had no personal investment in the hypothesis they were testing. Believers showed an additional bias in their use of the information received. As a group, they said the horoscope was accurate whether their probing of the confederate produced strong or weak support for that conclusion.

Just as selective memory can make a coincidence seem especially unlikely, so can it help to maintain our beliefs. The supporter of a political candidate can more readily recall the candidates strengths and accomplishments than her weaknesses and failures. Once again, merely having a viewpoint biases our thinking. Psychologists Dan Russell and Warren Jones demonstrated the effect of selective memory on the maintenance of belief in extrasensory perception in a simple study of college students.[58] First, two groups of students were selected, one made up of believers in ESP and the other of people who were skeptical about the existence of ESP. These groups were further divided, so that half the believers and half the skeptics received information supporting the existence of ESP. The other half of each group received information not supporting the existence of ESP. Thus, there were four groups in all. Each student was asked to read an abstract reporting several ESP experiments. All of the abstracts were identical except that in the support-for-ESP groups, the studies showed significant ESP effects and in the no-support-for-ESP groups, they did not. Next, the students filled out a mood questionnaire to assess their current level of emotional arousal, and finally, they were given a short test on the content of the abstracts.

The experimenters found that all of the students remembered the abstract well *except* ESP believers who read the unsupportive version. This group remembered significantly less of the abstract and in some cases actually reversed the conclusion, saying that the results supported rather than challenged the existence of ESP. The mechanism underlying this biased memory of contradictory information may be *cognitive dissonance*, a psychological theory introduced by former University of Minnesota psychologist Leon Festinger. According to Festinger, when a person receives information that is in conflict with a strongly held belief, a kind of dissonance is created that produces heightened emotional arousal. This arousal can, in turn, motivate the individual either to defend or to alter the original belief. Consistent with this view, the students in the ESP study whose beliefs were not confirmed by the abstract reported greater emotional arousal on the mood questionnaire. Thus, the poor memory of ESP believers who read the unsupportive abstract may have been a defensive reaction motivated by cognitive dissonance.

Festinger used cognitive dissonance theory to understand one of the most dramatic examples of belief maintained in the face of unsupportive information. In 1956 he published a book, with Henry Riecken and Stanley Schachter, titled *When Prophecy Fails.*[59] It was a nonfiction account of a small religious group that predicted the destruction of the world by flood on a specific day. Leaders of the group said that faithful members would be saved by spacemen who would appear just before the apocalypse. In preparation for their trip, several people quit their jobs and discarded valuable possessions. When the flood did not occur on the appointed day, many group members became even more devoted to their leaders, not less. Having committed themselves so completely to the group, it was easier to diminish dissonance by reaffirming their beliefs than by admitting they had been wrong.

Television interviewers often reveal their attitudes toward their subjects by the kinds of questions they ask. If the interviewer is favorably inclined, the questions are often friendlier. The less favorable interviewer's questions are more critical. We exhibit a similar bias when examining evidence that is either consistent with or inconsistent with our beliefs. In a study conducted at Stanford University, two groups of students were selected: one consisting of people who believed that capital punishment was an effective crime deterrent and one of people who did not.[60] All of the students were asked to read and evaluate summaries of two studies of the death penalty, one supporting the deterrent effect and one not. All of the students, regardless of their position, tended to be more critical of the disconfirming study—the one contradicting their own view—than the confirming one. Confirming studies were judged "more convincing" and "better conducted." Of course, everyone read the same research summaries, so the different results were the product of biased evaluation. Furthermore, after reading the studies, both groups said that they felt stronger belief in their initial position and that they were even more convinced of the correctness of their view. Rather than being drawn together by exposure to information supporting both positions, the two groups were pushed further apart.

This kind of skewed judgment is common wherever strongly held beliefs are found, and in many of these cases, belief in superstition or the paranormal is quite strong. Although it has not been tested directly, the Stanford study suggests that both skeptics and believers would be more critical of evidence that opposed their viewpoints. Interestingly, skeptical authors writing about the paranormal have often made this bias explicit, arguing that "extraordinary claims demand extraordinary proof."[61] For example, the assertion that Transcendental Meditation (TM) makes you feel good might be accepted on the basis of testimonial. If several people who had tried it said it felt good, we would not require further evidence. However, if several people said they had used Transcendental Meditation to levitate their bodies several inches above the ground, we would need more proof. This second claim contradicts the law of gravity, which, for those of us who live on Earth, is a constant. Paranormal claims, by definition, contradict accepted principles of science, and therefore, skeptics argue—perhaps justifiably—that a higher standard of proof is required than would be needed for more conventional claims. For their part, believers in ESP and other paranormal phenomena have often taken the opposite position, arguing that the methods of "conventional scientific knowledge" need to be relaxed and that other evidence must be allowed into court.[62] This controversy suggests that the biased evaluation of information about paranormal phenomena helps to maintain strongly held beliefs on both a conscious and an unconscious level.

When Only Superstitious Thoughts Come to Mind

For many people, traveling by air is an anxious experience. They tense up during the takeoff and landing, and their hearts race at just a hint of turbulence. When the fear grows serious enough to affect a person's business or family life, he or she may seek help from a clinical psychologist. Fear of flying is quite common, even among those who know that air travel is one of the safest forms of transportation. Driving your own car is much more dangerous, yet driving phobias are relatively rare. Why? Because it is easier to recall images of spectacular airplane crashes than examples of fatal car crashes. When an airliner full of passengers falls from the sky, many people die at once, and the event draws national media attention. In contrast, individual car accidents affect far fewer people and are given only routine coverage by local news media. Thus, because memories of spectacular air disasters come more readily to mind—are more *available*—they have greater influence on the thoughts and emotions associated with flying. As previously noted, people tend to underestimate the frequency of suicide, and here, too, the availability heuristic and unbalanced reporting are to blame.

Fear of flying is maintained by other factors as well. For example, most people drive or ride in cars more often than they fly, and their fears of driving diminish as they become accustomed to the experience. In contrast, flying is an infrequent, somewhat special, event that rarely becomes as commonplace as driving. Some people also suggest that their anxiety about flying comes from the relative lack of control. Drivers have greater control over their vehicles than airplane passengers do, and for some it is this diminished influence that makes air travel unpleasant. Later in this chapter, we will see how important a sense of control is to the human psyche. We want to be in charge—or at least feel as if we are—even when our control is more imagined than real.

Whenever the information we receive is unbalanced, the availability heuristic affects our thinking and judgment, and the information we receive about superstition and the paranormal is unbalanced in at least two ways. First, when we experience unlikely events, the scientific and mathematical explanations discussed in this chapter are not generally close at hand. Anyone who has successfully negotiated high school can apply mathematics to problems of household finance and engineering (e.g., calculating a monthly budget or estimating the quantity of fabric needed to make a set of curtains), but most people are ill-prepared to estimate probabilities. Because probabilistic explanations are less available, a mental search for the cause of a particularly fortuitous or unfortuitous event often leads to "luck" instead of "chance." Someone once said, "when the only tool you have is a hammer, everything begins to look like a nail." In a sense, the bits of information we hold in memory are our tools of explanation. If, because of unbalanced or deficient exposure, we lack relevant information, our judgment may suffer. Unfortunately, popular culture provides more-than-adequate exposure to superstitious and paranormal theories and less-than-adequate exposure to science and mathematics.

The availability heuristic also plays a role in choosing a course of action. Although advertising executives probably do not think in these terms, one of their most important goals is to use the availability heuristic to influence consumer behavior. Advertisements teach us the name of a product and what it looks like. Repeated exposure is used to strengthen these verbal and visual memories so that, when the need arises, the consumer will draw upon them in making a purchasing decision. If we cannot remember the product, it is not available for decision-making. Thus, the Coca-Cola Company hopes that our memories of Coke will be both numerous and salient when we are thirsty.

Obviously, commercial advertising is designed to achieve other goals as well. Advertisers promote a positive attitude toward their product by pairing it with music, attractive people, and beautiful scenery. And in many cases, the advertisement makes a logical appeal to the consumer, outlining the product's benefits over the competition and stressing its relative value. But the basic goal is simply to make us remember the product.

Advertising and the availability heuristic have similar effects on decisions to engage in superstitious behavior. For example, many lovelorn individuals—most of them women—consult an astrologer, numerologist, tarotcard reader, or psychic in the hope of finding out what their futures hold. In exchange for the fee, these people undoubtedly receive a number of benefits: the personalized attention of a caring individual, a sense of entertainment and wonder, and a feeling of hope and reduced uncertainty about the future. There are a variety of other ways—many of them less expensive— to gain these same rewards, but if the customer has not been exposed to them, alternative strategies will not come to mind. In our increasingly urban society, loneliness is a growing problem, yet we receive little instruction in constructive methods of coping. In contrast, our exposure to paranormal methods of coping is extensive and multifaceted. Most newspapers print daily horoscopes, and many women's magazines publish a regular astrology column. Films, television, and popular literature present psychic prediction and other paranormal events as if they were genuine phenomena. And with the introduction of "900-line" telephone services advertised in newspapers, magazines, and on television, the market for psychics and astrologers has expanded to include anyone who has a telephone. Media exposure and effective advertising have also led to greater word-of-mouth marketing for psychics and astrologers.[63] As long as these methods of coping are aggressively promoted, they will continue to affect the choices we make.

Confusing Chance and Skill

Despite its negative image (Aristotle placed gamblers in the same category as thieves and plunderers),[64] gambling has become a pervasive feature of American culture, primarily due to the spread of state lotteries. In colonial times, legal lotteries were often used to finance public projects, and in the nineteenth century, they remained popular as fundraising vehicles for church and civic groups. Eventually, however, unscrupulous commercial operators entered the scene and opposition to lotteries began to grow. In 1890, Congress prohibited the use of the mail to conduct or advertise lotteries and thus effectively eliminated them. This prohibition continued until New Hampshire introduced the first legal lottery of this century in 1964. Today three fourths of the states offer lotteries, and for most Americans, the opportunity to gamble for substantial cash prizes is as close as the corner store. Soon it may become even more convenient with the appearance of in-home games that can be played via telephone and cable television. This form of state-sponsored gambling and others, such as keno and video poker, are likely to spread further because they are seen as a painless way to increase state revenue. Politicians and their constituents alike tend to prefer the potential social and moral ills of gambling to the unpleasantness of raising taxes.[65]

The growth of modern lotteries is a dazzling story of marketing success. On April 26, 1989, the jackpot of the Pennsylvania lottery rose to $100 million, and the news appeared on the front pages of newspapers throughout the country. Hopeful players flocked to the state from Illinois, Ohio, and New York, and on the day prior to the drawing, a single-day record of 24 million tickets were sold.[66] Today, these stories of "lotto fever" are commonplace, but at the beginning, lottery participation was less than overwhelming. Despite its novelty, the 1964 New Hampshire lottery failed to create a gambling sensation; it was not until New Jersey introduced its lottery in 1971 that sales began to improve. Why? What transformed a minor curiosity into the booming, billion-dollar industry that it is today? To be sure, better marketing was important; nowadays, state lotteries are often promoted in television commercials and print ads, and tickets can be purchased at restaurants, grocery stores, gas stations, and pharmacies. But the most important innovation of the New Jersey lottery was a simple change in the way the game was played. The New Hampshire lottery was a passive game, similar to a sweepstakes or a common raffle: participants bought a numbered ticket that represented a chance to win the jackpot. Drawings occurred relatively infrequently, usually twice a year, and the bettors won when the number on their tickets matched the number drawn. For the first time, New Jersy introduced a computer-controlled system that allowed players to pick their own numbers. Because the method of drawing winning numbers was completely random, the ability to choose a lottery number had absolutely no effect on the odds of winning, but it had a profound influence on the popularity of the game.

By allowing the player to choose a number prior to the drawing, the New Jersey lottery capitalized on a cognitive bias known as *the illusion of control*. Psychologist Ellen Langer first demonstrated that when a game of chance includes some of the features of a skilled activity, players tend to believe they have greater influence over the outcome. In one experiment, office workers were given the opportunity to play a lottery. Half the players chose their tickets—football cards showing pictures of various athletes—from a box containing several candidates; half were merely handed a ticket. Although their chances were no better than the others, players who chose their own tickets expressed greater confidence in their ability to win.

Giving a game of chance the flavor of a competitive sport also leads to unwarranted confidence. In another study, Langer devised a simple and completely random card game (similar to the child's game War), then put Yale students together to play against each other. Unknown to the other, one "competitor" in each game was a confederate. When the confederate in Langer's experiment was awkward and wore sloppy clothes, the naive student players felt they were more capable of winning, but when the the confederate was confident and dapper, competitors felt their chances were not as good.[67]

The Illusion of Control

Viewed objectively, playing the lottery is an activity governed completely by chance. There is nothing the player can do to improve the odds that a particular number will win. And, of course, the odds are very bad. Although for obvious reasons they do not emphasize the figures in their advertising campaigns, many states now disclose the probabilities of winning each lottery prize. Even when probabilities are not provided, however, they are usually quite easy to calculate. Most big jackpot lotteries determine the winning number by placing a group of numbered balls in a drum, mixing them up, and allowing six or seven balls to roll out at random. The result is referred to as the winning combination.[68] The probabilities for each individual ball are not independent, because as each one rolls out of the drum, it slightly alters the probability that the next ball will match one of the numbers on the player's ticket, but the changing probabilities are easy to determine.

Consider the case of the New York State Lotto. It consists of fifty-four numbers, from which the player must pick six. Imagine that, having chosen your numbers and purchased a ticket, you are poised at the edge of your seat, watching the drawing on television. Off-stage someone throws a switch, and the fifty-four balls begin to bounce gaily in a Plexiglas drum. With the air of a carnival barker, a tuxedoed lottery official says a few encouraging words, then opens a trap door from which the first ball slowly emerges. If this ball matches one of the six numbers on your ticket, you are still in the running. As a result, the probability of a match on the first ball is simply 6/54. But now, assuming the first ball *was* a match, there is one less ball in the drum and one less number on your ticket for the next ball to match. As a result, the probability that the second ball matches one of the remaining numbers on your ticket is 5/53. The fractions continue to descend accordingly as the remaining balls tumble out, with the sixth ball having a probability of 1/49. Since you are interested in matching all six numbers (the outcome that wins you the big prize), we must calculate the probability of the intersection of these six events by multiplying the individual probabilities. Thus, the probability of winning the top prize with a single ticket is:

$$\frac{6}{54} \times \frac{5}{53} \times \frac{4}{52} \times \frac{3}{51} \times \frac{2}{50} \times \frac{1}{49} = \frac{6 \times 5 \times 4 \times 3 \times 2 \times 1}{54 \times 53 \times 52 \times 51 \times 50 \times 49} = \frac{720}{18,595,558,800} = \frac{1}{25,827,165}$$

You have one chance in approximately 26 million. Actually, a minimum bet in the New York State Lotto is one dollar, which entitles you to pick two combinations of numbers. Therefore, the probability that one of these combinations will win is 2/25,827,165 or 1/12,913,583. Economists use the concept of *expected value* to help analyze risky decisions, such as whether or not to buy a lottery ticket. They suggest that the value of a wager is equal to the amount of the prize multiplied by the probability of winning it. Thus, for the New York State Lotto the value of the ticket is equivalent to its actual price ($1.00) when the jackpot rises to $12,913,583.[69]

When no one picks the winning number for a particular drawing, the jackpot "rolls over" and continues to build. Unfortunately, when the top prize rises to a dizzying figure, another factor begins to affect the value of a lottery ticket. As the Pennsylvania case makes clear, multimillion dollar prizes create a sensation that fuels massive sales. When many millions of tickets are sold for a particular lottery drawing, there is an increased probability that more than one player will have chosen the winning combination. Since multiple winners split the top prize, this situation further reduces the expected value of the ticket. For many players, there is an intangible entertainment aspect to playing the lottery that increases its value, but taken as a simple financial investment, lotteries are a bad bet.

This is the sad fact—in most cases, to say that winning the lottery is a million-to-one shot is an understatement. Furthermore, the process of determining a winning number is completely random and unaffected by any strategy the player may use. Nevertheless, bettors employ a number of personal strategies for picking numbers (Some refuse to reveal their methods, saying: "Does Macy's tell Gimbels?"[70]), and there is a substantial industry in lottery advisors and betting systems. A wide variety of books, magazines, and computer programs claims to offer proven methods for winning. In marketing their products, many state lottery commissions capitalize on the popular fascination with numbers and numerology. Although carefully avoiding the suggestion that such systems improve the player's odds, lottery advertisements sometimes highlight the mystique of numbers and encourage the use of birthdays and lucky numbers. Much of the appeal of these methods derives from the sense of control they provide.

But "instant-ticket" lottery games offer little player involvement and still remain popular. In these games, the bettor purchases a scratch-off ticket that is already either a winner or a loser. The retailer merely hands the ticket over the counter. These games remain popular for two reasons. First, they generate interest through the use of seasonal themes and changing formats. Second, and more important, they offer immediate feedback and reward. The player can determine whether or not he or she has won before leaving the store, and in many cases, winning tickets can be exchanged for cash at the same location. Whereas the computerized Lotto and Daily Numbers games rarely change and typically involve delayed feedback and payoff, instant tickets offer novelty and immediacy.

The influence of the illusion of control is most obvious in lotteries, but many games of pure chance are affected by this psychological phenomenon. If they are fairly constructed and used, roulette wheels, decks of cards, and dice are merely random-number generators. The games constructed around these machines of chance are usually more sophisticated than a simple lottery, and as a result, certain betting strategies are objectively more rational than others. For example, putting one's entire stash on a single number at a roulette table can, theoretically, lead to a tremendous windfall, but the narrow odds make it a reckless bet. Nevertheless, much of what people do while playing these games is affected by the illusion of control. Whether integral to the progress of the game (e.g., craps and card games) or limited to the selection of a betting strategy (e.g., roulette), the player's role is often large enough to blur the line between chance and skill.

The importance of player involvement in dice-rolling was strikingly demonstrated in a study of psychokinesis and the illusion of control. The process of altering physical events through mental effort alone is called psychokinesis (PK), and most scientists, both psychologists and physicists, agree that it has yet to be convincingly demonstrated.[71] Yet, as the Gallup polls indicate, 7 percent of Americans report having witnessed PK firsthand. Undoubtedly many others, who have not witnessed it, believe it is possible. To examine a number of influences on belief in PK, psychologists Victor Benassi, Paul Sweeney, and Gregg Drevno from California State University at Long Beach conducted a series of studies on dice-rolling.[72] The experimenters devised a simplified die, green on three of its six sides and red on the other three, and a "die funnel" into which the cube was thrown. After being shaken in a dice cup and tossed into the funnel, the die would roll to a stop inside a closed box that prevented the participants from seeing the outcome. The experimenters were interested in the level of confidence people had in their ability to influence the roll of the die, and they did not want their participants to be either encouraged or discouraged by seeing the outcome. To examine the effects of personal involvement on belief in PK, pairs of Cal State students were asked to concentrate on rolling a particular color on the die. Before each roll, the students were given a target color, and prior to tossing the die, the pair were to concentrate on that color for ten seconds. Both students tried to use mental energy to influence the roll of the die; however, only one person actually rolled it. After each roll, both members recorded how confident they felt about their effect on the die. Benassi and his colleagues found that, although the active member of the pair was determined by a coin toss, students who actually rolled the die had significantly greater confidence in their PK abilities than those who merely concentrated on the target color. Just as the illusion of control produced by the freedom to choose one's lottery number increases gamblers' confidence, active involvement in dice-rolling increases belief in PK. In other experiments, Benassi found that, as might be expected, students who had greater belief in paranormal phenomena in general were more confident in their PK abilities than nonbelievers. In addition, students who had a stronger internal locus of control—felt they had personal control over the events in their lives—had greater belief in their PK abilities.[73]

When games of pure luck require some action of the player, however small, the psychological line between between chance and skill begins to blur. Dice and lottery players start to believe in magic. But success can also be intoxicating. Investigating the illusion of control, Ellen Langer and Jane Roth discovered that common misunderstandings of randomness can make us believe we have power over chance.[74] Yale University undergraduates were asked to predict the results of thirty coin tosses. An experimenter tossed a coin, the student called out a prediction while the coin was in the air, and the experimenter reported the outcome. In fact, the feedback given to participants followed one of two predetermined patterns of "wins" and "losses." Both sequences contained fifteen wins and fifteen losses, but one series had most of its wins near the beginning and the other had most at the end. Langer and Roth found that students who were told they were successful on several early tosses were significantly more confident in their predictions than those who got little positive feedback early on—despite both groups having the same total "success." Langer and Roth concluded that their students judged their ability to predict very early in the series of coin flips and clung to this initial assessment in the face of opposite results near the end. As we have seen, truly random sequences of coin tosses often produce long strings of heads or tails that seem nonrandom. If that perceived nonrandomness occurs in the form of early success at predicting coin tosses, we may begin to believe we are psychic.

The Importance of Control

The research on the illusion of control leads us to a more general statement about human beings: we need to feel that we are in control. The famous psychological theorist Alfred Adler referred to control as an intrinsic "necessity of life."[75] The value of this necessity can be seen in a variety of areas. Psychologist Martin Seligman suggests that the feelings of helplessness that accompany clinical depression stem, in part, from a sense of diminished control over the world.[76] Looking at the problem of control somewhat differently, Ellen Langer and Judith Rodin found that when nursing-home residents were given the power to decide how their rooms would be arranged, where they would entertain visitors, and how they would occupy themselves, they were happier than those who were not given control over these decisions.[77] Another poignant study looked at a group of women suffering from breast cancer. In this research, psychologist Shelley Taylor discovered that most of the women were able to improve their circumstances by giving their condition some meaning and by attempting to exercise control over their disease. For example, almost all of the patients had developed a theory about how they were stricken.[78] Many attributed the disease to stress; others attributed it to contact with carcinogens, such as birth-control pills. One woman believed that her cancer stemmed from being hit in the breast with a Frisbee. Although understanding the precise cause of any individual case of cancer is an impossibility, these women appeared to have gained a sense of order from their theories—a sense of order that, despite being illusory, helped them adapt to their disease.

In addition, the majority of Taylor's patients believed they had some control over the recurrence of their cancer. Many expressed the view that maintaining a positive attitude would help them stay well; others gained a sense of mastery by learning as much as they could about the disease. Although their feelings of control were often more imagined than real, Taylor found that those who felt in control made better adjustments than those who did not. This conclusion is consistent with a large body of research demonstrating that a sense of control, either real or illusory, is associated with a more favorable response to a variety of setbacks.[79]

In her book *Positive Illusion*, Taylor persuasively argues two rather counterintuitive points. First, she proposes that, rather than being unusual or abnormal, positive self-deception is typical of normal human functioning. In every aspect of our lives, we tend to put a rosier spin on our attributes and achievements than is justified by fact. In contrast, realistic self-assessment is more common among depressed people.[80] Recent research suggests that those suffering from depression do not have a negatively biased view of the world; they see many things quite clearly and realistically. This disorder might thus be more accurately described as a loss of positive illusions. Second, Taylor suggests that, although much of traditional psychiatry and clinical psychology is based on the assumption that mental health springs from a realistic understanding of both the positive and negative aspects of one's circumstances, the promotion of an optimistic attitude of self-deception is more effective. A sense of meaning and control can have important beneficial effects, even when they are illusions. Thus, in Taylor's opinion, therapy should be aimed at fostering a sense of optimism and positive self-deception.

Superstition and Control

The research on control and its benefits leads to two important conclusions about superstitions based on illusions of control. First, the pervasive human desire for control is an important motivation for superstitious behavior. Superstitions provide a sense of control over the uncontrollable. Second, Shelley Taylor's research suggests that when superstitions are exercised in the context of stress or threat, the illusory control that results may be of psychological value. Further evidence of this can be found in a series of laboratory studies showing that when gamblers were under stress, they preferred games that provided a sense of illusory control.[81] Using a dice-rolling apparatus that (like the one described above) hid the outcome from view, researchers gave participants a choice between predicting the outcome before rolling the dice or reporting what they believed the outcome was after rolling the dice ("postdicting"). Gamblers who played under normal conditions tended to guess the outcome after the roll, but those who played under stress (having been told that they would receive an electric shock for each incorrect guess[82]) were more likely to predict before rolling—a choice that provided a greater sense of control. Because dice-rolling is a completely random enterprise, success is equally likely (or unlikely) under either strategy. Similar results were obtained in two additional studies, one involving betting on the spin of a roulette wheel and another involving the purchasing of lottery tickets. In each case, stress made the illusion of control more attractive. The authors concluded that stress threatens a person's sense of control and that, conversely, any improved sense of control—even if it is an illusion—can help alleviate stress.

A field study conducted in Israel during the 1991 Gulf War provides even stronger evidence that, for some people, superstition serves as a method of coping with stress.[83] In the early weeks of the war, a large number of SCUD missles were fired on Israel, and it soon became apparent which cities were in danger of attack and which were relatively safe. For example, Tel Aviv suffered several missile attacks, whereas Jerusalem suffered none. Giora Keinan of the University of Tel Aviv hypothesized that the greater stress experienced by those living in the more dangerous areas would encourage superstitious thinking about the attacks. To test this view, he developed a questionnaire that included true-false items such as "The chances of being hit during a missile attack are greater if a person whose house was attacked is present in the sealed room"[84] and "To be safe, it is best to step into the sealed room right foot first." Keinan went door-to-door asking people in high- and low-danger areas to fill out his questionnaire and to report their levels of stress. His hypothesis was confirmed: those living in the more dangerous areas reported higher levels of both stress and superstitious belief. An important additional finding of this study involved a personality trait known as tolerance for ambiguity, which is characterized by the ability to accept ambiguous situations without feeling threatened. Keinan found that people with lower tolerance for ambiguity were more superstitious, regardless of where they lived, and that those who were both lower in tolerance for ambiguity *and* living in a high-stress area were especially superstitious. The author concluded that low tolerance for ambiguity may itself be a stressful condition that encourages superstitious belief.

Obviously, this group of studies shows that, both in and out of the laboratory, people often resort to superstition when placed under stressful conditions that are beyond their control. But this research does not prove that superstitions are a beneficial coping strategy. Evidence for this conclusion would be difficult to gather because it would require placing people under threatening conditions and then randomly assigning them to superstitious and nonsuperstitious conditions. Finally, after some period of time had passed during which the participants were presumably exercising or not exercising their superstitions, we would need to measure the level of stress they were experiencing. Obviously, such a study is impossible because people cannot be randomly assigned to hold superstitious beliefs. Nevertheless, this group of studies bolsters the view that some superstitions are a useful adaptation to the combination of stress and a lack of objective control. When we are pressured and at loose ends, the sense of control that a superstition provides may be a positive illusion.

The P. T. Barnum Effect

The personality descriptions given in horoscopes and psychic readings are usually rather ambiguous and abstract:

> Some of your aspirations tend to be pretty unrealistic. At times you are extroverted, affable, and social, while at other times you are introverted, wary, and reserved. You have found it unwise to be too frank in revealing yourself to others. You pride yourself on being an independent thinker and do not accept others' opinions without satisfactory proof. You prefer a certain amount of change and variety, and become dissatisfied when hemmed in by restrictions and limitations. At times you have serious doubts as to whether you have made the right decision or done the right thing. Disciplined and controlled on the outside, you tend to be worrisome and insecure on the inside. Your sexual adjustment has presented some problems for you. While you have some personality weaknesses, you are generally able to compensate for them.[85]

Handwriting analyses and, yes, even personality assessments conducted by clinical psychologists can have a similar vacuous quality. Nevertheless, when told that such a personality profile was constructed expressly for them, most people will say it is very accurate. Psychologist Paul Meehl called this the "P. T. Barnum effect," after the circus magnate's famous maxim "There's a sucker born every minute."[86]

Several studies have examined the influence of the Barnum effect on belief in astrology. In one case, experimenters posing as astrologers constructed horoscopes for two groups of people.[87] Prior to offering their results, the astrologers asked participants in one group for the year, month, and day of their birth; participants in the other group were asked only for the year and month. Everyone in both groups received the same handwritten profile constructed from statements found in the bestselling book *Linda Goodman's Sun Signs*.[88] Consistent with the Barnum effect, people from both groups thought the horoscope was an accurate description of their personalities, but those who were asked for more detailed information thought it was more accurate than those who were not. Thus, the request for specific information enhanced the illusion that a general description was constructed for the recipient. Many professional astrologers do ask for very detailed data prior to constructing a horoscope, and according to these findings, their diligence is rewarded—not by more accurate readings, but by clients who believe more strongly in the accuracy of their readings.[89]

Lawrence University psychologist Peter Glick and his colleagues conducted a study of the susceptibility of both skeptics and believers to the Barnum effect.[90] Glick assembled two groups of high-school students, one made up of those who believed that horoscopes accurately describe a person's personality and another of students who did not believe horoscopes were accurate. Students in both groups were given personality descriptions that they were told were created by a "professional astrology service" based on birth information they had provided earlier. In reality, of course, the horoscopes were not individually prepared. All the students received one of two versions of the horoscope. Half the students in each group were given a horoscope that was generally positive in its description of the recipient's personality and character (e.g., "sympathetic," " dependable," and "sociable"), and the other half of each group was given horoscopes that were negative (e.g., "undependable," "unrealistic," "overly sensitive"). Later, when the students were asked how accurate their horoscopes were, those in the believers' group said it was very accurate, regardless of whether it was flattering or unflattering. However, skeptics who received the flattering version said it was accurate, and those who received the unflattering version said it was not. Thus, both skeptics and believers were susceptible to the Barnum effect—as long as the feedback they received was complimentary.

Finally, to assess changes in belief, Glick asked the students to report their level of belief in astrology both before and after receiving their horoscope. Of course, the believers began the experiment with greater faith in astrology, and their confidence remained high regardless of the content of their horoscope. Similarly, skeptics who received a negative horoscope were unchanged by the experience. However, the skeptics who received the flattering version reported significantly greater belief in astrology at the end of the experiment than at the beginning. Therefore, the Barnum effect created by a complimentary horoscope helped convince these skeptics that astrology is valid. Similar effects could be expected for psychic readings, handwriting analysis, and psychological assessments.

Seeing What You Believe: Placebo Effects and Superstition

Earlier I said that medical experiments are usually designed to compare a group of people who have received a certain treatment (the experimental group) to a group who have not (the control group). In the case of most drug research, this is not strictly the case. For example, if one wished to determine whether or not daily doses of aspirin were effective in preventing heart attacks, the standard procedure would be to give the experimental group a pill that contained aspirin and the control group an identical-looking pill that contained no active medicine—a placebo. None of the participants would know which group he or she was in; as a condition of their inclusion in the study, everyone would be told that they might be assigned to take either the active drug or the placebo. Typically, if the drug is shown to be effective, it is offered to members of the control group at the completion of the experiment, but until the end, everyone is kept in the dark.[91]

Why all this elaborate deception? Because sometimes, just believing that you are taking an effective drug is enough to cure your illness. Our thoughts and beliefs about a medical remedy can have a profound effect on our recovery. In fact, although the technique has fallen out of favor, physicians have long prescribed placebos to patients who might benefit from a sham treatment—a practice known as the "benevolent deception."[92] Thus, the mere fact that a particular treatment has led to improvement does not prove its effectiveness. There are hundreds of documented cases of simple sugar pills producing significant improvement in a wide variety of maladies. As a result, the improvement brought about by a new drug is always measured against the changes brought on by taking an inert placebo.

Placebo effects are thought to be produced by *response expectancies*.[93] Whenever recipients believe that a drug will have a particular physiological, behavioral, or psychological effect, they are susceptible to placebo effects. Interestingly, although research shows that alcohol decreases sexual arousal, the common folk wisdom holds that it is an aphrodisiac, and consistent with the expectancy hypothesis (and not the true pharmacological effect), people who are given an alcohol placebo show *increased* arousal. Placebo effects can also be produced in decaf drinkers who think they are drinking caffeinated coffee. For example, in one experiment, college students who were told that they were drinking caffeinated coffee said they felt more alert and more tense, when in fact the coffee they had drunk was decaffeinated. Furthermore, these deluded (diluted) coffee-drinkers showed significant changes in blood pressure.[94] Indeed, the role of expectancies in drug reactions is so important that University of Connecticut psychologist Irving Kirsch was moved to write, "the placebo component of drug administration can be as powerful or more powerful than the pharmacological component of drug effects."[95]

And placebo effects are not limited to drugs. Kirsch's research suggests that the changes in behavior observed in people under hypnosis are also produced, in large part, by the participant's beliefs about what hypnosis does. Since the discovery of hypnosis by the eigtheenth-century Viennese physician Franz Mesmer, the role of the "mesmerized" individual has gradually evolved. In the eighteenth and nineteenth centuries, hypnotized people sometimes coughed, laughed, or increased their breathing rate. In modern times, the expectations for the behavior of the hypnotist's subject have become more standardized, and most contemporary people under hypnosis conform well to the role. That expectancies are a powerful influence on one's response to hypnosis is further supported by research showing that participants who are told that spontaneous amnesia is a characteristic of hypnosis are more likely to forget what happened during the trance. Other suggestions produce similar effects.[96]

Placebo effects are both powerful and pervasive, and they play a role in beliefs involving faith healing, unsubstantiated medical remedies, and all manner of cures and quackery.[97] If we truly believe that a homeopathic medicine or a psychic healer can improve our condition, it may. Ironically, most homeopathic drugs are, in fact, placebos. Yet, if testimonials or the persuasion of a homeopathic practitioner produce the expectation of positive results, significant and real changes can occur. In the case of religious faith healers, such as Kathryn Kuhlman, the expectancy effects are often intensified in an atmosphere of uplifting emotional arousal.

If all of this is true, what is so bad about placebo effects? Improvement is improvement. Is this such a bad superstition? In some cases, perhaps not. Belief that a homeopathic remedy is a good treatment for the common cold is harmless and may, in fact, bring about a speedier recovery. But more serious conditions make placebo effects, as well as the misinterpretation of variability, more troublesome. If an individual is persuaded to avoid more conventional (i.e., more effective) forms of treatment, then the self-delusion of placebo effects and the misinterpretation of variability are very troublesome. These phenomena can maintain belief in useless treatments. There are well-publicized cases of people choosing homeopathy over conventional medicine and paying for this decision with their good health and, in some cases, their lives. Even when the illness is not serious, belief in unproven medical remedies can be a consumer issue. As placebos go, many of these therapies are very expensive. On the other hand, if, for example, a cancer patient follows the traditional medical treatment for her condition and combines it with placebo-like New Age therapies such as crystal healing, there may be some benefits. Superstition may have its place, but when the stakes are high, choosing magic over science holds great risks.

• • •

The fallibility of human reason is the greatest single source of superstitious belief. We are the most intelligent of all species, yet our powerful minds are prone to systematic bias and error. Research in this area is quite active and will undoubtedly lead to further understanding of our misunderstandings. But what about our superstitious beginnings? How and at what age are superstitious beliefs first formed? To answer these questions, we must look at the psychology of the developing child and the social psychology of superstition.

5
Growing Up Superstitious

Outwardly the children in the back streets and around the housing estate appear to belong to the twentieth century, but ancient apprehensions, even if only half believed in, continue to infiltrate their minds. . . . With simple faith they accept beliefs which have not changed since Shakespeare's day: that if a dog howls outside a house or scratches at the floor someone is going to die in that house; that if owls screech at night it is a sign of death; that if a person hears of two deaths he will assuredly be the third; and in the evening places where children meet, the telling of each dark precept is supported with gruesome instances.

—Iona and Peter Opie, *Lore and Language of Schoolchildren*

See a pin and pick it up
All the day you'll have good luck
See a pin and let it lay
Bad luck you'll have all that day

—J. O. Halliwell, *Nursery Rhymes of England*

In the mid-1950s, Philip Goldberg was a young Dodgers fan growing up in Brooklyn. He and his friends played stickball in the streets with mop handles and hairless pink rubber balls known as "spaldeens." As many as fifteen times a season, he passed through the gates of Ebbets Field to see the great Jackie Robinson take the field, and he watched many other games on television, either at home or at a neighborhood luncheonette. But Goldberg was not merely a passive observer. He helped the Dodgers win. He had a lucky blue Dodgers hat that he wore during every game, and a yellowed Dodgers T-shirt that was imbued with magical powers. Like many boys, he was concerned that the bill of his cap have just the right degree of curl, so at the end of the day, he would roll it into a cylinder and stick it in a drinking glass overnight. Soon he came to believe that this nightly ritual maintained the hat's power to make the Dodgers win.

Although Goldberg's own baseball magic benefited the Dodgers, his mother was a jinx. On several occasions, when he and his father were watching crucial games, such as those against the Giants in the 1951 National League playoffs, the team's fortunes changed as soon as Mrs. Goldberg entered the room. Bobby Thomson hit a home run to win the pennant for the Giants, or some other calamity befell the home team.

Thirty years later, having followed the Dodgers to Los Angeles, Philip Goldberg memorialized the Brooklyn of his youth in an autobiographical novel, *This Is Next Year*.[1] The main character, a young boy named Roger Stone, has a lucky hat and a mother who is a jinx, and he believes that if he sits on a particular stool at the local luncheonette and drinks an egg cream just before the start of the game, the Dodgers will win. At a dramatic point in the novel, which takes place during the 1955 championship season, Roger goes to Jackie Robinson's house and gives him his lucky hat.

The adult Philip Goldberg is still a Dodgers fan and still has a lucky hat. He wore it during every game of the 1988 stretch drive and throughout the playoff series with the Mets. He was wearing it when Kirk Gibson hit his famous home run, and he wore it during all the World Series games of that winning season.[2] He claims he does not believe as strongly as he did as a child, but he takes no chances: "The old saying is that there are no atheists in foxholes. Well, there aren't any in the bleachers either."[3]

• • •

At the turn of the century, the most prominent psychologists of the day thought children were savages. Throughout the nineteenth century, even before Darwin's *Origin of Species* appeared in 1859, evolution was widely debated in scientific circles. Several theories of the development of species were proposed, but it was not until after Darwin that the theory of natural selection—the survival of those individuals who are physically and behaviorally adapted to their environments—took hold. Among the evolutionary ideas that were popular at the time was the law of recapitulation.[4] Although this principle was independently proposed by several theorists, it is most closely associated with the German zoologist Ernst Haeckel, who called it the "biogenetic law." The law, as he stated it, was "Ontogeny is the short and rapid recapitulation of phylogeny."[5] Simply put, the biogenetic law holds that as an individual develops from embryo to adult (ontogeny), it mirrors the evolution of its species (phylogeny). Thus, for example, the human fetus passes through a stage at which it resembles a fish—presumably an evolutionary ancestor.

The biogenetic law remained popular through the early decades of this century, exerting important influences outside the field of zoology. For example, before World War II, the concept of recapitulation was used as a scientific basis for the inequality of the races. African adults were said to resemble European children, a view that justified treating blacks as children, members of an ancestral race.[6]

The biogenetic law exerted a particularly strong influence on theories of child development. G. Stanley Hall, the most noted child psychologist of his day and founder of the American Psychological Association, believed that evolutionary recapitulation was a central theme of child development and was particularly evident in childhood play:

> I regard play as the motor habits and spirit of the past of the race, persisting in the present, as rudimentary functions sometimes of and always akin to rudimentary organs. The best index and guide to the stated activities of adults in past ages is found in the instinctive, untaught, and non-imitative plays of children. . . . Thus we rehearse the activities of our ancestors, back we know not how far, and repeat their life work in summative and adumbrated ways.[7]

Although psychologists no longer hold this view of children (it insults both children and our ancestors), two related points are important to our topic. First, we must treat children fairly. Youngsters move within our grownup society but are not yet bona fide members of it. As a result, their lapses in rationality can be excused as the products of their prescientific intellects. What children—particularly younger children—do and say cannot, in good conscience, be classified as true superstitions or paranormal beliefs.[8] Nevertheless, the curiosities of childhood belief often grow into genuine adult superstitions. For example, many of the traditional social superstitions, such as the fear of black cats, are first acquired in childhood—when our critical skills are not well honed—and are maintained through maturity—when we ought to know better. Thus, a full accounting of the psychology of superstition must include an examination of the beginnings of superstitious belief in childhood.

Second, although the world of developing children does not mirror the cultural evolution of Western society, as Hall believed, it does represent a rich and unique culture filled with distinctive literature, songs, customs, and systems of belief. Although almost every aspect of childhood has been studied in great detail, very few investigators have examined the society of children the way a cultural anthropologist would approach a different culture. The primary exceptions to this rule have been Peter and Iona Opie.

The Magical Lore of Schoolchildren

In 1959, the Opies published their landmark work, *The Lore and Language of Schoolchildren*. For this study, schoolteachers, headmasters, and headmistresses served as informants, reporting observations of five thousand children from England, Scotland, Wales, and Ireland, which the Opies collected and categorized. The final product paints a detailed portrait of the child's world complete with rhymes, songs, riddles, games, epithets, and customs, many of which are magical pieces of childhood superstition.

Oaths

Perhaps the simplest form of children's magic described by the Opies is the oath. These ritual declarations of the veracity of a statement or the intention to perform an act are extremely common, and they are often sealed by a gesture, such as spitting, crossing the fingers, or touching cold iron. Of course, religious oaths are quite common. For example, the Opies found that the most popular of all oaths among English schoolchildren was "God's honor," sealed by licking the tip of the index finger and making the sign of the cross on the swearer's throat. Other religious oaths included "God's word," "Hate God if I tell a lie," and "May I sell my God if I am not telling the truth."

If, after an oath is made, there remains some residual doubt, the inquisitor may test the oath-giver's truth. For example, the truth might be tested by peering into the swearer's mouth, because according to legend, if you tell a lie, a blister will appear on your tongue. Another truth test reported by the Opies involved drawing two fingers along the ground. If both remained clean, a lie had been told; if one became dirty, the truth had been told.[9] (It is not clear what two dirty fingers would mean.)

Once completed, an oath has a kind of legal status, such that if the contract is broken, important consequences will follow. For example, the Opies found that children would frequently demand of a cohort: "spit your mother's death."[10] Such a gesture would presumably lead to the parent's demise if her child was not true to his or her word. Often the terms of the contract were stated in rhyme. In the town of Ruthin, in northern Wales, the Opies heard the following couplet:

Cross my heart and hope to die,
Drop down dead if I tell a lie.[11]

Growing up in the Midwest, I heard the more gruesome American version:

Cross my heart and hope to die,
Stick a needle in my eye.

In this case, it is not clear whether the second line was meant to be a truth test that the doubting listener was urged to employ or a particularly grizzly way to accomplish the "hope to die" part of the bargain.

The importance of keeping an oath is often supported by stories of those who failed to be true and died instantly. The Opies reported one particularly dramatic case:

> A Somerset writer for instance has recalled that, in his day, schoolboys had a story in which a sinner was not only immediately struck dead when he perjured himself but became rooted to the spot where he stood so that no power on earth—not even a team of horses attached by ropes and chains—could move the body, which stood (like Lot's wife) as a terrible warning to other men and women.[12]

Childhood Superstitions

In addition to a belief in magical oaths, children hold genuine juvenile superstitions. Most of us have personal experiences with childhood superstitions, but again, the Opies provide the most organized collection and analysis of what they called "half-beliefs." They also recognized the peculiar social source of childhood superstitions:

> The beliefs with which we are concerned here are those which children absorb through going about with each other, and consequently mostly involve happenings out-of-doors: people met in the street, objects found in the road, and mascots carried with them to school. We find, what is understandable, that the younger schoolchildren treat the beliefs and rites of their companions more seriously than those practiced by their parents.[13]

In the United States, perhaps the most famous of all childhood superstitions is recited while walking the sidewalk on the way to school:

Step on a crack
You'll break your mother's back.

This couplet is recited all over the country with only minor variations, such as "you'll break your grandmother's back" or "you'll break the devil's back."[14] The Opies also found this ominous belief expressed throughout England, with several colorful variations:

If you tread on a nick
You'll marry a brick (or a 'stick')
And a beetle will come to your wedding.[15]

One version, heard in Portsmouth, also required that attention be paid to places where water ran across the pavement:

> If you tread on a crack, or tread on a spout,
> It's a sure thing your mother will turn you out.[16]

Many of the childhood superstitions reported to the Opies involved finding lucky objects: buttons, pins, four-leaf clovers, coins, or stones. In most cases, finding something was not, in itself, enough; to tease luck from a newly discovered treasure the child must "step on it, threaten it, spit on it, implore of it, or, very often, throw it away."[17] Interestingly, English children placed special significance on finding particular cigarette packages. In Aberystwyth and Swansea, for instance, the Opies found that children looked for empty packs of Player's Navy Cut, and when they were lucky enough to find one they recited:

> Sailor, sailor, bring me luck
> Find a shilling in the muck.

The four-leaf clover is perhaps the most famous of all lucky found objects, and the Opies recount what must be the world record: on May 13 (was it Friday?), 1953, Joan Nott of North Finchley, London found nine four-leaf clovers near her home.

Both children and adults make wishes from time to time. Indeed, most public fountains are quickly filled with spare change.[18] On Thanksgiving, many a carver has taken the extra steps necessary to carefully extract the bird's wishbone in a single piece; later, often while the dishes are being cleared away, the familiar wish-making duel ensues. But the practice of making wishes is most strongly associated with children. Birthday cakes with candles are an important symbol of childhood, marking the passing of a milestone, and the ritual singing of "Happy Birthday" combined with the blowing out of candles is an almost universal ceremonial practice. As I learned the birthday wishing spell, to be successful you must (1) silently make a wish, (2) blow all the candles out with a single breath, (3) not tell anyone what the wish was (no matter how much they tease you about it), and (4) not speak again until you have eaten your first bite of cake. Another wishing procedure was the subject of Jiminy Cricket's famous song from the Disney version of *Pinocchio*, "When You Wish upon a Star."

The Opies found a number of circumstances that their young subjects hold propitious for the granting of wishes. Seeing a white horse was said to be lucky, and some said that after seeing such an animal your wish would be granted. In some versions of this belief, the wisher had to perform an additional ritual, such as spitting or crossing her fingers and keeping them crossed until she saw a dog.[19] A particularly charming wish procedure reported by the Opies involved the chance occurrence of simultaneous speech. If two children accidentally say the same thing at the same instance, "they instantly stop what they are doing and, without uttering a further word to each other or making any sound, glide into a set ritual which varies only according to the part of Britain or, for this is an international performance, the part of the world in which they live."[20] For example, children in Alton, Hampshire, touched wood and said, "My letter in the post come quick," and then named a poet, usually Shakespeare.[21] In Carbondale, Illinois, children "lock the right-hand little fingers, wish silently, and then unlock simultaneously, each child giving the name of some animal or bird."[22]

Two categories of children's superstitions observed by the Opies closely parallel beliefs and practices used by adults. For example, like Canadian and American college students, English schoolchildren employ superstitions to give them luck in examinations. They often bring in "mascots," small toy pigs, elephants, frogs, dogs, or other animals, which they "set up in front of them on their desks (and tactfully ignored by the examiners), or are worn as brooches or pendants."[23] Others try to gain an edge by bringing a piece of coal in their pocket. The Opies make a particularly interesting observation about the kinds of students who used lucky objects when the stakes are high:

> They are particularly conscientious about bringing charms to the 11-plus examination, the "scholarship" as they call it, which, determines whether they shall go on to a grammar school or to a secondary modern; and it may, perhaps, be reflected that grammar school children (the children who were successful in the examination) are more likely to be superstitious than secondary modern school children, for children at grammar schools are children who have found that lucky charms work.[24]

Although the Opies seem to offer this view more as speculation than as fact, it is supported by the finding that successful athletes are more likely to be superstitious than less successful ones (see chapter 2). Furthermore, it is consistent with the win-stay/lose-shift pattern of superstition exhibited by gamblers.

The Opies found that, like Henslin's crapshooters, children often use magical incantations to improve their luck in games. When tossing a coin, some were heard to chant, "Lucky tails, never fails," or, when drawing a third playing card or hoping to roll a three at dice, "Lucky three, bring luck to me." Apparently marbles was a game that schoolchildren felt they needed a little luck to win. The Opies reported a number of verbal spells used by players, including one heard in East Orange, New Jersey:

Roll, roll, tootsie roll,
Roll, marble, in the hole.

Other techniques involve making marks in the dirt (which—although I am a nonplayer, it seems to me, might change the course of a speeding cat's eye). For example, some children protected a marble from being hit by drawing a ring around it. These rituals are reminiscent of the practices of adult baseball players and gamblers.

• • •

Peter and Iona Opie's study of schoolchildren is a window onto a culture that adults have forgotten. Americans reading their reports in the 1990s will find that some details differ from their own youthful experiences, but the basic framework is universal. Children live in a unique world filled with songs, oral literature, beliefs, and half-beliefs. But we cannot help noticing the similarities between these childhood superstitions and those of adults. Many of us acquire our belief in magic as children and retain it long after we have adopted grownup sensibilities. This observation begs the question: how do children learn to be superstitious? To see if we can find an answer, we must look at two primary forces in the child's world—the development of thought and the process of socialization.

Magical Thinking in Childhood

The study of intellectual development in children is dominated by a single figure. Jean Piaget's theory of cognitive development is criticized by some contemporary researchers who believe several of its details to be inaccurate, but it is the most complete account we have of the development of thought. Furthermore, because Piaget was a tireless and careful observer, his theory faithfully portrays many important features of the real lives of children. His work, which filled many volumes, describes how children come to understand the world, as well as how they misunderstand it along the way. One of these misunderstandings is magical thinking, a superstition-like phenomenon of early childhood.

Piaget was a something of a prodigy. Born on August 9, 1896, in Neuchâtel, Switzerland, he had an early interest in biology. His prolific publishing career began when, at age ten, he published an article in a natural-history magazine describing an albino sparrow he had observed in a local park. A series of articles on mollusks, written when Piaget was between fifteen and eighteen, led to an invitation to serve as curator of the mollusk collection at the Geneva natural-history museum (an invitation he had to refuse because he had not yet completed high school). By the age of twenty-one, Piaget had completed his Ph.D. in biology, and his interests turned to psychology. He continued his studies in Zurich and later at the Sorbonne University in Paris, where, in 1920, he accepted a position with Teophile Simon at the Binet Laboratory. Simon and Alfred Binet had developed the Binet-Simon intelligence test, and Piaget was chosen to help develop standardized items for intelligence tests.[25]

As legend has it, Piaget was less interested in children's correct responses to test items than he was in their errors. He noticed that older children were not just smarter than younger ones; they reasoned in a qualitatively different way. He began to publish articles on children's thought and soon took a position as research director for the Jean-Jacque Rousseau Institute in Geneva, where he continued his research in cognitive development. Having settled on his life's work, Piaget began publishing a long series of books outlining his theory of cognitive development, but he did not completely forsake his training in biology. His theory of child development was strongly influenced by biological and evolutionary processes, emphasizing children's methods of adaptation to the environment. According to his theory, as children grow, they pass through a series of cognitive stages, ending at the *formal operational stage* when they are approximately twelve years old. At this point, the child can engage in abstract thought and can reason using purely verbal and logical statements (see Table 5.1).[26]

Before children arrive at this point, their intellectual development is incomplete, and they make predictable reasoning errors. Piaget detailed these errors and used some of them as evidence for his stage-theory approach to cognitive development. Perhaps the most famous example is the so-called problem of conservation. From age two to approximately age seven, children are in Piaget's *preoperational stage*. During this period, children are beginning to use symbols and images but have not yet begun to think logically. If, for example, an adult places before a child two balls of clay of the same size, the child will agree that they are the same. However, if one of the balls is then rolled out into a long cylinder, the preoperational child will say that the cylinder is bigger. The child fails to understand that the clay retains (or conserves) its volume regardless of its shape. My four-year-old son once demonstrated this error by asking me to cut his grilled-cheese sandwich into four pieces "so there will be more." After the age of seven, children enter the *concrete operational* stage and understand the concept of conservation.

Another characteristic of children in the preoperational stage (but not limited to it) is *egocentrism*—the inability to take another's point of view.

Table 5.1   *Piaget's Stages of Cognitive Development*

Stage	Ages	Activities and Accomplishments
Sensorimotor	Birth to two years	Infants discover the world through sensory impressions and motor activities. They learn to differentiate the self from the outside world, and that objects continue to exist even when not visible. They begin to understand cause and effect.
Preoperational	Two to seven years	Children are unable to manipulate and transform information in logical ways or make general logical statements, but they can use images and symbols. They acquire language and play pretend games.
Concrete operational	Seven to eleven years	Children can understand logical principles that apply to concrete external objects. They understand that objects remain the same despite changes in appearance; they can sort objects into categories.
Formal operational	Over eleven years	Adolescents and adults can think logically about abstractions and can imagine other worlds. They reason about purely verbal or logical statements and reflect on their own activity of thinking.

Source: Bernstein, Clark-Stewart, Roy, and Wickens (1994). Copyright © 1994 by Houghton Mifflin Company. Adapted with permission.

According to Piaget, this attribute is the basis of several forms of magical thinking in young children. The classic demonstration of egocentrism is the three-mountains task, in which a child is seated in front of a three-dimensional model of a mountain range.[27] A doll is placed so that it also appears to be viewing the model, but from a different angle. Finally, the child is asked to select, from a number of pictures, that view that the doll sees. Piaget found that children under the age of approximately eight tend to choose the view that they see, rather than what the doll sees. More recent research suggests that children younger than eight can be successful on a similar task, but it is clear that various forms of egocentrism are common to children of this age group. Furthermore, this youthful self-centeredness is responsible for two other cognitive errors that lead to magical thinking: *realism* and *animism*.

Realism and Dreams

Piaget described young children as realists, by which he meant that they are unable to make the distinction between themselves and the external world and between thought and reality. The child's description of the nature of dreams is an interesting example of this problem. Piaget and his collaborators interviewed children of different ages about their dreams and identified three distinct stages of development. At approximately five to six years of age children report that a dream comes from outside them and remains external. At seven to eight children believe that a dream comes from within them but exists in the room in front of or around them. Finally, children of nine to ten years describe a dream as coming from them and residing in their heads or behind their eyelids.[28]

The following dialogue with one of Piaget's subjects, the six-year-old Sci, demonstrates the first stage, in which dreams come from and exist apart from the dreamer:

> Where does a dream come from?
> *From the night.*
> What is it?
> *It's the evening.*
> What is the night like?
> *It is black.*
> How are dreams made?
> *Out there* (pointing to the window).
> What are dreams made of?
> *Black.*
> Yes, but of what?
> *Of light.*
> Where do they come from?
> *From lights outside.*
> Where are they?
> *There are some out there* (pointing to the street lamps).
> Why do dreams come?
> *Because the light makes them.*[29]

Piaget's second stage, in which the dream comes from within the dreamer but exists outside, is demonstrated by Schi, who is described as a "very intelligent" six-year-old boy:[30]

> Do you sometimes have dreams? What is a dream?
> *You think of something during the night.*
> What do you dream with?
> *With the soul, with thought.*
> Where does the dream come from?
> *During the night. It is the night that shows us the dream.*
> What does that mean? Where is the dream whilst you're dreaming?
> *It is in the*—[he was about to say "head"], *it is between the night and the head.*
> While you are dreaming, are your eyes open or shut?

Shut.
Then where is the dream?
It's when you see black that the dream comes.
Where is it?
When you are not asleep it's in the head. While you are asleep it comes out.
When it's night, it's night, but while you're asleep it isn't night any more.
When the dream comes, where is it?
In front of the eyes and it goes against the wall.
Could your father see it?
No.
Only you?
Yes, because it's me that's asleep.

It is as though Schi has distinguished between daydreams (waking dreams) and sleeping dreams. He knows that while he is awake his dreams exist inside him, but he believes that as he descends into sleep, his dreams leave his body, at least sometimes. Yet his father would not be able to see his dreams because they are somehow produced by and connected only with him.

Older children acquire a more mature understanding: that dreams come from inside and remain internal. Tann, an eight-year-old, retains some unusual ideas about dreams, but he shows the important features of Piaget's third stage.

Where do dreams come from?
When you shut your eyes; instead of its being night, you see things.
Where are they?
Nowhere. They aren't real. They're in the eyes.
Do dreams come from within you or from outside?
From the outside. When you go for a walk and you see something, it makes a mark on the forehead in little drops of blood.
What happens when you are asleep?
You see it.
Is the dream inside the head or outside?
It comes from outside, and when you dream of it, it comes from the head.
Where are the images when you are dreaming?
From inside the brain they come into the eyes.
Is there anything in front of the eyes?
No.[31]

Realism and Participation

Dreams are magical. In a dream, the physical limitations of waking life are stripped away to reveal a world of pure imagination and wonder. But they are common to both children and adults, and although a small child may need to be reminded in the middle of the night that nightmares—and all dreams—are not real, most children soon learn to distinguish dreamscapes from waking landscapes. Thus dreams do not represent the kind of magical thinking we associate with childhood superstition. For this it is necessary to have magical beliefs about cause-and-effect relationships in the everyday, waking world. Here, also, the problem of realism plays a role.

For his discussion of magical thinking in children, Piaget borrowed anthropologist Lucien Lévy-Bruhl's term "participation" to describe a child's belief that there is a causal link between two unconnected people or events. His observations of children led him to identify four forms of magical participation.

Magic by Participation between Actions and Things

The childish magical beliefs recounted by Piaget are very similar to those described by the Opies. Most represent the superstitious hope that some act or thought will bring something good or stave off something bad. The following story of an anxious boy is typical.

> A boy who lived in a somewhat lonely house was always very frightened on the evenings when his parents were out. Before going to bed he used to draw the curtains by unwinding a sort of roller. He had always the idea that if he could succeed in drawing the curtains very quickly the robbers would not come. But if the curtain took some time to unroll the house was in danger.[32]

Many of the magic prescriptions of schoolchildren described by the Opies fall into this actions/things category—avoiding cracks in sidewalks, finding four-leaf clovers, and picking up pins.[33] According to Piaget, belief in the magical participation between actions and things is produced by a form of realism that confuses a symbolic action with the cause of a subsequent event.

Magic by Participation between Thoughts and Things

When something is wanted very badly, many children—and even some adults—will avoid thinking about their desires, sometimes thinking the opposite, to keep from "jinxing" themselves. This kind of behavior represents Piaget's second kind of magical participation. Here, the principle of realism leads children to believe that their private thoughts have an external reality that can affect objects and events in the physical world. Piaget recounted the memory of a colleague which demonstrates this kind of magical thinking. As a young girl, this colleague would play school, imagining that she was the teacher giving various grades to her friends. In general, she gave better grades to her friends and worse ones to children she did not like. When later she went to school, the young girl was convinced that she had influenced the actual questions asked by her teacher. She believed that somehow she had helped her friends and hindered her enemies.[34]

Magic by Participation between Objects

Children often see certain events or objects as ominous or emblematic. Thus, a shooting star or a white horse may be seen as lucky. But children may believe that physical entities share some occult connection—that objects themselves interact. Piaget offers the following recollection by a young girl as an example:

> When I had just won certain marbles (by taking them from my opponent), I never used these marbles to play with again, because I thought I was more likely to lose these than the others, since I had the idea that they would be in some way attached to their former surroundings and have a tendency to be returned to their former owner.[35]

As in the case of participations between thoughts and things, participations between objects come from a failure of the child's realistic—literal—mind to separate signs from events or thoughts from objects.

Animism

Some children believe that inanimate objects are living things, or even that objects are obedient. This form of participation is called animism. In its most extreme form, it leads children to believe that they are "masters of the universe" controlling all that they survey, but the most famous examples concern the behavior of the sun, moon, and clouds. A four-and-a-half-year-old answered the following question:

> Can the moon go wherever it wants, or does something make it move?
> in this way:
> *It's me, when I walk. It comes with me, it follows us.*[36]
> A seven-year-old, when asked,
> Does the moon move or not?
> answered:
> *It follows us.*
> Why?
> *When we go, it goes.*
> What makes it move?
> *We do.*
> How?
> *When we walk. It goes by itself.*[37]

Origins of Magical Thinking

Having identified these categories of magical thought, Piaget offers some explanations for the development of these superstition-like phenomena. At the core, is the concept of egocentrism. Piaget goes so far as to describe the infant's egocentrism as being a form of solipsism—the belief that only one's self exists and all else is imaginary. The baby makes no distinction between self and the world—indeed, the baby feels it *is* the world. It takes delight in watching the movement of its hands and feet and the movement of a mobile bouncing above the crib. But according to Piaget, these are the same to the child. Internal and external are one.

Soon children learn that the world is responsive to their commands. Limbs and objects move as they direct. Even parents appear to behave as if they were extensions of the child's body, supplying food, toys, and physical comfort at the slightest whimper. This kind of experience leads the child, in later stages, to make magical commands to the world and expect that they will be obeyed. The development of symbolic behavior further contributes to magical thinking. As children learn the names of objects, they often exhibit what Piaget called *nominal realism*—the confusion of the name with the object itself. It is this principle that Rozin and his colleagues observed in college students who were uncomfortable eating sugar from a container marked "sodium cyanide" (see chapter 1, page 9). In children, nominal realism leads to the expectation that names and thoughts are connected with objects and can influence real world events. Thus, a practice such as thinking the opposite of what is desired can emerge.

Piaget also suggested that in some instances, gestures or actions with innocent beginnings later take on a magical role. For example, the lowering of the window shade described above may have begun as a simple action to protect against robbers and other undesirables by making peo-ple and things in the house less visible. Later, the precise manner in which the action is completed took on a supernatural function. Similarly, a child who is walking on a sidewalk may begin to walk in a particular way—hopping over the pavement lines, for example—purely as a game or for aesthetic reasons. Then one day, while walking in this characteristic way, the child is possessed by a particular fear or strong desire. This accidental contiguity of action and desire gives rise to the ritualization of the walk.[38]

• • •

Piaget's account of magical thinking has come under some criticism. Some have questioned the basic premise that children are unable to distinguish between the internal and external worlds, and others point out that adults—who are presumably in the formal operational stage of cognitive development—often exhibit religious and philosophical beliefs that share features with the magical thinking of younger children.[39] To examine adults with such magical beliefs, Ronnie Lesser and Marilyn Paisner of the City University of New York compared women who were members of the Institute of the New Age, a nonsectarian spiritual community that denied the existence of chance and attributed great control to the individual, to a second group of women who were not involved with a spiritual community.[40] Members of the New Age group believed in reincarnation, karma, and the notion that, prior to birth (or rebirth), one chooses one's parents. First, Lesser and Paisner measured the developmental level of both groups using a permutations task developed by Piaget and Bärbel Inhelder.[41] The study participants were asked to find all possible reorderings of the four letters ABCD (ABDC, ADBC, etc.). (Successful performance on this task is associated with the rule-based, abstract reasoning of the formal operational stage.) The results indicated that both groups were firmly rooted in the formal operational stage and equally adept at the permutations task. Next, Lesser and Paisner assessed the level of supernatural belief in both groups and, as expected, found significantly higher levels of belief in ESP, plant consciousness, UFOs, magic, and witchcraft in the New Age group.

Although the presence of formal operational thought in combination with magical thinking appears to contradict Piaget's theory, the authors resurrected Piaget's account by making a distinction between the magical thinking of preoperational children and that of the New Agers. Lesser and Paisner argued that when young children say they make the moon move, it is a naive statement of fact. In contrast, when one of the New Age participants said that people's actions collectively affect the weather, she understood this to be a statement of belief. This woman's awareness of the different status of her ideas reflects formal operational, rather than preoperational, thought.

The Socialization of Superstition

When we critically consider Piaget's explanation of the ritual of avoidance of cracks in sidewalks, it is clear that his theory is insufficient. The avoidance of cracks and most of the other beliefs reported by the Opies are social superstitions that, in all but a very few instances, must have been passed from person to person. Given the wide popularity of these beliefs across diverse areas of England, the United States, and other countries, it is extremely unlikely that each superstitious child went through a parallel process of accidental contiguity between a habitual practice and a current fear. Cognitive maturation is undoubtedly important to the development of personal superstitions in children, but those who acquire a fear of sidewalk cracks and other social superstitions need the help of others to do so.

Critics of Piaget's theory suggest that many of a child's most common beliefs are established through socialization—the process by which parents, teachers, and other authority figures teach the skills and social norms that children will need to function in their social environment.[42] As they grow and develop, children acquire the language, social customs, and ethical systems of those around them, and for most children, this educational process includes learning about a number of traditional superstitions. Several processes—some more fully researched than others—are responsible for the transmission of social superstitions, but the two most important ones are direct instruction and social learning.

Superstitious Instruction

Children believe what they are told. Skepticism is an adult characteristic acquired, if at all, with age. As a college professor, I spend much of my time prodding students to critically evaluate what they have been told, to question authority. Even at their relatively advanced ages, college students and other adults are often more accepting than is justified. But when we are young, we trust those around us almost completely. This naiveté is so inherent to childhood that adults must routinely warn children about strangers who may not have their best interests at heart. The same youthful gullibility undoubtedly allows the word-of-mouth transfer of superstitious beliefs. Schoolchildren, like those whom the Opies' chronicled, teach each other what they have learned from others. In addition, just as Nancy Reagan's parents taught her the magical rituals of the theater, superstitious adults teach their offspring to be superstitious children.

Perhaps because the effects of direct instruction on children seem so obvious and uncontroversial, there has been little research into this mode of spreading superstitious behavior, but one study clearly shows how misinformation can produce simple superstitions in preschool children. Edward Morris and his colleagues at the University of Kansas, who in chapter 3 employed Bobo the clown to condition superstitious behavior, recruited him again in a test of social transmission of superstitions.[43]

In this case, individual preschool children were observed in a small room with Bobo, who, as before, was simply a mechanical toy clown mounted on the wall. The children were told that whenever Bobo's red nose lit up he would dispense marbles from his mouth, and that if they collected enough marbles they would be able to take home a toy. All of the children who participated were prompted to press Bobo's nose once during this early instructional period, but only some of the children were told that Bobo would give marbles if "you press his nose a lot."[44] In fact, Bobo coughed up his prizes on a variable time schedule averaging one marble every fifteen seconds—*irrespective of the child's behavior.*

The effect of this subtle difference in instructions was dramatic. Those who were told that pressing made Bobo give his marbles responded rapidly and consistently whenever his nose was lit. The children were observed for ten minutes a day, five days a week, and one four-year-old girl pressed Bobo's nose for more than four weeks—averaging sixty-seven responses per minute on some days. The children who did not receive the instructions to press a lot merely collected the marbles as they arrived and never pressed Bobo's nose again. They were dismissed from the experiment after five sessions—presumably with a new toy in hand.

This experiment is a simple yet clear demonstration of how superstitions can be passed from person to person. The kind of behavior engendered by adult instruction was an essential feature of the study. Because the instruction was to press "a lot" and because the trusting children did as they were told, Bobo's programming guaranteed that each marble appeared shortly after a nose-pressing response. Not every press was followed by a marble (in fact, the children made hundreds of responses per session in return for approximately forty marbles), nor did the children press the same number of times for each marble. Nonetheless, rapid pressing guaranteed that each marble would appear shortly after a press, and the temporal contiguity of response and reinforcement maintained the apparent power of Bobo's nose.[45]

The relationship to everyday superstition is clear. If a schoolchild is told that bringing charms to an examination will bring good luck, the potential for coincidental reinforcement is established. A good grade is likely to encourage the use of charms at future examinations. Even if the magic fails on the first try, other factors—such as witnessing another child's success with charms—may sustain the behavior until it is accidentally reinforced.

This leads us to the second important form of social transmission: social learning.

Social Learning

Parents are their children's first and most important teachers, and the sheer scope of their job is daunting. If children are to learn to walk, speak, and take care of themselves, adults cannot simply wait for a time-driven process of cognitive development to unfold. Neither can they wait until children exhibit desirable behaviors by chance, and then lavishly reinforce these lucky episodes.[46] Of course, parents do reinforce and punish the behavior of their children all the time, but most of these pokes and prods are aimed at altering the future likelihood of some already established behavior. Children are praised for playing together without conflict and admonished for running with scissors. Without social learning, the task of educating children would be painfully slow.

Simply put, what psychologists have come to call social learning or observational learning is imitation. The child observes someone else engage in an action (e.g., an adult placing a videotape into a VCR) and later attempts to do the same thing. For more than fifty years, psychologists have given much attention to imitation, and three primary theories of social learning have emerged from their work. Perhaps the longest-held theory is that imitation is a form of instinctive behavior. In 1890, in his classic text, *The Principles of Psychology*, American psychologist William James asserted that "imitativeness is possessed by man in common with other gregarious animals, and is an instinct in the fullest sense of the term."[47] Others also expressed this view, but it was not until almost a century after James's text was published that convincing evidence emerged. In a famous series of experiments, Andrew Meltzoff and M. Keith Moore tested newborn infants, some only hours old, under controlled conditions and found that babies could imitate facial movements (e.g., pursing the lips or sticking out the tongue) that had been modeled by an adult.[48] Because Meltzoff and Moore's children showed this behavior at such an early age, well before any learning could have taken place, many developmental psychologists came to believe that humans are born with the ability to imitate some simple gestures. These findings created a sensation in the field of developmental psychology because they revealed that the newborn infant has the remarkable ability to take a visual stimulus—the sight of an adult's face—and, despite being unable to see its own face, connect it with a set of parallel muscular movements. These results were particularly impressive because Meltzoff and Moore's children were too young to have had any experience watching themselves in a mirror and had probably not seen their own faces before.

A second view of observational learning holds that it is simply another form of operant conditioning. In the middle decades of this century, operant conditioning was psychology's dominant theoretical model. In 1941, Neal Miller and John Dollard published *Social Learning and Imitation*, promoting the view that imitation was a conditioning process like that studied by B. F. Skinner and others except that in this case, the antecedent condition that set the occasion for learning was the behavior of another person. Such an interpretation might hold for those cases in which someone observes a particular action, immediately imitates it, and then receives reinforcement, but as the critics of this approach were quick to point out, not all imitation occurs immediately after observing a model.[49]

In contrast, Bandura's social learning theory provides a mechanism for both immediate and long delayed reproduction of the models actions. Albert Bandura, the Stanford University psychologist who is most strongly associated with social-learning theory, is also responsible for increasing the sales of Bobo dolls. (Edward Morris's Bobo was named in honor of the doll used in Bandura's experiments.) The Bobo is an inflatable plastic clown approximately four feet high, with a weighted bottom that cries out to be hit. Once hit, poor Bobo rocks backwards on his heels, often banging his airy head on the ground, and then, thanks to the sand in his shoes, returns to an upright position, ready for more abuse. In his most famous series of experiments, Bandura and his colleagues used a beleaguered Bobo as the object of children's aggression, and psychology professors who admire Bandura's work have kept Bobo dolls in their offices ever since.

In a typical experiment, children watched through a window while an adult in a playroom struck and shouted at poor Bobo in a ritualistic way.[50] Later, when the children had an opportunity to go into the playroom, they mimicked the same forms of aggression they had seen demonstrated by the adult minutes before. Children who watched a nonaggressive model behaved more temperately in the same playroom. This research has been replicated many times under a variety of conditions with essentially the same results. When children observed the model's actions being reinforced (or at least not being punished), they imitated the behavior when given the opportunity to do so. It is this line of research that is largely responsible for the continuing concern about the effects of violent television programming on the behavior of children.[51]

Bandura's research demonstrated delayed imitation. In most of his experiments, the time between observation and reproduction was brief, just a few minutes, but the children did show delayed imitation in the playroom after the adult model had left the scene. To bridge this temporal gap, Bandura developed a theory of observational learning built on four processes that combine to produce the final mimicking action:[52]

Attentional processes. For learning to take place, the observer must observe. He or she must be able to perceive what the model is doing and must have the cognitive ability to interpret what is seen. Models, too, can enhance the observer's attention, by being interesting, by being emotional, or by engaging in simple, rather than complex, actions.

Retentional processes. To exhibit the model's behavior at some later point, the observer must remember it. Retention is affected by the observer's cognitive abilities and the use of strategies such as rehearsal (i.e., mentally replaying the scene).

Production processes. If one has attended to and retained the memory of the model's behavior, imitation may still not result. The observer must be capable of the necessary motor behavior to reproduce the observed action. I have witnessed countless NBA and college basketball players slam dunk a basketball through the hoop, yet I remain stricken with a life-long inability to imitate such behavior.

Motivational processes. Finally, when the opportunity to imitate presents itself, one must be motivated to do so. The behavior must have intrinsic reinforcement value—as dunking would for me—or the local environment must offer external sources of reinforcement for such behavior.

Thanks in large part to Bandura's research and his several books on the topic, social-learning theory has emerged as one of the most important accounts of personality development.[53] The effects of social learning have been observed in all manner of human activity, and at least one study has attempted to demonstrate that children will imitate superstitious behavior. Using their marble-dispensing version of Bobo again, Edward Morris and his colleagues attempted to produce superstitious nose-pressing in preschoolers through the observation of a peer.[54] During the previous study of the effects of instructions on children's superstitious behavior, the experimenters videotaped one child rapidly pressing Bobo's nose. In this second experiment, five children watched this videotape as part of their introduction to the task of obtaining a toy by collecting the requisite number of marbles. They were given no other information about how the marbles were produced. Five other children assigned to the control group watched a videotape that simply showed Bobo.

The videotape did not lead to nose-pressing in all of the children who watched the child from the previous study, but three of the five did press the clown's nose consistently over three weeks of daily sessions. The five children in the control group were observed for three sessions, during which one child pressed Bobo's nose a few times in one day. None of the others ever pressed Bobo's nose. Thus, according to this study, observation of a peer model can engender simple superstitions in children.

Of course, imitation is not limited to young children. Using a procedure similar to the one Roger Boshier used in his Auckland ladder study (see chapter 2), an experiment conducted at the University of Maryland demonstrated the imitation of *non*superstitious behavior by college students.[55] The researchers placed a fourteen-foot, free-standing step ladder in the lobby of a dormitory so that it straddled the most popular exit. Students exiting the dorm had to choose between walking under the ladder or going nine feet out of their way to an adjacent door. The ladder did not block the door, and both doors were propped open during the experiment. In half of the trials, when a student approached the exit, a confederate in full view of the unsuspecting walker went under the ladder and out the main entrance. On the other half of the trials, no model was provided. The result was a significant decrease in superstitious behavior when students observed a nonsuperstitious model: sixty percent of those who had observed the model walked under the ladder, as compared to only 24 percent of those who had not. Interestingly, the effect of the model disappeared when there was a rational reason to avoid walking under the ladder. When the investigators placed a window washer with a bucket and sponge on top of the ladder, approximately the same number of walkers went under the ladder in the model and no-model conditions.[56]

There are no other published experimental studies of social learning and superstition, but these demonstrations and the hundreds of other studies showing the power of imitation in the acquisition of a wide variety of behaviors make it safe to assume that social learning is an important path to superstition. The child who watches his Catholic mother light a candle for good fortune or her father repeatedly wearing his "lucky socks" on the golf course is likely to engage in similar superstitions. In actual practice, parents or peers may combine instruction ("cat's-eye marbles are lucky") with modeling (demonstrating the use of cat's eyes) —undoubtedly a particularly effective method of teaching magical practices.[57]

Social Influence and Superstition

In addition to the social and developmental processes we have already touched on, children—like adults—are susceptible to social influences, such as conformity and obedience. The most important theory of social influence is the Bibb Latané's Law of Social Impact.[58] His is a field theory, in the tradition of Gestalt psychologist Kurt Lewin, which suggests that we are influenced by social forces that vary in intensity in relation to the number of people (or sources of influence) around us, their intensity, and their immediacy. Thus, several people have a greater impact on an individual than a single person does, and someone far away has less impact than someone nearby. If, for example, you wished to convince someone of a particular point of view, the law of social impact would suggest that you should summon a group of people who hold your point of view, assemble them in the same room as the person you hope to persuade, and collectively argue with the poor individual as forcefully as possible. Such a strategy employs the principles of number, immediacy, and intensity (forcefulness of each persuading individual) to maximize the chance for success.

Inspired in part by the famous case of Kitty Genovese, who in 1964 was brutally murdered in the Kew Gardens neighborhood of New York City, Latané and co-investigator John Darley conducted several studies of the influences on altruistic behavior. The Genovese case had drawn considerable attention because it was soon discovered that thirty-eight neighbors had seen the murder in progress through their windows over the course of half an hour, yet none had intervened or even called the police. In their book *The Unresponsive Bystander: Why Doesn't He Help*,[59] Latané and Darley outlined the results of several experiments examining the problem of altruistic behavior in natural settings. Among other things, they discovered that multiple witnesses decrease the likelihood that any one witness will act. This principle, known as the diffusion of responsibility, is created by the division of impact (see Figure 5.1). Here, one individual or source (Kitty Genovese) is exerting influence on several targets (the thirty-eight witnesses); thus, the influence on any one target is reduced. The diffusion of responsibility can be felt in our different reactions to a person in need. If an elderly person stumbles and you are the only other person present, you will probably respond unhesitatingly. If, on the other hand, the same episode occurs in the middle of a small group of people, the possibility of hesitation—or complete inaction—is much greater. Further-

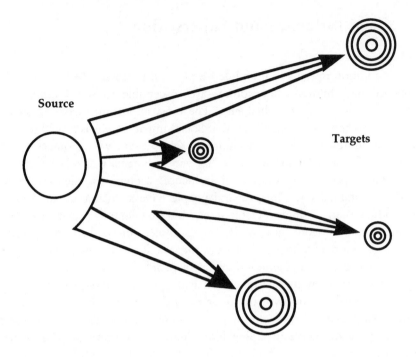

Figure 5.1   Division of impact. *Source:* Latané, (1981). Copyright (1981) by the American Psychological Association. Adapted with permission.

more, the principle of immediacy usually compels the bystander closest to the person in need to react first.

Conformity

At least some of the time, other people have the power to make us say things we would not normally say and do things we would not normally do. In most of these cases, we say what they are saying and do what they are doing: we conform to the group. Imagine the following situation. You and six other people have been asked to participate in an experiment on "visual judgment." You all sit around a table, and a psychologist presents pictures of lines of different lengths. In something of a multiple-choice format, you are presented with two white cards. The first contains a single vertical line, the standard line. The second contains three comparison lines. One of these matches the standard line, but the other two are substantially different.

At the beginning of the experiment everything is routine. The job seems exceedingly easy. Everyone agrees on the answers to the first few sets of cards, and you begin to wonder why anyone would bother to conduct such a silly experiment. Then something rather troubling happens. When the third or fourth set of cards is presented, the first participant chooses a line that is clearly different from the standard. Amazingly, when the others around the table chime in, they agree with him—making an obvious error. Then it is your turn. If you give the correct answer, you will have to contradict the six other participants. This is precisely the situation in which several Swarthmore College students found themselves in the early 1950s when Solomon Asch conducted his classic experiments in conformity.[60] What was unknown to the participants was that six of the students were confederates, following a script designed by Asch. Only one person—the hero of our scenario—was a true participant.

Asch's findings were dramatic. Despite the concrete nature of the judgments in these experiments, Swarthmore college students made errors in keeping with the majority—they conformed—on up to 35 percent of these trials. A number of factors affected the degree of conformity. For example, consistent with Latané's Social Impact Theory, the larger the opposing group of confederates, the greater the conformity observed in the true participants.[61] But in many replications of Asch's original studies, large numbers of participants expressed judgments that—we can be certain—they would not have made under different circumstances. Did the students actually believe what they were saying when they went with the majority and chose the wrong line? Not all of them. Conformity is defined as "a change in behavior or belief toward a group as a result of real or imagined group pressure."[62] When the change is in behavior only, it is called *compliance*; when it is a change in belief, it is called *private acceptance*. Asch's college students appear to have shown both kinds of conformity. Some came to believe that the group was right and they were wrong. Others told Asch they went along with the majority to avoid "spoiling your results."[63]

Asch's experiments focused on conformity as behavior under the control of social forces, but it can also be studied as a trait: a conformity disposition. In children, this disposition is thought to follow an inverted U-shaped developmental trend. In the early years, conformity is relatively absent, but it increases steadily to a peak during adolescence, when the need for affiliation with a group is greatest.[64] With further maturity, this need diminishes and, with it, so does the conformity disposition. Studies of adolescents have found that both social forces—peer pressure, for example—and a disposition for conformity increase the likelihood of "misbehavior" (drug and alcohol use, sexual behavior, and delinquency).[65]

Although no one has explicitly examined the relationship between conformity and childhood superstition, the link is undoubtedly there. The behavior and beliefs documented by the Opies are part of the culture of schoolchildren, and for any individual child, the adoption of this behavior is likely to be affected by subtle (and not-so-subtle) peer influence, as well as the child's disposition toward conformity. The research also shows that if one wishes to be liked—as most of us do—going along with the group is the best strategy. The famous social psychologist Stanley Schachter conducted a classic study in which he engaged small groups of people in discussions.[66] Three of the participants in each group were confederates: *the deviant*, who was instructed to oppose the group unswervingly, *the slider*, who disagreed with the majority at the beginning but gradually switched sides as the discussion progressed, and *the mode*, who consistently agreed with the majority. As you might expect, groups arranged in this way spent much of their time trying unsuccessfully to recruit the deviant, but Schachter also discovered that when the discussion was ended, group members found the deviant significantly less attractive than either the slider or the mode. Thus, the study suggested that if you dare to buck the majority, you can expect both to be the focus of much peer pressure and to be disliked, each of which are strong incentives to conform. To the extent that children want to be accepted and liked, they are often willing to adopt the magical practices of their social group, even when—like Asch's line-judging college students—they know better.

Obedience to Authority

Conformity, again, is a change in belief or behavior in response to peers. When the social influence comes through request of someone of a higher status, it is called obedience. One of the most famous of all psychology experiments demonstrated very dramatically the extent to which average people will obey an authority figure.[67] Yale University psychologist Stanley Milgram asked people to participate in an experiment that would look at the effects of punishment on human learning. In one version of the study, two people were recruited and greeted in the laboratory by a male scientist dressed in a gray lab coat. Straws were drawn to determine which participant would be the "learner" and which the "teacher;" however, because the drawing was rigged and one of the participants was actually a trained actor working for Milgram, the same friendly gentleman who said he had a "heart condition" was always the learner. Only one person, the teacher, was a true participant in the experiment.

The experimenter escorted the learner into a room, strapped him into a chair, and attached an electrode to his wrist. The teacher was seated at a table in an adjoining room. On top of the table was a large shock generator equipped with a row of thirty switches, each labeled with a voltage ranging from 15 volts on the left to 450 volts on the extreme right. In addition, verbal indicators were given for various voltages: starting with "Slight Shock" on the left, "Moderate Shock" in the middle, "Danger: Severe Shock" on the right. The final switch was designated simply "XXX." To give the teacher an appreciation for what his pupil would be experiencing, the experimenter gave him[68] a sample shock at 45 volts and said, "Although the shocks can be extremely painful, they cause no permanent tissue damage." Of course, the generator was not real, and the only shock actually given throughout the experiment was the "sample" received by the teacher.

The experimenter then explained that the teacher would be reading multiple-choice questions to the learner over an intercom system, and the learner would indicate his choice by throwing one of four switches that lit colored lights in the teacher's room. Whenever the learner made an error, the teacher was to shock him by throwing one of the switches on the panel, starting with the low voltages on the left and moving up with each successive error.

The learner followed a standard script. As you might guess, he made many errors, which meant that, to satisfy the scientist, the participant had to administer many shocks. As the voltages went up, the learner—who was not visible in his adjoining room—made a number of sounds. At 75 volts he began to grunt with each shock. At 120 volts he shouted that the shocks were becoming painful, and at 150 volts he pleaded with the experimenter to stop the experiment, saying that he refused to go on. At 270 volts (if the teacher continued to this point), the learner gave out a loud scream, and at 300 volts he announced that he would no longer answer. The experimenter indicated that no response must be considered a wrong answer and that the shocks must continue. For the next few questions, the learner screamed loudly after each shock, and eventually there was no sound at all from the learner's room.

The experimenter also followed a script. If the teacher, the true participant in the study, hesitated, the experimenter would say, "The experiment requires that you continue" or "You have no choice; you *must* go on." Thus, in the framework of Latané's Law of Social Impact, the participant in Milgram's experiment was being squeezed between the forces of the learner and the experimenter. The experimenter had several advantages in this conflict of social influences. He was more immediate than the learner because he was in the same room as the teacher, and he drew intensity from his status as an authority figure. Latané's third concept, number, was even in this case, since there was only one learner and one experimenter.

For his part, the learner was less immediate, but his influence grew (through increased strength) as his tortured performance progressed. The experimental question was, of course, Would people keep shocking this poor man with the heart condition, or would they act humanely and defy the evil scientist?

Milgram's research in this area is important because the results were unexpected. To get a sense of what professionals might expect from his experiment, Milgram described it to a group of forty psychiatrists and asked them to predict how many participants would obey the experimenter all the way to the 450 volt level at the end of the panel. They said only approximately one person in a thousand (0.125 percent) would be pathological enough to continue to the end. In fact, a full 63 percent of the teachers obeyed to the bitter end.[69] Most people in Milgram's study, and in replications of his study in other locations in the United States and other countries, never defied an authority figure who would have to be described as cruel and unreasonable.

Milgram's findings were also important because they challenged common notions of evil. They suggested that someone like Adolf Eichmann, who presided over the murder of millions of Jews during World War II, might not be the monster we think him to be, but rather a more ordinary person behaving under the influence of powerful social forces. Indeed, descriptions of Eichmann support this view.[70] To be sure, the situations experienced and actions taken by Eichmann and the participants in Milgram's study were quite different. For example, Eichmann's deeds were done over several years, whereas Milgram's experiment lasted only an hour. Nonetheless, Milgram's research and that of Latané, Asch, and other social psychologists shows that behavior which we think results from stable personality characteristics or dispositions is often caused by more immediate social forces.

To what extent does obedience to authority figures contribute to the development of superstition? By virtue of their youth, children are of relatively low social status. To a child, almost everyone is an authority figure, and parents are particularly important authority figures. When, as a young girl, Nancy Reagan was instructed not to put her hat on the bed, the greater social status of her parents played a role in her compliance. What is unknown is the role of authority figures in the lasting acquisition of superstitious behavior. Does compliance with an authority lead to sustained behavior later in life? Does direct instruction in superstition by a parent lead to greater levels of adult belief than instruction by a peer?

These questions will not be answered without additional research, because existing evidence suggests that children have a fairly sophisticated view of parental authority. Piaget thought children viewed adults as monolithic authority figures who derived their status from advanced years, superior size, and greater power.[71] More recent research suggests that children view parental authority in a more detailed fashion. For example, according to one study, children felt that parents had legitimate authority to make rules regarding stealing and the completion of household chores, but they described their choice of friends as outside the bounds of parental influence.[72] Children place similar boundaries around the authority of other adults.[73] In addition, changes in our culture since Milgram conducted his research in the 1960's may have altered the view of authority figures. Thus, the role of authority figures in the social transmission of superstition represents a complex and largely unanswered question.

Imagination

When I was in elementary school, my teacher wrote a comment on my report card that became a source of lasting amusement for my family: "Stuart is a pleasant child, but he daydreams too much." Although waking dreams may have been my downfall in second grade, those who study childhood imagination and make-believe suggest that this kind of behavior has many positive effects.[74] Pretend play, like other forms of play, provides both immediate benefits and preparation for later life. According to various theorists, imaginative play helps children assimilate new information, modulate their emotions, and define their identities.[75] Children express their imagination to varying degrees, but the absence of pretend play in young children is a source of some concern.

It has long been thought that imaginative play in children is related to creativity in adulthood. Imagination opens the child to the "realm of the possible,"[76] which is a prelude to divergent thinking—the ability to generate alternative possibilities. In turn, divergent thinking is an important constituent of intelligent and creative behavior. Although no one has studied the relationship between make-believe play and superstition, it seems reasonable to suggest that a such a relationship might exist. Unfortunately, there is some ambiguity about its nature. Being open to the "realm of the possible" sounds remarkably close to the attitude taken by New Agers and others who are willing to believe in various unscientific and paranormal phenomena. "Keep an open mind," they implore. Those who are more imaginative than others may be more accepting of alternate realities and unusual cause-and-effect relationships. For example, in his book *Supernatural on stage: Ghosts and Superstitions of the Theatre*, Richard Huggett asserts that "of all professional bodies, actors are the most superstitious," and in an effort to explain this characteristic he cites actors' "strong imagination and sense of fantasy."[77] This is not scientific evidence, but it does support the common view that imagination promotes superstitious belief. On the other hand, a talent for divergent thinking—a common form of creativity and imagination—enables one to generate alternative explanations for various phenomena. Psychic predictions are not so impressive if we can think of other ways they might have been accomplished.[78] Of course, there is a third possibility: that childhood imagination is not related to superstitions at all. The answer awaits future research.

• • •

Both our own personal experiences and the Opies' careful documentation make it clear that superstitious behavior is a common feature of childhood. Underdeveloped reasoning abilities and social learning are important determinates of early superstition, and a number of other psychological forces—conformity, obedience to authority, and imaginative play—may further contribute to its development. Nonetheless, much is unknown about the early emergence of superstition. For example, there are no longitudinal studies to tell us whether childhood superstition leads to adult superstition. Common sense and the testimony of believers, such as Nancy Reagan, suggest that it does, but we have no direct evidence.

The superstitions that are typical of schoolchildren seem harmless enough. They have the quality of games or amusements shared by youthful playmates. But can superstitions be harmful? Can superstition or belief in the paranormal be a form of abnormal behavior? It is to these, and related, questions that we now turn.

6

Is Superstition Abnormal, Irrational, or Neither?

Who in the rainbow can draw the line where the violet tint ends and the orange tint begins? Distinctly we see the difference of the colors, but where exactly does the one first blendingly enter into the other? So with sanity and insanity.
—Herman Melville, *Billy Budd*

He remembers that it began on August 28, 1965, when he was thirteen years old. He and his father were watching *Tea House of the August Moon*, on NBC's Saturday Night at the Movies. Eventually he went to bed and was struck with a profound fear that he was "queer." Things seemed unreal to him, and he was aware that his feelings were not normal. From this point on, his life was filled with irrational fears and obsessive thoughts. The onset of his difficulties on August 28 gave the number twenty-eight special significance. He engaged in rituals twenty-eight times for fear that not doing so would lead to the death of a loved one or would make time run backwards. Living in the San Francisco area, he was obsessed with the fear not just that an earthquake would occur, but that he would do something to *cause* an earthquake. On occasion, he was afraid that simply touching an object might be enough. He was haunted by the belief that Pepperidge Farms products could cause earthquakes because an earthquake occurred on Thanksgiving Day in 1974, shortly after he had eaten a Pepperidge Farms turnover.

His parents eventually divorced, and his mother moved to the East Coast. When it came time to go to college, he chose Carleton College in Minnesota, both to avoid his earthquake fears and to be halfway between his parents. For a time, the hot- and cold-water taps of his sink began to symbolize to him his parents' differing political views, mother on the left and father on the right, and whenever he used the sink he felt compelled to turn on both the hot and cold water.

Now in his mid-forties, he continues to fight against the irrational thoughts that plague his daily life, and he often writes about his struggles with mental illness. This passage, written for a mental-health association's newsletter, describes his efforts to defeat the irrational ideas and impulses that invade his mind:

> Based on long experience, I believe that it may be best to treat magical thinking as an internal enemy, a treasonable bully who should not be appeased. I say that because I've learned that, once I act on the basis of an admittedly irrational view of cause and effect, it becomes harder to summon up the rational part of me.[1]

* * *

Are superstitions abnormal? Can they be indicative of a psychological disorder? Should we be concerned about our mental health if we are superstitious? We will approach these questions in two ways. First, we will try to define abnormal behavior and measure examples of superstitious behavior against our definition. Then, taking the question from a different angle, we will identify known mental disorders that have features resembling superstitious behavior or paranormal beliefs and attempt to determine what, if any, relationship they have to common superstitions. Somewhere between these two approaches we should find an answer to our questions.

What Is Abnormal?

As you might expect, this question is more easily asked than answered. Although mental-health professionals and laypeople agree that certain forms of behavior are abnormal or pathological, there is little agreement on a general definition of abnormality. The *Diagnostic and Statistical Manual of Mental Disorders (4th Edition)*[2], known as *DSM-IV*, is the American Psychiatric Association's catalogue of psychopathology. It contains the current list of mental disorders recognized by the American Psychiatric

Association and the criteria for their diagnosis. As the Roman numeral suggests, this manual is a work in progress. It has gone through many editions, each one changing the method of diagnosis and adding and subtracting disorders from the list. In an earlier version, homosexuality was considered a mental disorder; today it is not. New disorders, some controversial, are introduced to replace the ones that fall by the wayside; still others merely change their names or reproduce, splitting into several smaller disorders. As fluid and impermanent as it is, the *DSM-IV* has become the accepted clinical manual used by mental health professionals to diagnose mental disorders.

At 886 pages, *DSM-IV* contains almost everything you would want to know about identifying mental health problems, yet its authors devote only four brief paragraphs to the problem of defining mental disorder. The authors admit that "the concept of mental disorder . . . lacks a consistent operational definition that covers all situations"[3]; nonetheless, they propose the following:

> a clinically significant behavioral or psychological syndrome or pattern that occurs in an individual and that is associated with present distress (e.g., a painful symptom) or disability (i.e., impairment in one or more important areas of functioning) or with a significantly increased risk of suffering death, pain, disability, or an important loss of freedom.[4]

This, too, is rather vague. Things always get difficult when one is asked to judge what is "significant" and what is not; what does the phrase "clinically significant" really mean? However, the American Psychiatric Association definition does rest on three possible criteria for inclusion and several for exclusion. An observed syndrome or pattern of behavior may be a mental disorder if it meets any one of three criteria. First, the syndrome may be distressful to the individual who has it. Second, the syndrome may create problems in "one or more important areas of functioning," such as health, career, or family relationships. Finally, the syndrome may involve "significantly" increased risk of death or disability. Such a condition cannot be considered a mental disability if it is an understandable response to tragedy or if it is a form of deviant behavior that is primarily a conflict between the individual and society (e.g., unusual political or religious beliefs). Furthermore, many disorders in the *DSM-IV* specifically rule out syndromes that result from a general medical condition.

Although the American Psychiatric Association has attempted to make *DSM-IV* atheoretical, the language of the manual is as one might expect, reminiscent of a biomedical view of abnormal behavior. Psychological problems are organized into "syndromes," which are detected by the presence of "symptoms" and assumed to have some "etiology," a source. Without question, biological factors, such as genetics and brain chemistry, are important causes of behavior, but our actions are also determined by other variables. The biomedical model is only one of several ways of conceptualizing normal and abnormal behavior.[5] Furthermore, for our examination of superstition and belief in the paranormal, the biomedical model is overly constraining. Abnormal superstition—if it exists—may not appear in the form of a well-organized syndrome, and it may not have a biological cause. We will return to the *DSM-IV* when we examine known psychological disorders that have features resembling superstition or belief in the paranormal, but for now, let us move to a definition of abnormal behavior that is less theoretically laden and, perhaps, a bit more specific.

David Rosenhan and Martin Seligman[6] have proposed a "family-resemblance" approach to abnormal behavior. Acknowledging that a uniform and consistent definition of abnormality is difficult to establish, they have identified seven elements or properties of abnormality. A person's behavior may not show all seven elements, but if several are present with sufficient severity, then the label *abnormal* can be applied with some confidence. Two different forms of behavior (e.g., paranoia and depression) may both be legitimately classified as abnormal and yet show different elements of abnormality. Rosenhan and Seligman compare this method to the judgment of family resemblance. People from the same family are all said to resemble each other, even though a brother and sister may have similarly shaped noses and the same hair color and two other individuals may have very different features in common.

Rosenhan and Seligman's seven elements of abnormality are:
- Suffering
- Maladaptiveness
- Irrationality and incomprehensibility
- Unpredictability and loss of control
- Vividness and unconventionality
- Observer discomfort
- Violation of moral and ideal standards

Suffering and maladaptiveness are different names for the *DSM-IV*'s distress and disability criteria. Behavior that does not serve the individual and is poorly suited to his or her life circumstances is considered maladaptive. Irrationality and incomprehensibility are demonstrated when a person acts in ways that seem meaningless or absurd. For example, people who are stricken with schizophrenia exhibit thought disorders and hallucinations that, by all appearances, have no understandable pattern or theme.

Many mental disorders include a feature of unpredictability and loss of control. The individual may show sudden changes in personality or erratic and unexpected shifts in behavior. While suffering from manic depression, a person may impulsively leave on a Hawaiian vacation and spend all of his savings. Later, he may become so depressed that he is unable to get out of bed for several days. Although spontaneity may be typical and even desirable under certain circumstances, a number of psychological problems include examples of severe unpredictability and dramatic loss of control.

Rosenhan and Seligman's concept of vividness and unconventionality is one that must be judged with some care. The vividness of a behavior is related to its statistical infrequency. A raggedly dressed man who stands on the street corner shouting at people who are not there appears abnormal in part because we see so few people behaving this way (except, perhaps, in large cities). Yet, infrequency alone is not sufficient cause to label behavior abnormal. The genius of an Isaac Asimov or the athletic ability of a Michael Jordan is extremely rare, but because these are socially desirable behaviors, we do not label them abnormal. Conversely, infrequency is not necessary for abnormality. Depression is relatively common; yet if serious enough, it is considered a mental disorder.

The shouting man appears abnormal because his behavior is unconventional. Social norms dictate that, under most circumstances, we should conduct conversations only with people who exist and are actually present to hear what we are saying. There are exceptions to this rule, of course, such as when we rehearse what we are going to say in an important conversation, but it is interesting to note that we often joke about people "talking to themselves" and feel embarrassed when we are caught doing so. But our view of conventional and unconventional behavior changes frequently with time and point of view. Behavior that is common and acceptable in one culture would appear bizarre in another. Similarly, many of the clothes we feel quite comfortable wearing today would have appeared extremely unusual a hundred years ago. Moreover, the judgment of unconventionality can be a dangerously subjective activity. I can remember a girl from my high school who used to sing and perform a solitary ballet-like dance in the park across the street from our school. Although I knew her to be a very good student, in my adolescent view, she was crazy. Looking back today with a more mature eye, I think she seemed a bit lonely but not abnormal. I suspect she was a very creative person.

People whose behavior is abnormal often create discomfort in those around them (observer discomfort). They may be unusually needy and demanding, or they may violate unwritten rules of social behavior. For example, in most contexts it is not acceptable to stand very close to a person who is not a family member or lover. Crowded subway cars and other congested locations are excepted from this rule, but in open environments where adequate space is available, people choose to stand a comfortable distance apart. The actual boundary of one's personal space may vary from person to person and across cultures, but most people have a distinct line that, when crossed, causes them some discomfort. There are many other social conventions, such as those defining private versus public behavior, that, when not adhered to, can make us feel uncomfortable.

Finally, Rosenhan and Seligman suggest that behavior may be abnormal if it violates moral or ideal standards. It is widely believed that people should love, be supportive, and be kind. They should work, as long as they are not independently wealthy and work is available. So the person who is cruel, disloyal, or unusually shy may be judged abnormal.

Rosenhan and Seligman's family-resemblance approach to labeling abnormal behavior avoids the theory-laden language of the *DSM-IV* definition while providing adequate detail to capture the varied forms of psychopathology we encounter. Furthermore, in applying this approach we are using a process similar to that used to diagnose a specific mental disorder. Most of the psychological problems in the *DSM-IV* are defined by a list of typical "symptoms." If enough of the symptoms are present in an individual, the diagnostic label may be applied. Unfortunately, diagnosis using any method can involve difficult decisions. As we have seen, several of Rosenhan and Seligman's elements of abnormality require judgments that are susceptible to bias and error. Bearing this caveat in mind, let us apply this seven-element definition to superstitious behavior.

Is Superstitious Behavior Abnormal?

Based on Rosenhan and Seligman's criteria, most superstitions are not abnormal. Trying to be as objective as possible, I have provided the scoring in Table 6.1. In most cases, superstitious behavior does not produce suffering. Ill-advised actions may lead to suffering or other difficulties, but most common superstitious behavior does not itself produce distress. In contrast, some appears to produce some psychological benefit.

Again, most superstitions are not maladaptive. The athlete who uses a lucky item or performs a pregame ritual probably does not adversely affect either her play or her life in general. Most popular superstitions, both socially shared and personal superstitions, are of this benign variety. Yet, some examples are clearly maladaptive. For example, the student mentioned in chapter 2 who felt compelled to find a penny before taking an exam wasted time that could have been spent studying or resting. As you

Table 6.1 An assessment of the abnormality of typical superstitious behavior using Rosenhan and Seligman's criteria

Criteria	
Suffering	No
Maladaptiveness	Yes/No
Irrationality and incomprehensibility	Yes
Unpredictability	No
Vividness and unconventionality	Yes/No
Observer discomfort	No
Violation of moral and ideal standards	No

recall, he sometimes found it necessary to visit local bus stops in search of his lucky token. In some cases, at least, he might have performed better on the exam had he not engaged in this ritual.

Superstitions are irrational. At least, they are irrational if we look at them objectively and scientifically. There is no objective way known to physics or psychology that finding a penny can improve test performance. There is no scientific evidence to support the usefulness of a rabbit's foot or the evilness of black cats. Yet, most superstitions are not perceived by observers as being the kind of irrational and incomprehensible behavior that is typically associated with mental illness. Schizophrenia is a serious mental disorder that usually includes behavior that is dramatically at odds with what seems normal. Many schizophrenic patients have what are called "thought disorders," which may lead them to hear voices or say that other people are controlling them in some way. The irrationality of most superstitious behavior is mild compared to this kind of psychopathology.

Unpredictability and loss of control are clearly not features of superstitious behavior. In most cases, superstitions are employed with deliberateness and purpose, often quite ritualistically. Indeed, as we have seen, superstitious behavior most often appears during uncontrollable circumstances as an effort to exert greater control.

Rosenhan and Seligman's concept of vividness is related to its statistical rarity. When behavior is common, it is not particularly remarkable; but if it is rare, we notice it. Unusual behavior seems unconventional and abnormal. In the case of superstition, the behavior is often quite typical. As we have learned, the traditional, socially shared beliefs are quite prevalent. Personal superstitions are more idiosyncratic. Using an Internet discussion group, I recently surveyed other teachers of psychology about exam-related superstitions they had encountered. Although I expected to get stories of rituals they had observed in their students, most of the responses were about superstitions that friends or spouses used in college. One network participant told the story of taking a course in a semi-submerged basement classroom. On exam days, a friend insisted on entering the classroom through a basement window. This behavior is quite rare, and must have appeared vivid and unconventional to the other people in the class. Yet, the unconventionality of this behavior is drastically diminished when it is identified as a superstition. People often do unusual things to increase their luck. A particular personal superstition (e.g., entering rooms through windows) may appear vivid and unconventional, but the general category of superstitious behavior is quite common.

Observer discomfort is an unlikely feature of superstitious behavior. If anything, a friend's lucky charm or superstitious ritual is a source of amusement and teasing. Furthermore, the potential for ridicule may push some believers to hide their superstitions, making both teasing and observer discomfort less likely. Finally, in most cases, superstitious behavior does not violate moral or ideal standards. Some religious believers hold that superstitions are a form of paganism and an affront to God, but this is not a popular attitude. Superstitious beliefs are far more prevalent than this particular religious view. As we learned in chapter 1, throughout history, magic and religion have coexisted quite comfortably. Even today, faith healing and other magical religious beliefs are very common. The violation of ideal standards is also quite rare. Superstitions rarely interfere with normal standards of behavior. People who are superstitious maintain love relationships, jobs, and families, and as a group they are no more aggressive, depressed, or shy than the general public. As we have seen, superstition is correlated with a number of negative personality dimensions (anxiety, depression, fear of death), but no study has determined that the levels of these traits are abnormal. On average, those who are superstitious show higher levels of these traits, but judgment of abnormality must be based on the intensity of the problem and the extent to which it is in conflict with ideal standards. Casual observation of superstitious people suggests that, in the great majority of cases, their levels of anxiety and depression are not abnormal.

So, of the seven elements of abnormality proposed by Rosenhan and Seligman, only three apply to superstitious behavior, and even these are not as strongly represented as in most mental disorders. Irrationality is probably the most obvious feature of superstition, but the irrationality of superstitious and paranormal beliefs is typically less problematic than, for example, the hallucinations of a person stricken with schizophrenia. In sum, we have to conclude that common superstitious behaviors and paranormal beliefs are not abnormal. One need not seek psychological services for the treatment of belief in astrology. Nevertheless, the converse is not true.

Some serious mental disorders do include forms of superstition and magical thinking.

Superstition and Mental Disorders

Obsessive-Compulsive Disorder

The mental disorder with features most akin to normal superstitious behavior is obsessive-compulsive disorder. It is this condition that afflicts the earthquake-fearing man described at the beginning of this chapter. Obsessive-compulsive disorder is a member of the larger category of anxiety disorders. Some anxiety disorders, such as panic disorder, are so called because anxiety is the primary disturbance; in other cases, including obsessive-compulsive disorder and phobias, anxiety is experienced when an individual attempts to resist his or her compulsions or confront a feared object.

Obsessive-compulsive disorder is equally common in boys and girls, but it appears earlier in boys. In boys, its onset comes between six and fifteen years of age, and in girls (young women) between twenty and twenty-nine years. The primary features are *obsessions*, unwanted, often disturbing, thoughts or impulses that occur repeatedly and are difficult to control, and *compulsions*, behavioral responses to these obsessions that frequently take the form of repetitious, rigidly executed movements that are difficult to resist.[7] Fears of germs and contamination are very common, and hand-washing or other forms of cleansing rituals are by far the most popular form of compulsive behavior, found in 85 percent of one sample.[8] In her book *The Boy Who Couldn't Stop Washing*, National Institute of Health psychiatrist Judith Rapoport tells the story of a boy named Charles who, at age fourteen, spent three hours a day in the shower and two hours a day dressing.[9] Other people with similar compulsions may wash their hands with strong soaps and cleaning fluid until the skin is raw and chapped.[10] Often children initially hide their rituals by making more frequent trips to the bathroom or executing their rituals in private. Eventually their parents discover their unusual patterns of behavior and seek help.

Howard Hughes is said to have had a lifelong fear of contamination that resulted in elaborate rituals. His aides wore special pads on their hands to avoid touching things they brought to him, and he had lengthy instructions for the preparation of foods.[11] For example, the simple opening of a can of fruit required a nine-step procedure that included the use of sterile utensils and an elaborate method of washing the can prior to opening.[12] The famous eighteenth-century literary figure Samuel Johnson also appears to have suffered from an obsessive-compulsive disorder that took the form of checking rituals (e.g., repeatedly checking lights and locks) and excessive routines involving comings and goings. Johnson approached doorways with a certain number of steps and always stepped across the threshold with the same foot (it is not clear which one). When walking on the street, Johnson never stepped on the cracks between paving stones but would touch every post he passed. According to his biographer, James Boswell, Johnson's behavior had a truly compulsive quality. If felt he had missed a post, he would go back to touch it. [13]

For people with obsessive-compulsive disorder, sometimes the simple activity of walking down stairs can involve a process of repeatedly going up and down the stairs counting each step in a proscribed manner. If for some reason the ritual is interrupted or the person is disturbed by a sound or some other event, the sequence must be started again. Often those who engage in this kind of behavior believe—as the earthquake-fearing man did—that, if they do not complete these compulsive rituals, some horrible event, such as the death of a loved one, will result. In some cases, these rituals can take several minutes, and those afflicted with them complain that they get "stuck."

The causes of obsessive-compulsive disorder are not well understood, but most researchers believe there is some inherited component to the condition. Immediate family members of people with obsessive-compulsive disorder are more likely to exhibit psychiatric problems than those in the general population.[14] In addition, anomalies of brain chemistry are implicated, specifically abnormal levels of the neurotransmitter serotonin. But as with many mental disorders, obsessive-compulsive disorder is probably produced by genetic and biological factors combined with environmental forces. Many people with this disorder can be helped by behavior therapy, medication, or a combination of the two. Nevertheless, in a large number of cases, problems with obsessions and compulsions persist into adulthood. In addition, by the time they are adults, many people with obsessive-compulsive disorder develop other, associated psychological problems, the most common of which is depression.

Magical Thinking and Obsessive-Compulsive Disorder

Many of the thoughts and actions of people with obsessive-compulsive disorder resemble common superstitions, especially superstitions that involve "bad luck": avoiding black cats in your path and stepping on cracks in the pavement, for example. People with obsessive-compulsive disorder do not engage in rituals aimed at enhancing their luck; they hope to avoid imagined dire consequences. Often the compulsions and obsessive thoughts do not seem directed toward a particular feared event. Instead, the afflicted individual simply feels that he or she must engage in rituals; if there is any positive effect at all, it is a temporary reduction in anxiety. Yet some do say that they engage in their compulsions because they are afraid of what will happen if they fail to do so. Sometimes the fear is nonspecific, as in the case of a boy who avoided certain numbers because he felt they were unlucky—a practice that sounds very much like a superstition.[15] Others, like the man who feared he might start a California earthquake, have a specific, magical purpose for their actions. But are these behaviors normal superstitions gone bad, or are they distinct features of mental disorder that have an unrelated cause?

Henrietta Leonard and her colleagues at the National Institute of Mental Health have studied this question as part of a larger investigation of obsessive-compulsive disorder.[16] They selected a group of thirty-eight children with obsessive-compulsive disorder ranging in age from seven to eighteen and a comparison group of twenty-two children obtained through newspaper advertisements. The children from this nonclinical control group were of the same average age as the children with obsessive-compulsive disorder and were screened for psychological problems. Leonard conducted structured interviews with the children of each group and their parents. They were asked about the child's belief in particular superstitions (e.g., "Do you [does your child] have a lucky number?") and about early developmental rituals commonly observed as part of normal development (e.g. arranging stuffed animals in a particular way each night before bed).[17]

Both groups had low and equivalent levels of superstition. However, developmental rituals were significantly more common in the group with obsessive-compulsive disorder. Only 27 percent of the control group had a marked childhood ritual, in contrast to 70 percent of the group with obsessive-compulsive disorder. Furthermore, the extent of rituals, both during preschool ages (two to five years) and grade school (six to twelve years) was greater in the clinical group. But many of the developmental rituals remembered by the children in the obsessive-compulsive group and their parents appeared related to the child's major obsessive-compulsive symptoms. For example, one fifteen-year-old girl had an early ritual of arranging her toys in a certain way and not wanting to disturb them—to the extent that she avoided playing with them. Her current compulsions involved checking, arranging, and straightening. When the developmental rituals that resembled clinical symptoms were eliminated from the analysis, the two groups were no longer significantly different.

Leonard and her colleagues drew a number of conclusions from these results. First, their findings suggest that childhood superstitions are not related to obsessive-compulsive disorder. There were no differences between the groups on this dimension, and furthermore, all of the children with obsessive-compulsive disorder reported that superstitions were "what everyone did" and were "different from [obsessive-compulsive disorder]."[18] The relationship of developmental rituals to obsessive-compulsive disorder was not as clear from the results of this study. The more frequent childhood rituals among the clinical group might be caused by biased reporting (parents of diagnosed children may remember these behaviors more distinctly than parents of typical children) or by the occurrence of early, mild bouts of obsessive-compulsive disorder. The more extensive developmental rituals may be precursors of obsessive-compulsive disorder, but a more complete understanding of the relationship between childhood rituals and obsessive-compulsive disorder awaits future research.

Magical Thinking and Schizophrenia

Obsessive-compulsive disorder used to be called a neurosis, a term no longer used to classify mental disorders. People with neurotic disorders were said to experience emotionally distressing symptoms and unwelcome psychological states, but their behavior was reasonably within the boundaries of social norms.[19] In contrast, psychosis—a term still in use—refers to a disorder characterized by profound disturbances of thought and emotion.[20] For example, psychotic patients often suffer from hallucinations or delusions that indicate a serious break in their contact with reality. Because psychotic disorders are of greater severity than neuroses, people with psychoses more often require hospitalization.

The most prominent psychotic disorder is schizophrenia. Often schizophrenia is misconstrued as "split personality" (a description more consistent with multiple personality disorder). There are actually several schizophrenic disorders, all of which share the features of a substantial break from reality, such as delusions, hallucinations, seriously disorganized speech. The delusions of schizophrenia may include the belief that one is Jesus Christ, royalty, or some other grandiose figure. Other delusions may lead to the belief that one's thoughts are being controlled by outside forces (a delusion of control) or that someone is "out to get me" (a delusion of persecution). Hallucinations are perceptual disorders that may be auditory, such as the common schizophrenic symptom of "hearing voices," visual, or tactile. Even hallucinations of smell and taste are possible. Of course, to be considered psychotic symptoms, hallucinations must occur when the individual is awake and sober; dreams and pharmacological experiences are exempted. Disorganized schizophrenic speech often involves "loosening of associations," a condition that leads its sufferers to bounce inexplicably from topic to topic. When questioned, the individual may respond with a completely unrelated answer. Finally, people with schizophrenia may show few outward signs of emotion. Their faces may appear expressionless and unresponsive, they may avoid eye contact, and they may express little through body language.

Schizophrenia has serious implications for its victims. Prior to the 1950s, most schizophrenics were simply warehoused in barren institutions such as those depicted in the famous documentary film *Titicut Follies* and the novel and feature film *One Flew Over the Cuckoo's Nest*. But beginning in the mid-1950s, the growing use of neuroleptic drugs produced dramatic changes in the prognosis of many schizophrenic patients. In 1955, approximately half a million Americans were living in psychiatric hospitals, and 50 percent of all hospital beds were occupied by psychiatric patients, many of whom were schizophrenic. By 1977, the psychiatric inpatient population had dropped to less than 160,000.[21] Yet, despite the revolutionary effects of psychopharmacology on the treatment of schizophrenia, its therapeutic course is rarely smooth. The condition itself is quite variable, with periods of remission and relapse. Complete remission is rare, and of those discharged from inpatient facilities, many will later be readmitted. For example, in 1972, 72 percent of all schizophrenics admitted to hospitals had been there before.[22] Although much progress has been made in recent years, schizophrenia remains a serious psychiatric problem and the subject of much research.

In addition to the investigation of pharmacological and psychological treatments for schizophrenia, much current research has focused on identifying the causes of the disorder and predicting its occurrence. These efforts may someday lead to strategies for preventing schizophrenia or minimizing its effects. It is this research, particularly research in the identification of people at risk for development of schizophrenia, that has revealed the strongest relationship between superstition and this (or, in fact, *any*) mental disorder. Whereas the relationship of superstitious behavior to obsessive-compulsive disorder seems to be one of mere appearance rather than substance, the evidence for a real connection between superstition and schizophrenia is stronger. But before we understand this connection, we must address the origins and development of the disorder.

The Beginnings of Schizophrenia

Schizophrenia is a classic example of the combined influences of nature and nurture, heredity and environment. The disorder runs in families, with the children of schizophrenics having increased risk of developing the disorder themselves. But this alone does not prove a hereditary link. Schizo-phrenia might be genetically transmitted, or growing up with schizo-phrenic parents might create a chaotic environment that produces the dis-order through a form of social contagion. In fact, both of these hypotheses are true. Adoption studies have shown that the children of schizophrenics are more likely to develop this disorder if they are raised by their own par-ents than if adopted by unaffected parents.[23] Thus, the environment pro-vided by schizophrenic parents has some influence on their children's men-tal health. However, these and other adoption studies reveal a hereditary link as well. Even when raised by unaffected parents, the children of schiz-ophrenics show higher rates of the disorder than children of unaffected parents.[24]

Although these hereditary and environmental factors are thought to be important influences, it should be remembered that we are in the realm of risk factors, not complete answers to the question of cause. For example, approximately 90 percent of those who develop schizophrenia do not have schizophrenic parents.[25] Therefore, the best scientific evidence suggests that genetics supplies a predisposition for schizophrenia which must be combined with other experiences (stressful life events or disruptive social relationships) to produce the disorder. It will be some time before our understanding of the roots of schizophrenia is complete, but in the mean-time, some additional indicators of risk have been identified. One of the most important of these involves *magical ideation*—a condition related to superstition and paranormal belief.

Several theories have been proposed to explain the appearance of schiz-ophrenia in some people at risk but not others.[26] These theories are com-plicated and somewhat speculative, and we need not be troubled with them here. But one risk factor recognized by a number of experts is the presence of *schizotypal personality disorder*, a condition that resembles a less severe version of schizophrenia.[27] Although the great majority of people with schizotypal personality disorder will not go on to develop genuine schizo-phrenia, the two conditions are thought to be genetically related, with schizotypal individuals at greater risk of developing schizophrenia. People with schizotypal personality disorder are sometimes referred to as "psy-chosis prone."[28]

Personality disorders are stable, enduring, and pervasive patterns of behavior that deviate markedly from "the expectations of the individual's culture."[29] In the case of schizotypal personality disorder, the individual often exhibits *ideas of reference*, the unjustified belief that people are speaking to you, or noticing you—in particular, a condition that can lead to suspiciousness and paranoia. Difficulties in establishing and maintaining social relationships are very common, as are suspicious or paranoid thoughts, excessive social anxiety, and oddities of speech and behavior. Among the list of diagnostic criteria for schizotypal personality disorder, of particular interest to us is the criterion "superstitiousness, belief in clairvoyance, telepathy, or 'sixth sense'"[30] It is this feature, referred to as *magical thinking* or *magical ideation*, that is both an important aspect of schizotypal personality disorder and a useful predictor of eventual psychosis.

Superstitiousness and Psychosis

For thirty years, Loren Chapman of the University of Wisconsin has directed a research effort aimed at identifying individuals at risk for serious mental disorders such as schizophrenia. He and his colleagues have developed a number of paper-and-pencil tests that are designed to detect important psychological symptoms. One of the most heavily studied of these is the Magical Ideation Scale, developed with Mark Eckblad in 1983.[31] This thirty-item true-or-false questionnaire checks for the presence of the kind of unusual thinking that is common to people with schizotypal personality disorder. Over the last few years, the Magical Ideation Scale has been an instrument of considerable clinical and research value.

Of greatest importance to us is that the concept of magical ideation as defined by Eckblad and Chapman's questionnaire includes several beliefs and actions that fall within our definition of superstition. Table 6.2 presents those items from the scale that probe for superstitious beliefs. The first four items represent common socially shared superstitions, and the fifth item (number 18) addresses a form of psychokinesis (mind over matter) that falls within our definition of superstition. Finally, item 26 asks about the kind of ritual that would constitute a personal superstition. It is interesting to note that, except perhaps for the somewhat malevolent psychokinesis question, these superstition items are fairly innocuous. Taken by themselves, they do not appear to be assessing abnormal behavior.

In addition to these superstitious items, there are a number of questions that do not meet our definition of superstition but do represent common paranormal beliefs. These are also presented in Table 6.2.[32]

Superstition and paranormal beliefs are not the only features of magical ideation measured by Eckblad and Chapman's scale. The concept of magical thinking as defined by this questionnaire includes a number of unusual forms of thought that are consistent with schizotypal personality disorder. For example, there are several items that address ideas of reference: "I have sometimes had the passing thought that strangers are in love

Table 6.2   *Selected Items from the Magical Ideation Scale*

Superstition Items

3. I have sometimes been fearful of stepping on sidewalk cracks (T).
5. Horoscopes are right too often for it to be a coincidence (T).
7. Numbers like 13 and 7 have no special powers (F).
13. Good-luck charms don't work (F).
18. It is not possible to harm others merely by thinking bad thoughts about them (F).
26. At times I perform certain little rituals to ward off negative influences (T).

Additional Paranormal Items

4. I think I could learn to read other's minds if I wanted to (T).
16. I almost never dream about things before they happen (F).
24. If reincarnation were true, it would explain some unusual experiences I have had (T).
27. I have felt that I might cause something to happen just by thinking too much about it (T).
28. I have wondered whether the spirits of the dead can influence the living (T).

Note: The responses that are indicative of magical ideation (T = true and F = false) are indicated.
Source: Eckblad and Chapman (1983). Copyright © (1983) by the American Psychological Association. Reprinted with permission.

with me." Other questions tap the suspicious/paranoid dimension of schizotypal thinking: "I have sometimes sensed an evil presence around me, although I could not see it." Still others describe unusual perceptual experiences, such as "I have had the momentary feeling that I might not be human." Finally, some questions combine features of several schizotypal characteristics—"The government refuses to tell us the truth about flying saucers"—combines the features of suspiciousness and belief in paranormal phenomena.

What is interesting for our discussion is that Chapman and others have found that college students who scored high on the Magical Ideation Scale also showed a greater number of psychotic and psychotic-like symptoms than students with lower scores.[33] In addition, in a study of psychiatric patients, those with schizophrenia had higher Magical Ideation scores than nonschizophrenic patients or than normal control participants.[34] Thus, Eckblad and Chapman's Magical Ideation Scale appears to measure a personality dimension that is present in both schizotypal nonpsychotic individuals and people diagnosed with schizophrenia who already show symptoms of psychosis.

The most important study of magical ideation and its relation to psychosis was a recently published longitudinal study conducted by Chapman and his colleagues.[35] In the 1970s and early 1980s, a total of 7,800 students from introductory psychology classes at the University of Wisconsin were given the Magical Ideation Scale and a number of other assessment instruments. From this sample, several groups of students were identified, including a group who scored particularly high on Magical Ideation and a control group that did not show high scores on any of the assessment instruments. Ten to fifteen years later, using a variety of detective techniques, the authors were able to locate and interview the participants from each group. The results indicated that students who scored high on Magical Ideation in college showed more symptoms of schizotypal personality and other schizophrenia-related disorders a decade later. In addition, these participants showed more psychotic experiences than others. Somewhat unexpectedly, Chapman's longitudinal study did not show a link between magical ideation in college and later schizophrenia, but when other forms of psychosis, such as manic depression, were considered, the link emerged. Ten years later, the number of people who had developed some form of psychosis was significantly greater in the group that had scored high on Magical Ideation.[36]

If Magical Ideation Is Psychotic, Is Superstition Abnormal?

While some studies have found that people who are superstitious or believers in the paranormal score higher on the Magical Ideation Scale, we cannot conclude that these people are mentally ill or even on their way to future mental illness.[37] As noted above, Eckblad and Chapman's Magical Ideation Scale includes some questions about very popular superstitions and paranormal beliefs. Given that many people in the general population endorse these beliefs, some correlation between magical ideation and superstitions is likely to be detected. On the other hand, the Magical Ideation Scale also contains a number of questions that tap more psychotic forms of thought ("It is not possible to harm others merely by thinking bad thoughts about them" [F]). No one has attempted to determine which questions in the scale are most effective in identifying schizotypal individuals, but it is possible that questions revealing more innocuous superstition and paranormal beliefs are unimportant and that the more pathological items are the most valid—for example, "I have sometimes felt an evil presence around me, although I could not see it." Without further research, there is no way to know.

Interestingly, an Australian study examined this issue by comparing the cognitive styles of four groups of participants: schizophrenics, "schizotypes" (people with schizotypal personality disorder), paranormal believers (members of the Australian Institute of Parapsychological Research), and a control group.[38] Although the two pathological groups and the paranormal believers group all showed similarly high levels of paranormal belief, they differed in their view of cause-and-effect relationships. The paranormal-believers group had a greater sense of personal control in their lives, whereas the schizophrenic and schizotypal groups believed that their lives were more often governed by chance. As a result, the authors concluded that the different groups arrived at their paranormal beliefs through different frames of reference. For the parapsychological group, paranormal beliefs were a way—if a somewhat magical way—to order their lives. In contrast, for the psychopathological groups, the same paranormal beliefs were an expression of their "impaired psychological functioning" and the perceived role of chance in their lives.

A View from the Inside

While writing this book, I was contacted by Stephen Weiner, the earthquake-fearing man whose story is presented at the beginning of this chapter. Although we were both in our early forties and had shared many of the common experiences of our generation, as I listened to him, I was quickly convinced that our histories were very different. Like many people struggling with mental illness, he had gone through a progression of diagnoses, therapies, and drug treatments. At various times, he was labeled hyperactive, schizophrenic, and obsessive-compulsive. He was hospitalized for a brief period, but most often he was treated as an outpatient. The list of medications he had taken was quite lengthy, including many powerful neuroleptic drugs, such as Melaril and Stelazine, and a variety of antidepressants. After transferring back West, he completed his bachelor's degree at Stanford University. He believed his condition was most accurately described as obsessive compulsive disorder with major depression and schizotypal features. He still faced a number of struggles on a daily basis, including the allure of magical thinking and periodic bouts of depression, but he found drug therapy with Prozac very helpful. He lived on disability and did not work, but he had close friends and wrote very articulately about mental illness.

Because he had given me the opportunity, I asked Stephen the central question of this chapter: were his superstitions like those common to people who were not afflicted with mental illness? Without hesitation, he said no, and he gave me two reasons for his assertion. First, he said, "It is a quantitative difference that becomes qualitative."[39] That is, magical thinking was such a pervasive, haunting concern in his life that it could not reasonably be compared to typical, everyday superstition. In addition, he said, the unafflicted "do not experience superstition as suffering." He had never derived a sense of joy or satisfaction from his rituals. Thus, we have confirmation of our conclusion from someone who has firsthand experience with magical thinking.

If Superstition Is Not Abnormal, Is it Irrational?

Psychologists, economists, philosophers, and political scientists have spent much time debating the definition of rationality. Although we know it when we see it, establishing a clear definition of rational behavior—and, by extension, irrational behavior—is quite difficult. There are many issues to consider, and some are quite thorny. For example, deliberately placing oneself at risk of injury or death seems irrational; yet in times of war, a society expects its soldiers to do just that.[40] Thus, considering only the individual's personal desires, an action may seem irrational despite being completely rational—indeed essential—at a higher level of analysis. Under the right conditions, littering, theft, and even murder could make rational sense for the individual, but extended to large numbers of people, such behaviors are quite damaging.

The difference between rationality on the individual and societal levels is not our primary concern. In the next chapter we will address the societal implications of widespread superstition and belief in the paranormal, but the most meaningful level of analysis for the question of rationality of superstition is the individual. Does superstitious behavior make sense for the person engaging in it? Unfortunately, even this more restricted question is difficult to answer.

On the individual level, rationality is a label that can be applied to both actions and beliefs. Behavior is rational if it is appropriate to a person's beliefs and desired goals. Beliefs are rational if they follow from the evidence available. But the relationship of one's beliefs to truth depends on the evidence at hand. In many cases, the true nature of events is hidden by a lack of information, making it possible that one's beliefs may be based on the best of what is known and still be false. Yet the superstitious person has another problem.[41] According to our definition, superstitious behavior is irrational because it is based on beliefs that are inconsistent with the available scientific facts. To do justice to this claim, we must look a bit deeper.

Principles of rationality place great importance on the logicalness of beliefs, and logical beliefs result from what cognitive psychologist Jonathan Baron calls good thinking. Good thinking and good decision-making require a thorough search for possible solutions and a fair evaluation of the evidence for a belief or a course of action. In his book *Thinking and Deciding*, Baron identified three obstacles to good thinking:[42]

1. Our search misses something that it should have discovered, or we act with high confidence after little search.
2. We seek evidence and make inferences in ways that prevent us from choosing the best possibility.
3. We think too much.[43]

Baron suggests that we should be actively open-minded, searching for all possible views of a problem and evaluating the evidence in support of each. An energetic search for and evaluation of the available theories should lead to beliefs that are more likely to be truthful and, thus, more likely to lead us to our goals. Naturally, the effectiveness of our actions in actually producing the desired outcome—even when based on good thinking—is limited by the availability and quality of information. Often there are unknowns in the equation, and yet some action must be taken. Under these circumstances, we may encounter Baron's third pitfall—becoming lost in thought. In the course of battle, our soldier must not sit down to ponder the alternatives. Unless he chooses quickly, the consequences will be disastrous.

In their book *Theory of Games and Economic Behavior* economists John von Neumann and Oskar Morgenstern described an economic theory known as *expected utility*—first encountered in chapter 4—that is widely used by economists and psychologists to evaluate decisions involving uncertainty.[44] In its simplest sense, expected-utility theory combines the probability of the possible outcomes with the value placed on them. When the outcomes are purely monetary, we calculate expected values. For example, consider the following wager. You are offered the chance to win $5 by getting heads on the single flip of a coin, but if you flip tails, you must pay $5. Based on these simple rules, there are only two outcomes, winning or losing. The expected value of the wager is calculated by multiplying the probability of each outcome by its monetary effect and adding these individual expected values together:

$$\frac{1}{2} \times \$5 = +\$2.50 \text{ (win)}$$

$$+ \ \frac{1}{2} \times -\$5 = -\$2.50 \text{ (lose)}$$

$$\text{Expected Value} = \$0.00$$

An important premise of this analysis is that the expected value of the gamble is what an individual should average in the long run—after many trials. Of course, on any individual flip of the coin, the player will either gain $5 or lose $5, but after many plays, he or she should walk away even.

The game I have described is an even bet, often called a "fair gamble," and if we based our decision to play on expected values only, we would be indifferent about it.[45] We would be equally as likely to take the bet as not. However, most people will not accept such a proposition because the potential satisfaction from a gain of $5 does not match the dissatisfaction of a loss of $5. For most people, money has what economists call diminishing marginal utility: the more we get, the less it makes us happy. This phenomenon demonstrates the distinction between value and utility. Although the term value (or expected value) refers to the actual change in wealth, utility describes the satisfaction derived from that change. The principle of diminishing marginal utility is one that makes intuitive sense. Consider this senario. Without warning, a poor woman is handed a check for one million dollars. Naturally, she is extremely happy, and, as soon as she recovers her composure, she runs to the bank. Now imagine that a few days later, our friend has the exceptional good fortune to be given a second check for a million dollars. Of course, she would be very happy, but this time, her bliss—her utility—would probably not be quite as great as it was the first time. After all, when she received the first check she was a mere mortal, but by the time she got the second one, she was already a millionaire. Again, money has diminishing marginal utility: the more we have, the less satisfied it makes us. In fact, most things in life have diminishing marginal utility. When a hungry person digs into a new pint of ice cream, the first spoonful tends to taste the best; subsequent bites provide less satisfaction. It is too much of a good thing.

The concept of diminishing marginal utility affects the attractiveness of gambles such as our coin-flipping example. Although the change in expected value is the same for winning or losing ($5), diminishing marginal utility makes the change in utility greater for losing. Assuming one starts with some wealth, although the expected increase in wealth from winning is equal in size to the decrease from losing, the changes in actual satisfaction (utility) are not equal. It hurts more to lose than it feels good to win. In other words, the expected value of the bet is 0, but the expected utility is negative. As a result, people tend to be risk-averse and refuse an even bet. Furthermore, to have a wager that is worth making, it is not sufficient that it have a positive expected value. It must have a positive expected utility. The amount of money we win must be large enough to overcome the diminishing increases in satisfaction we get from increases in wealth.

This probabilistic algebra is relatively clear and useful in assessing simple monetary transactions; yet purchases often bring us more than can be summarized in a balance sheet. For example, buying a lottery ticket can be, on one level, a simple financial investment, and on another level, fun. If the individual derives some pleasure from choosing the numbers and waiting for the results of the drawing, then the dollar spent has done double service. The utility of playing is greater than the utility of the financial transaction alone. It is more difficult to quantify the entertainment component of the gamble, but it is assumed that there is a separate utility curve for the enjoyment value of the game. Thus, the expected utility of the financial transaction might not justify the purchase of a lottery ticket; but the expected utility of the bet as a whole, including the entertainment it will generate, might make it worth the price.

Once we recognize that the concept of utility can be applied to things other than money, it becomes a very useful tool for the evaluation of a wide range of decisions. Indeed, Jonathan Baron and others argue that rational decision-making can often be aided by the careful analysis of all the possible outcomes of a decision, their probabilities, and the utility of each outcome for the decision-maker.[46] It is an important part of avoiding obstacle number two to good thinking: seeking evidence and making inferences in ways that preclude sound decision-making. Of course, in some cases there is no time for this kind of analysis, and we must act quickly to avoid pitfall number three: getting lost in thought. But if we have the time, a reasonable estimation of the probabilities and utilities of various choices can lead to good decisions.

To demonstrate this approach using an entirely different kind of gamble, we can create a simple decision table for Pascal's Wager. As described in chapter 3, Pascal proposed that it made sense to live a Christian life because the potential gain was so great. The possible outcomes of each choice of action are summarized in Table 6.3.[47] To assess the choices more clearly, we can assign numerical weights to each outcome using an arbitrary scale of utility, as in Table 6.4. These values are meant to be estimates

Table 6.3   Decision table for Pascal's Wager

| | State of the World | |
Choice of Action	God exists	God does not exist
Live a Christian life	Saved (very good)	Small inconvenience
Live otherwise	Damned (very bad)	Normal life

Table 6.4   *Utility weights for each outcome of Pascal's Wager*

Choice of Action	State of the World	
	God exists	God does not exist
Live a Christian life	+1,000,000	-100
Live otherwise	-1,000,000	0

of the actual satisfaction—or relative satisfaction—we would feel if we obtained each outcome. By starting with a neutral value of zero for living a normal, nonreligious life when God (and presumably heaven and hell) does not exist, we can then give a modest negative value of -100 to having wasted one's time practicing a Christian life only to discover that there is no reward in the hereafter. Next, if we assume that God does exist, we can give going to heaven a weight of 1 million and going to hell -1 million. These weights might not be valid for everyone, but they are a reasonable starting point for our example. Finally, by applying probabilities to the existence of God, we can calculate the expected utility of each decision. As Table 6.5 indicates, even when we set the probability of God's existence as low as 1/100, living a Christian life has greater utility than living otherwise. As long as the relative arrangements of the utility weights are the same as in Table 6.4, choosing a different set of numbers still produces an advantage for a Christian life, and setting a higher probability for the existence of God just makes the advantage greater. For example, reversing the probability of the existence of God to 99/100 makes the expected utility of a Christian life +989,999 and living otherwise -990,000.

Although this example rests on a number of assumptions about religion and the nature of the world which not everyone would be willing to grant, it demonstrates how expected utility theory can provide a useful framework for evaluating decisions. Many psychologists and economists believe it represents a standard against which the rationality of decisions can be

Table 6.5   *Expected utilities for each choice of Pascal's Wager*

Choice of Action	State of the World		Expected Utility
	God exists	God does not exist	
Live a Christian life	$1/100 \times +1,000,000$ +	$99/100 \times -100 =$	+ 9,901
Live otherwise	$1/100 \times -1,000,000$ +	$99/100 \times 0 =$	-10,000

measured. After making a few more assumptions, it can be used to judge the rationality of superstitious behavior.

Expected Utility and Superstition

Let us begin with the assumptions. First, we must assert that any benefits derived from superstitious acts are not the result of magic. Chicken does not actually make Wade Boggs a better hitter; Nancy Reagan's astrologer could not really predict the future. Until there is convincing scientific evidence to the contrary, we will begin with this assumption.[48] Second, although in our first assumption we ruled out the possibility of a direct, cause-and-effect relationship between the superstition and the desired outcome, it could have indirect effects. Those superstitions that are meant to affect one's performance, such as the lucky rituals of athletes and college students, could conceivably produce a positive emotional effect that leads to improved performance. We do not have direct proof of this assumption, but there is adequate evidence from other areas of psychology, such as Taylor's research with cancer patients, to grant it here. Finally, even if the practitioner does not actually believe that the superstition has an effect on performance (or some other outcome, such as winning the lottery, that is not dependent on performance), he or she may derive some secondary gain in the form of entertainment or positive emotion in the time prior to the event in question. Thus, someone concerned about an approaching operation might bring a lucky charm to the hospital not because he expects it to affect the success of the procedure, but because it makes him feel better.

One of the exam-related superstitions I learned about through the computer network for psychology professors was described by the wife of a man who, as a college student, used to buy an instant lottery ticket before each exam. His theory was that as soon as he scratched the ticket and determined that he had lost, he had used up his bad luck for the day. This ritual worked well enough until the day he had a winning ticket!

In this case, although there are two choices—to buy the ticket or not to buy the ticket—buying the ticket has several potential outcomes. First, it could have a direct magical effect on the believer's exam performance; however, our working assumptions rule this possiblity out. Second, the superstition could produce an emotional boost that indirectly affects exam performance. For example, the illusion of control could provide an enhanced feeling of confidence that provides the right emotional context for optimal performance. Finally, our exam-taker may merely be hoping to entertain himself or to provide a temporary distraction that will help fill the time before the exam. Based on the way this purchase was originally described, we will ignore the possiblity that our believer has purchased the ticket to win the lottery. If our young man bought the ticket purely out of a belief that it directly affected his exam results, we must label his action irrational: it was based on an irrational belief. If the ticket was not purchased out of belief in magic, the rationality of the superstition rests on the expected utilities of the other benefits. Assuming that it was inexpensive, this pre-exam ritual is reasonable as long as there is sufficient potential for the other positive effects. To demonstrate how this purchase might be just such a rational superstition, we can follow procedures similar to those used with Pascal's Wager.

First, we can list the possible outcomes and assign utility weights to each.[49] In this case, for the single choice of action there are four possible outcomes: the three potential effects and the expense, which is a certainty. A set of utility weights for these is presented in Table 6.6. The cost of of the ticket is given the arbitrary utility of -3, and a direct effect on exam performance, were it possible, is given +300. The other effects are given more moderate positive weights. Next, we simply assign a zero value to the absence of each effect. In this senario, not receiving any of the hoped-for beneficial effects merely leaves one in a neutral position—relying on more typical means (studying, rest, etc.) of getting a good grade. Finally, we assign likely probabilities to each event and calculate the estimated expected utilities (see Table 6.7).

The values we use in this case give a positive utility to buying the lottery ticket—it represents a rational action! Of course, the result would be different if money were judged to have greater utility or if the positive effects of buying the ticket were assigned lower probabilities or lower utilities. Changes in this direction would lead to a negative utility for the decision to buy the ticket, indicating that, according to expected-utility theory, this is an irrational superstition. Conversely, many people would assign a probability of greater than zero to the possibility of a direct magical effect.

Table 6.6   Utility weights of the potential outcomes of a lottery ticket pre-exam superstition

Potential Outcomes	Present	Absent
Direct effect on performance	+300	0
Indirect effect on performance	+80	0
Emotional/entertainment value	+30	0
Cost	-3	0

Table 6.7   Decision table for lottery ticket pre-exam superstition

Potential Outcomes	Present	Absent	Expected Utility
Direct effect on performance	0/100 x +300	100/100 x 0	0
Indirect effect on performance	25/100 x +80	75/100 x 0	20
Emotional/entertainment value	75/100 x +30	25/100 x 0	22.5
Cost	100/100 x -3	0/100 x 0	-3
			Total = +39.5

If someone would derive sufficient satisfaction from a magical effect, a small probability of success might be sufficient—even in the absence of other hypothesized effects—to produce a total utility that was positive. Would this mean the superstition was rational? Yes and no. It would be rational action with respect to the individual's beliefs. If a person truly believes in magic, then acting upon that belief is rational. But the belief itself is irrational. In forming this belief, the individual has failed to evaluate the available evidence accurately.

In chapter 2 we encountered the college student who had to find a coin on the day of an exam.[50] On some occasions, when he had difficulty finding one, he would spend time "scrounging around bus stops" in desperation. Here the student's choice is between engaging in superstitious behavior and doing something more productive with his time. An expected-utility analysis of this superstition would give a negative value to searching for lucky pennies. We would have to say that either resting or studying would be more rational, especially given that the young man in question sometimes spent so much time in search that he risked being late to the exam—something that might have had a serious effect on his grade. When superstitions interfere with more reasoned responses to a situation, we must put them in the irrational category. Thus, when a person responds to illness by visiting an herbalist rather than a internist, he or she is behaving irrationally.

When Time Is Short and the Stakes Are High

The expected-utility approach to these decisions changes somewhat when one is faced with a more desperate situation. If the potential gains—however improbable—are enormous, then some superstitious behaviors become more rational. Consider the case of the patient facing terminal cancer. As mentioned above, expected-utility theory is based on the effects of various decisions *in the long term*, but for the person in this situation, the horizon is very near. Furthermore, the potential gains have infinite utility.

We are bargaining not for a better grade on an exam but for life itself. As a result, Pascal's Wager provides the framework for rational superstition. Provided the patient is doing all that is possible using the recommended conventional treatments, even an extremely small probability of a positive result from the use of crystals, for example, might be rational.[51] Again, as in Table 6.5, the small inconvenience of the superstition is outweighed by the potential benefit. There are other arguments for not engaging in this kind of rational superstition, but we will save that discussion for the next chapter.

• • •

We are left with the conclusion that superstition is not a form of abnormal behavior, and under some circumstances, it is not irrational either. The best evidence indicates that the rituals and superstitions typical of obsessive-compulsive disorder are quite different from the behavior that is common to large segments of the general public. And while superstitions and paranormal beliefs are part of schizotypal personality disorder and schizophrenia, there is no proof that, by themselves, these behaviors are indicative of present or future psychopathology. Finally, although it is probably safe to say that most superstitions are irrational, an analysis of the expected utility of various decisions shows that, under some circumstances, superstitions can in fact be rational.

7

A Magical View of the World

It is no defense of superstition and pseudoscience to say that it brings solace and comfort to people and that therefore we "elitists" should not claim to know better and to take it away from the less sophisticated.

If solace and comfort are how we judge the worth of something, then consider that tobacco brings solace and comfort to smokers; alcohol brings it to drinkers; drugs of all kinds bring it to addicts; the fall of cards and the run of horses bring it to gamblers; cruelty and violence bring it to sociopaths. Judge by solace and comfort only and there is no behavior we ought to interfere with.

— Isaac Asimov, *The Humanist*

Sometimes it's better to be lucky than good. That's why I do things to create luck, like eating the chicken and running my sprints at 7:17 before night games. I want to feel lucky. I want to feel that if I hit a ball to the shortstop, it's going to hit a rock and go over his head.

—Wade Boggs, *The New York Times*

The basic question of this book has been: Why are people superstitious? Or, given that we observe many people to be superstitious, how do they become so? As we have seen, the answer is not simple. There are many factors that can contribute to the acquisition and maintenance of superstition. Not all of them apply to any particular individual, but each can lead us to hold beliefs or engage in acts that reflect a magical view of the world. Given the great number of psychological influences we have encountered—and there are undoubtedly others that have yet to be discovered and researched—we might expect everyone to hold some secret magical belief or practice some hidden superstitious ritual. But the sheer number of potential psychological influences is not a true indicator of the role of these forces in our lives. Some social and psychological phenomena are more important, pervasive, or powerful than others. The rest, while potentially influential when the necessary circumstances arise, are undoubtedly rarer or subtler in their action. The time has come to stand back and take a broader view. Now that we have enumerated the many sources of superstitious belief and behavior, it is time to reexamine the most important themes that have emerged in the foregoing chapters. In addition, having come this far without passing serious judgment on superstition, we must now assess the impact of superstitious beliefs and behavior in our current society. Do superstition and belief in the paranormal serve us well or ill? Where can we see the effects of superstition in our world? Finally, we will consider what, if anything, can—or should—be done about superstition.

The Paths to Superstition

Many Superstitions Come with Membership in a Social Group

If you were a detective who was assigned to determine whether or not a particular individual was superstitious and you could only choose a single line of inquiry (and you could not ask the obvious question), perhaps the most important data you could gather would be information about occupational and social groups. What does the person in question do for a living? Is he or she involved in sports, gambling, or the theater? How old and—less important—what gender is he or she? Membership in a group involves socialization by the group. The athlete acquires the language and skills of the game as well as the particular habits of the team. For example, during their very successful 1995 season, the Connecticut College varsity lacrosse team had a practice of going en masse to a local donut shop on the evening before a match. Many players expressed the belief that this practice helped the team win.[1] As we learned in chapter 2, similar socially shared superstitions become part of the culture of the group, and the individual member adopts them as part of his or her socialization to the culture. Being a member of a superstitious subgroup is important because it exposes one to a number of psychological forces: social learning (chapter 5), direct instruction (chapter 5), and reinforcement (chapter 4) by others in the group. If superstition is an active part of the group culture, these influences make it likely that new members will acquire them. Thus, for the detective who wants to predict whether an individual is superstitious or not, the best single piece of information is whether he or she is a member of one of the traditionally superstitious social or occupational subgroups.

In chapter 5, we discovered that perhaps the most important superstitious subgroup is inhabited by the youngest among us. As documented in great detail by Iona and Peter Opie, the culture of childhood is replete with characteristic songs, games, legends, and figures of speech, and because the superstitions of childhood are so widespread, we all share at least a vague memory of the quirky beliefs and practices that came with our member-ship.[2] They were not true superstitions. They were childish "half-beliefs" that resulted both from the same forces that affect grownup social groups and from an immature understanding of cause-and-effect relationships. Moreover, youthful superstitions are encouraged by the role of imagination and fantasy in children's play. We cannot expect children to be logical and scientific. And yet, when we are older and should know better, the magical experiences of youth may encourage adult superstitions.

Personality Is Related to Belief in Superstition, But Only Moderately

The most common lay explanation for any form of behavior is person-ality. People behave the way they do because they possess stable personal-ity traits that determine how they will act under a variety of circumstances. The shyness of a college student affects his choice of classes (large ones where he will be lost in the crowd), career path (minimal social contact and public speaking), and mate (approachable candidates preferred). A closer examination often reveals a more complicated picture. People do have measurable personality traits, but these traits often do not predict behav-ior. In chapter 2, we found that superstitious people have higher anxiety and a greater fear of death, feel less in control, suffer more from depres-sion, experience higher levels of neuroticism, and have lower self-esteem than nonsuperstitious people. In addition, the Gulf War study described in chapter 4 showed that a person's tolerance for ambiguity is related to superstition, with those less tolerant of ambiguous situations and events being more likely to adopt magical coping strategies. This does not present a very flattering picture of the superstitious person, but we must remember that, although these results were statistically significant (i.e., not mere chance relationships), in real terms the link between these personality dimensions and superstitious behavior is quite weak. It is true, for exam-ple, that on average, superstitious people are more anxious than those who are not superstitious, but there is much overlap between the two groups. As a result, there are undoubtedly many college students who, while remarkably calm and nonchalant most of the time, will, when confronted with an important test, bring a lucky object to the examination room to help them through the ordeal. Similarly, there are many anxious and fearful people who think superstitions are silly and would never consider them a viable method of coping. Nonetheless, the research in personality gives us another piece of our answer. People who show these characteristics are somewhat more likely to be superstitious.

Superstitions Often Emerge from Accidental Conditioning

Conditioning plays an extremely important role in our lives. Many people prefer to deny this notion because classical and operant conditioning seem like such basic and primitive forces; we would like to believe that they are limited to young children and other, less talented species. After all, the classic symbol of Pavlovian conditioning is a drooling dog, and the classic symbol of operant conditioning is a lowly white rat, the subject of thousands of cartoon caricatures. Yet many volumes of research make it clear that we are all susceptible: young and old, rodent and primate, biped and quadruped.

Operant conditioning often springs from contiguity.[3] After a period of struggle, the door lock responds just as we pull up on the key, and as a result we quickly pull the key the next time the lock sticks. Pulling up is reinforced by the immediate positive outcome, and in this example, it probably results from a true contingency. The lock responds because of an actual mechanical oddity that makes it operate in this fashion. But as we learned in chapter 3, contiguity can appear accidentally. Consider the basketball player who makes an important free throw after bouncing the ball a certain number of times before the shot. The bounces could not have affected his aim or the arc of the ball in space, but because they occurred just before the reinforced action, bouncing the ball in this manner is "stamped in." It is possible that a personal superstition—a shooting ritual—will result. Similarly, lucky hats, shirts, shoes, and underwear acquire magical powers when they are worn at the moment some significant reward is given. The reward is thought to depend on the presence of an antecedent stimulus: Bjorn Borg's beard or Lou Carnesecca's crewneck sweater.

A number of these examples may involve other kinds of psychological processes. The player who thinks his socks are lucky is obviously aware of it. He must make plans to preserve them in their unlaundered condition (if this is part of the superstition) and take precautions against loss. But the research reported in chapter 3 makes it clear that conditioning also plays a role. Operant conditioning is one of the most pervasive and irresistible forces in our psychological world, molding our behavior to the demands of our surroundings. But it sometimes goes awry, adapting our actions to contingencies that are not really there.

Reasoning Errors Often Maintain
Our Belief in Superstition

Once socialization and operant conditioning have established a superstition—perhaps with the help of a receptive personality—cognitive biases and errors help keep things going. Given the manifold evidence of the power of human intellect, it is surprising to discover so many apparent weaknesses in our abilities; yet there is something about many of our reasoning errors that is not completely irrational. A mistake is a mistake, and no one wants to make one if it can be avoided. But some mistakes sustain us in important ways. For example, when we consider all the biases and heuristics discussed in chapter 4, it is clear that several of them provide important benefits at the same time they lead us astray. In particular, these reasoning errors maintain our personal sense of self and give us a feeling of control.

When we are confronted with information that appears both reliable and contradictory to a belief we hold true, the rational response is to question our beliefs. We should discard the old or, at very least, acknowledge that we are now uncertain and seek additional information. But this is difficult to do. No one likes to be proved wrong, and to the extent that the prior belief is tied to our sense of self, it will be difficult to set aside. Furthermore, if we have acted on this belief in the past (e.g., exercised a superstition), adopting a new belief may create an uncomfortable dissonance between those past actions and this new idea. Indeed, it may be preferable to engage in a form of self-deception than to let go of the old belief.[4] Many of the cognitive errors that sustain superstitions also serve this function. When what appears to be a fortunate coincidence is attributed to a lucky charm, the misunderstanding of probability may be caused by simple mathematical naiveté, but the special meaning attached to the coincidence serves to maintain the belief that lucky charms work. Similarly, the different forms of confirmation bias all share the purpose of sustaining the individual's prior belief.

Superstition Is an Attempt to
Control the Uncontrollable

After the effects of socialization, probably the second most important determinant of belief in superstition is the universal human desire for autonomy and control. Psychological research in a variety of fields has documented a basic human motivation to have power over the important events in our lives. As we have seen, the elderly and those suffering from cancer seem to benefit from a perception of control—even when control is not possible. Moreover, the absence of a sense of personal control is an important feature of many psychological problems. For example, depression, one of the most common and problematic psychological disorders, is thought to result, in part, from the sufferer's perception that he or she is helpless and unable to act effectively upon the world. This condition, known as *learned helplessness*, was first demonstrated in laboratory studies of dogs who, when forced to endure shocks they could not escape, soon stopped trying. Later when the shocks could have been avoided, the dogs remained passive and continued to accepted them. The dogs had acquired an attitude of helplessness because they had learned that their actions had no effect on the shocks. Learned helplessness has come to symbolize an important aspect of depression—a perceived lack of control.[5] Similarly, the Australian study described in the previous chapter showed that people who suffered from either schizophrenia or schizotypal personality disorder had significantly less sense of personal control than believers in the paranormal did. If there is a universal truth about superstition, it is that superstitious behavior emerges as a response to uncertainty—to circumstances that are inherently random and uncontrollable. Malinowski's analysis of superstition based on observations of Trobriand fishermen is still valid: we are most likely to employ magic when we venture out into the dangerous outer waters of our world, where our fate is less secure.

Superstitions Help Pass the Time

From time to time, we find ourselves waiting for important events to happen. Sometimes, the thing we are waiting for dominates our attention and prevents us from doing anything else. We wait while a loved one undergoes surgery; we wait in our seat for the big exam to be passed out; we wait backstage for the curtain to rise on opening night. In these situations, we are anxious about the outcome of an uncertain event, yet there is little or nothing we can do to affect the outcome directly. This period of uncomfortable quiescence is one of the times when superstitious rituals are most likely to occur. This is why most athletes practice their rituals and superstitions before the contest or during breaks in the action. Pregame rituals and dugout superstitions abound, but players very rarely engage in such behavior during active play or when the game is over. As we have seen, the time-filling nature of many superstitions mirrors the quirky,

repetitive actions of animals waiting between reinforcements in an operant-conditioning chamber, or of the Australian university students playing
video poker whom we encountered in chapter 3.

Lucky charms and pieces of clothing are an interesting exception. They
are typically worn throughout the contest, and although much of the athlete's (or gambler's or student's) behavior with respect to these treasured
items is practiced as part of the pregame ritual (e.g., the dressing routine),
some relevant behavior must necessarily occur after the game. The hat
must be cared for and put in a place where it can be found the next time it
is needed. But the important initiation of the superstition occurs in the
anxious moments before the game, and once the hat is on or the charm is
safely tucked away in a pocket, it is typically not revisited until after the
game, when the athlete has the time to attend to it again. In this case, sensory conditioning or illusory correlation has given the object such significance that some of the superstitious behavior spills over into the postgame
period.

Superstition Is Not Limited to Traditional Cultures or People of Low Intelligence

Despite its popularity in our contemporary society, superstition is
thought to reflect low intelligence, and in many people's minds it is linked
to the magical practices of "primitive" cultures. Indeed, because intelligence is so integral to one's sense of self, it is likely that much of the social
stigma associated with superstition results from this aspect of its reputation. And there is some research evidence to support the view that superstition and belief in the paranormal are more common among people with
lower IQs and poorer academic performance. But we also know that the
New Age movement is particularly popular with college-educated people,
that college students—even Harvard students—employ exam-related
superstitions, and that, according to news accounts, many of the United
States' most prestigious writers and editors participated in a chain letter in
1990 and 1991. As a result, the relationship between superstition and
intelligence needs more clarification. The existing studies may have produced the results they did in part because they asked the wrong questions.
As we have seen, people in different social groups show different forms
and differing degrees of superstitious behavior. Intelligent, college-educated
people may be less likely to endorse the traditional socially shared superstitions, such as a belief in the influence of black cats, ladders, and four-leaf
clovers, but they may be more likely to have superstitions related to their

social and occupational groups, such as exam- or business-related superstitions. Without additional research, it is impossible to know. What we can say, however, is that superstition is far from rare among people at either end of the intellectual spectrum.

Superstition Is Not a Form of Psychopathology

Although it bears a resemblance to both the magical ideation of schizophrenia and the compulsions of obsessive-compulsive disorder, superstition does not appear to be a form of abnormal behavior, nor is it linked to psychopathology in any established way. Superstition is too common and, in most cases, too benign to be of concern to psychiatrists and clinicians. Magical thinking is both a feature of schizotypal personality disorder and an indication of increased risk of future schizophrenia, but the concept of magical ideation as measured by schizophrenia researchers is not identical to superstition. As a result, it is not clear whether superstition alone is related to schizophrenia. In the case of obsessive-compulsive disorder, both researchers and patients agree that the rituals of this psychological problem are something quite different from everyday superstitions.[6]

But we have seen throughout this book that superstition is a normal feature of everyday life. We have encountered college students, crap shooters, police officers, professional basketball players, children, and sidewalk strollers—all normal people. There are numerous psychological processes that are sufficient to produce superstition in people who are otherwise normal. Thus, given the wide popularity of superstition among the general populace, we must conclude that superstition is not abnormal.

Should We Be Concerned About Superstition?

We have determined that, in general, superstition and belief in the paranormal have their genesis in normal psychological processes, and they almost always provide some satisfaction to the believer. But as Isaac Asimov reminds us, the same can be said of alcohol and drug addiction, overeating, and many examples of violent behavior. Much that is human is, nonetheless, unwanted or self-destructive. What about superstition? Now that we understand it, what should we think about it? Are superstitions and belief in the paranormal social problems that are worth our attention? To answer these questions, we must consider how superstition and belief in the paranormal affect both the individual and the larger social group.

Superstition and the Individual

In the last chapter we used expected-utility theory to evaluate the rationality of superstition, and we decided that under certain circumstances, superstitious behavior can be rational. The actor who performs a simple ritual before going onstage may recognize that it has no truly magical effect, but it may make him feel better. It costs him little, and it may calm his nerves and help him through the worrisome moments before the performance begins. Thus, the actor's ritual is reasonable and beneficial.

Expected utility theory provides a useful framework for calculating the costs and benefits of individual superstitious acts, but when judging whether or not superstition represents a problem behavior, it is important to go beyond the individual act and consider how a pattern of behavior can affect a person's life. Here we can borrow a system from another field. In his book *The Alcohol Troubled Person*, Alan Willoughby proposes a functional definition of alcoholism that concentrates on how drinking affects an individual's life.[7] Rejecting traditional conceptions based on when, what, with whom, and how much a person drinks, Willoughby offers the following definition:

> An individual has troubles with alcohol if he or she continues to drink when to do so reduces the quality of his or her life in any one (or more) of the following areas:
> 1. Social (including, but not confined to, family)
> 2. Financial (including, but not confined to, job)
> 3. Physical
> 4. Emotional and cognitive[8]

This definition can easily be applied to any behavior. For example, you might ask yourself, does my obsession with exercise create a problem in any of these four domains? Or does watching television cause me difficulties? If so, exercise or television-watching may be problem behaviors that are worth changing. Willoughby also distinguishes among alcohol problems of differing severity. An example of severe, late-stage drinking problems might be drinking in the face of significant health problems, such as liver damage or delirium tremens. In contrast, a mild alcohol problem could involve spending too much of your income at the bar each night and fighting with your spouse about drinking.[9] Similarly, superstitious behavior can be assessed in relation to its effects on a person's life. Although superstition-related problems are far less common, they, like alcohol problems, can have a negative impact on these domains or can contribute to the damaging effects of other kinds of behavior.

Social. Although it is not impossible, superstitions probably rarely cause significant problems in the social domain. We have seen that superstitious behavior is often supported by one's social group, and thus, whether rational or not, superstition may actually improve some relationships by helping to build a connection with one's peers. We are more likely to see problems in another area—finances, which can soon become a source of marital conflict. Nevertheless, even though superstition carries a slight social stigma, serious problems in the social domain are probably relatively uncommon.

Financial. Superstitious behavior is much more likely to cause or contribute to financial difficulties. In recent years, the combined influence of cable television, the telephone, and easy credit have given us access to products and services that previously we could only obtain by leaving the house. Entire cable channels are devoted to selling products to the home viewer, and "infomercials" give half-hour-long pitches for kitchen products and cosmetics. One of the most popular of these television appeals has been for telephone "psychic advisors," who will counsel customers for between $3 and $5 a minute. Consulting a psychic is as convenient as a phone call (psychologists and conventional financial advisors are rarely this accessible), and the charges are simply added to one's phone bill. Here the potential for financial damage is great. A number of investigations have shown that psychics are no better at predicting the future than anyone else—perhaps worse.[10] If, on the other hand, one consults a telephone psychic for entertainment only or for emotional comfort, these benefits come at an extremely high price. Four dollars a minute (the most common fee at the time of this writing) represents $240 per hour. Even a Broadway play with a ticket price of $100 per seat is a better entertainment value. We tend to think that movie prices are outrageously expensive, but at $8 a ticket, a movie is approximately sixty times the entertainment value of a call to a psychic ($4 per hour versus $240 per hour).

Even compared to professional financial or psychological services that provide similar individual attention, the telephone psychic is extremely expensive. The psychic's $240-an-hour fee is approximately twice the fee of a psychologist or a psychiatrist—even more than twice the fee in some cases. The fee for individual financial advice varies, but it is likely to be anywhere from one tenth to one third that of a telephone psychic. Furthermore, these prices are based on the assumption that the professional advisor would meet the client face-to-face. Were these legitimate services available over the phone, we could expect them to be even less expensive.

Obviously, telephone psychics are a bad deal. Yet they appear to be popular enough to support expensive advertising campaigns featuring glowing testimonials and celebrity endorsements. The service is private, confidential, and extremely convenient, and the advertising suggests that the person on the other end of the line will be warm and encouraging. Bad news is undoubtedly bad for business. All of these features could make dialing a 900 number very appealing to the person who needs an emotional boost. Unfortunately, placing that call could make it difficult to pay the phone bill. Those who call primarily for entertainment purposes probably place limits on what they will pay for their experience, but if the caller is a true believer, use of the "psychic hotline" could become a problem behavior. Indeed, there have been reports of people accumulating phone bills as high as $5000 from calls to telepone psychics.[11] Even if these calls do not decrease the quality of one's financial life, it is clear that there are better ways to spend one's money.

Gambling is a behavior that often becomes a serious problem, much like drinking or drug abuse. Mental-health professionals routinely speak of gambling addictions, and most cities now have regular meetings of Gamblers Anonymous, a self-help group patterned after Alcoholics Anonymous. Gambling addictions will probably be an increasing social problem in the coming years due to the national proliferation of casinos and other gambling venues and the continuing popularity of state-sponsored lotteries. But what role does superstition play in the social problems associated with gambling? It is difficult to say. The gambler's superstitions probably help to sustain his play. Lucky charms and rituals give him confidence that something good will happen and reduce any trepidation he may feel about the financial risks he takes. At least one author takes this view, arguing that the superstitious strategies of bingo players, such as sitting next to certain players or using lucky "dabbers" to mark their bingo cards, help to encourage play and alleviate any moral trepidation the players might have about gambling.[12] On the other hand, the player who avoids the lure of superstitious belief is probably somewhat less prone to problem gambling and more amenable to efforts to curb his behavior. Without additional research, however, it is impossible to say how influential superstitions are in the maintenance of gambling addictions.

Physical. In the last chapter we concluded that the cancer patient who adopts a macrobiotic diet and uses crystals as adjuncts to chemotherapy and other standard treatments is merely hedging her bets. This is an understandable response to stakes that are very high—another form of Pascal's Wager. But the patient who avoids established treatments in favor of "alternative medical techniques" offered by a "healer" does so at great risk. This kind of superstition is clearly irrational—has low expected utility—and must be avoided. Moreover, the casual and less technical manner of many purveyors of alternative therapies may make office visits less intimidating than a trip to the hospital. Established, "traditional" medical procedures have the weight of scientific evidence to support their effectiveness, but they are often painful and sometimes bring unpleasant side effects. In addition, some alternative therapies have a spiritual flavor that many people find an appealing contrast to what they see as the cold technicality of conventional medicine. For the person facing the specter of chemotherapy and surgery, it might be very tempting to believe that cancer can be cured simply by changing one's diet and purifying one's thoughts. However, this temptation must be avoided; it is far from harmless.

Unfortunately, it is hard for the consumer of medical treatments to know whom to trust. Many quack therapies are promoted by physicians with medical degrees or by individuals with advanced degrees in other health related fields. For example, within the nursing profession, a new version of healing called therapeutic touch—which, ironically, does not involve touching—is gaining wide popularity. Believers suggest that there are "bioenergy fields" that surround the human body and that disease is caused by disturbances in these fields. By merely passing hands over the afflicted person a few inches above the skin, practitioners claim that they can smooth these fields and cure the patient. Yet there is little support for this technique. The entry on therapeutic touch in the American Medical Association's *Reader's Guide to Alternative Health Methods* reports that

> There is no scientific evidence that the "energy transfer" postulated by proponents exists. No study of therapeutic touch has been reported in a reputable scientific journal, but it is safe to assume that any reactions to the procedure are psychological responses to the "laying on of hands."[13]

Nevertheless, the technique is growing in popularity, in part because it has been so heavily promoted by people whom we trust to know what they are talking about. Therapeutic touch was originally developed by Dolores Krieger, Ph.D., R.N., a former professor of nursing at New York University, where she taught the technique to nursing students, and it continues to be a very popular, albeit somewhat controversial, therapy within the nursing profession.[14] As an example of the level of acceptance achieved by this healing method, a very positive article about therapeutic touch recently appeared in the *American Journal of Nursing*.[15] Unfortunately, it was based entirely on anecdotes and testimonials and presented no scientific data.

At best, we can say that therapeutic touch probably does no harm and may produce some desirable placebo effects (psychological responses), but at worst, it could encourage patients to defer more effective forms of treatment—with serious consequences. Therapeutic touch is closer to magic than it is to medicine; yet it is being promoted by respected heathcare professionals. If we cannot trust the medical establishment to promote scientifically valid treatments, how are we to choose a rational course of medical treatment?[16]

Emotional and Cognitive. We have already established that superstition is not a sign of madness or abnormality. It is not the manifestation of serious psychological problems. Indeed, it may have some positive effects. Although a person is more likely to engage in superstitious behavior while experiencing certain emotions, chiefly fear and anxiety, superstition is not usually the cause of emotional difficulties. Clinical psychologists are rarely, if ever, called upon to treat cases of excessive superstition. Obsessive-compulsive disorder is a real psychological disturbance that often produces symptoms resembling superstitions that have been taken to extremes, but the current evidence suggests that normal superstition and obsessive-compulsive disorder are unrelated. Common superstitions are not a reflection of psychopathology.

Similarly, superstitions often spring from reasoning errors, but these mistakes (illusions of control, misunderstandings of chance and probability, confirmation bias) are common to us all. As a result, superstitions that have their source in the frailties of human thought are normal and are not symptomatic of mental deficiency or defect. Reasoning errors are a natural feature of our humanity. Sometimes, however, superstition may create difficulties in our ability to think and act effectively. To the extent that superstitions distract us from the search for more effective methods of control and discourage us from energetically assessing our options, they will interfere with the process of problem-solving and diminish our level of functioning. If a businesswoman spends the time before an important presentation engaging in luck-enhancing rituals instead of preparing, she may sacrifice the quality of her performance. She may not speak quite as smoothly, or she may fail to discover a particularly effective way to make her case that would otherwise have occurred to her. Preoccupation with superstition, like any distraction, may interfere with good thinking. Nevertheless, most superstitions do not cause severe problems in a person's ability to think, function, and solve problems effectively. People who have difficulties in the emotional or cognitive domains of their lives are much more likely to have them for other reasons.

• • •

Our assessment of superstition as a potential problem behavior has revealed it to be much less of a worry than alcoholism. In most cases, the likelihood of serious problems in Willoughby's four domains is relatively modest. The greatest capacity for harm seems to be in two areas. In the financial domain, superstition could lead to diminished quality of life if one spends large sums of money on psychics, fortunetellers, numerologists, or Tarot-card readers, or if one's superstitious rituals help to maintain problem gambling. In the physical domain, adoption of magical therapies may delay or deter one from finding more effective treatment. Unfortunately, acceptance of baseless medical treatments appears to be a growing trend, and it probably represents the most serious problem associated with superstitious or paranormal systems of belief. Gambling and overspending on psychics are problems that are exacerbated by superstitious belief, but they are probably produced by other, more powerful forces. In these cases, superstition represents a contributing factor but not a sufficient cause. So our analysis of superstition on the individual level has revealed some reasons to avoid some superstitions, but no rationale for the complete rejection of superstition in all cases. Yet we may find reason for rejection when we examine the broader effects of superstition on our culture.

Superstition and Society

As we have noted, superstition and belief in the paranormal are surprisingly common in our modern, technologically sophisticated age. Their influence can be seen in the news and entertainment media, in sports, in business, in literature, and in our everyday lives. If you are not superstitious, then someone close to you is—a friend, relative, or coworker who routinely invokes magical forces in the hope of gaining some advantage. Despite the obvious power of science to shape and improve our lives, systems of belief that conflict with known scientific principles are quite popular. Superstition in modest doses may not create serious problems in the life of the individual believer, but does the general atmosphere of uncritical acceptance create a danger for the larger society? I think it does.

Now that we have reached the end of the twentieth century, it is clear that the demands of citizenship have changed dramatically in the last fifty years—not just generally, in the more technologically advanced countries, but particularly here in the United States. Although we are blessed with relative economic security, we are confronted with troubling social dilemmas not previously experienced by this or any other culture. For example, never before has widespread drug abuse had such a profound effect on life in the major cities of United States. Drug-related crime is now a common occurrence in most medium-sized and even some smaller communities.

Part of our modern challenge is produced by technology itself. During the first half of this century, transportation and communication were more difficult and less varied than they are today; the average citizen had access to relatively few sources of news and information; and as a result, daily life involved fewer temptations. Less travel and communication meant fewer opportunities to spend money. The practice of shopping at home via catalog, television sales, and direct phone solicitation had not yet been introduced, and the relative rarity of buying on credit provided another natural form of restraint. If you did not have the money to buy something, you could not buy it. Today, buying on credit is so popular that levels of personal debt are at their highest in history and personal bankruptcies are quite common.[17]

But it is not the social ills themselves that challenge us as citizens. We are affected by these problems, we worry about them, and sometimes our lives are touched by them. The problem of citizenship is in knowing how to respond. And yet our modern difficulties require social policies that cannot be adequately evaluated without a basic understanding of science and mathematics. For example, in the time of AIDS, what should be the policy for the evaluation of potential treatments? How should the Food and Drug Administration approach its role of protecting the consumer when this particular group of consumers is terminally ill and, at the moment, with little hope of a cure? Finding answers to these questions requires both a humane consideration of the plight of AIDS' victims and a basic understanding of the methods of science and the goals of the FDA. In this age of instant communication, legislators and government officials appear to be increasingly driven by the opinions of their constituencies. Issues that hold the attention of the electorate are acted upon, and those that do not are ignored—even when the consequences of the obscure issues are much greater. In the early 1980s, Congress deregulated the Savings and Loan industry and increased the government insurance on Savings and Loan deposits, but because these issues were foreign to most of us, the changes went largely unnoticed. By the end of the decade, after the real-estate boom had ended, many Savings and Loans collapsed, and the American people were forced to assume a financial burden of $250 billion.[18] The issues surrounding the Savings and Loan crisis *were* difficult to understand, but our lack of knowledge and attention cost us a greatly increased national debt. Other issues similarly challenge our knowledge and our capacity to choose among social policies. If a nation is to survive the hazards of the modern age, it is essential that its people—and not just its leaders—understand the issues that face them.

Many would prefer to resist the notion, but it is clear that as citizens in the twenty-first century, we will need to have greater knowledge of science and math. Magic is as old as civilization itself, and science is almost as old. But of the two, it is clear which has been more useful. It was science that cured polio and smallpox, made space travel possible, revealed the secrets of genetics, and produced the telephone, the television, and the computer. Of course, advances in technology sometimes bring us new challenges, such as environmental pollution and the insecurities of the nuclear age, but after centuries of investigation of the paranormal, it is difficult to point to a single practical effect. Psychics often offer their services to police departments working on high-profile cases, but, in general, the law enforcement profession has little respect for the value of psychics in the investigation of crime.[19] Similarly, much effort has gone into the study of alternative medical procedures. Indeed, the National Institute of Health has funded a department aimed at promoting such research, but most therapies involving paranormal mechanisms, like therapeutic touch, have yet to be supported by hard evidence.[20] Of course, it is important to encourage new ideas, but if we are to be successful as individuals and as a society we must be able to uncover the good ones and discard the rest. If superstition and the paranormal become integral parts of our beliefs about the world and about human nature, we are in danger of being mired in useless preoccupations—preoccupations that we cannot afford.

What Can We Do About Superstition?

Throughout this book I have adopted the stance that in many cases, superstition is a harmless and entirely natural form of human behavior. Given all of the ways an individual can acquire superstitious behaviors and beliefs, it is a wonder we are not all performing rituals and wearing lucky hats, and as we have seen, the possibility that superstition will be a substantial problem in the life of any individual is rather remote. Nonetheless, it is important that our understanding not lead to tacit endorsement. Magical thinking may have more serious repercussions on the societal level; and thus, it must be discouraged. Without making criminals of the believers, we must adopt policies that encourage people to choose reason over unreason. We must provide alternative methods of coping with life's uncertainties and promote other, more rational systems of belief. It will not be an easy task. Superstition and belief in the paranormal are well-integrated features of our culture, and perhaps because our contemporary world has heightened our sense of uncertainty, they appear to be gaining even greater acceptance. However, there is much we can do to buck this trend. Here are a few suggestions.

Teach Critical Thinking

Each year I begin my Research Methods course for psychology majors by outlining the ways of "fixing knowledge" as described by the American pragmatist philosopher Charles Sanders Peirce.[21] This is a standard opening for courses of this type, but it is a lesson that has meaning for us all, researchers and nonresearchers alike. According to Peirce, there are four basic methods of acquiring or maintaining knowledge: tenacity, authority, *a priori*, and the scientific method. In my own presentation of this list, I typically split the scientific method into two components, empiricism and rationalism or logic, for a total of five methods of fixing knowledge. The poorest source of knowledge is tenacity: holding onto an idea simply out of stubborn loyalty. For the tenacious believer, something is true because it is an eternal verity—regardless of evidence to the contrary. The second source of knowledge, authority, is not much better. Here we accept the word of another simply because we grant him or her the status of expert. A popular bumper sticker urges us to "Question Authority," and because authorities are often wrong, this is good advice. We should be particularly wary when authorities resort to their powerful status as support for the validity of their ideas. However, Peirce acknowledged that to make any progress we must accept some of what we learn from authority. No one can learn all he or she needs to know from direct experience alone. The third method, *a priori*, is sometimes called the *method of intuition*.[22] An idea is considered acceptable if it "makes sense" or "seems reasonable" to the individual. Unfortunately, what makes sense to one person can be completely nonsensical to another. The *a priori* method is a subjective assessment of ideas, a "gut reaction," that is far from infallible. Peirce called his fourth method the method of science; however, contrary to popular belief, there is no one scientific method.[23] The methods used by astronomers, for example, are primarily descriptive and quite different from the experimental methods of physicists and chemists. But all scientific methods of acquiring knowledge rely on empiricism and, to varying degrees, logic. Empiricism simply requires that ideas be tested. Seeing is believing, and if a thing is true, then we want to see the evidence. But seeing—even the seeing of scientists—is also a subjective thing. Scientists often disagree about the meaning of an empirical test. Nevertheless, empiricism is a highly valued source of knowledge. Finally, rationalism and logic give science rules under which to operate and methods of linking facts together. Today, most research in the behavioral sciences uses a "top-down" form of deductive reasoning that begins with a theory. Based on this theory, the scientist formulates a specific, testable statement: a hypothesis. Then, the scientist designs an experiment whose results will either support or contradict the hypothesis. As part of the self-correcting, nontenacious aspect of good science, if the results are inconsistent with the hypothesis, the theory may need to be modified or discarded. These and other accepted rules of science provide a rational method of linking empirically derived facts.[24]

My reason for presenting this material to my students is to distinguish the empirical methods of science from other, less valid methods of inquiry. But for me, there is a much broader message. It is my hope that the students will use Peirce's methods as a framework for evaluating their own beliefs about human behavior and about many other things. Toward this aim, at the beginning of the first class, before I have begun to talk about Peirce, I ask the students to fill out a questionnaire about their beliefs. The questions cover a wide range of topics, but several items ask about superstitious and paranormal beliefs.[25] I also ask my students to report any exam-related superstitions they had employed. During the second class, I present the results of the survey on an overhead projector. Table 7.1 pre-

Table 7.1   Percentage of psychology students in the Spring 1995 research methods class who endorse various beliefs

Percentage Endorsing	Item
81	The soul continues to exist though the body may die.
30	Some individuals are able to levitate (lift) objects through mental forces.
39	Black magic really exists.
11	Black cats can bring bad luck.
43	Your mind or soul can leave your body and travel (astral projection).
69	Dreams can provide information about the future.
44	During altered states, such as sleep or trances, the spirit can leave the body.
68	Some people have the ability to predict the future.
78	I believe in God.
26	A person's thoughts can influence the movement of a physical object.
23	The position of the star at the time of a person's birth determines, in part, his or her character.
89	The movement of electrons allow electric lights and appliances to function.
73	To preserve the environment, it is better to use paper bags rather than plastic bags.
95	Smoking causes cancer.
5	Abortion is wrong.
61	Democratically governed businesses and organizations are more productive than authoritarian ones.
66	Some people are born lucky.
37	War is wrong under all circumstances.
15	The number 13 is unlucky.
36	Crossing your fingers or knocking on wood can improve your luck.

Table 7.2   *Percentages of students reporting ever engaging in various exam-related superstitions*

Percentage Endorsing	Item
62	Used a lucky pen, piece of jewelry, or piece of clothing.
28	Wore sloppy clothes (dressed down).
33	Dressed up.
36	Touched a lucky object.
54	Sat in a particular seat.
38	Listened to special music or song.
26	Eaten a particular food.
23	Avoided a particular person, place, or action.
31	Performed a lucky action or sequence of actions.
13	Used another luck-enhancing strategy (e.g., perfume).

sents the totals on the beliefs section of the questionnaire for the 1995 spring-semester class, and Table 7.2 shows their totals on the exam-related-superstition section. Both are based on the responses of sixty-one psychology majors.

It is interesting to note the high levels of paranormal and superstitious beliefs, even among psychology majors, who, in some studies, have been shown to be more skeptical than other students.[26] Fully 85 percent of the class reported having used at least one of the exam-related superstitions from Table 7.2 at one time or another. Over half the class believed that dreams can foretell the future, that certain people can predict the future, and that some people are born lucky. Other unsubstantiated ideas also received remarkably high levels of endorsement. Over 40 percent believed in astral projection, and 30 percent in levitation.

But the purpose of this exercise is not to embarrass the students by revealing the strangeness of their beliefs. (Of course, the questionnaires are anonymous; no individual student can be identified.) It is to challenge them to think about where their ideas come from and to evaluate critically the sources of their beliefs. We begin by separating beliefs that are not properly within the realm of empirical inquiry. As a result, some religious views— "the soul continues to exist though the body may die" and "I believe in God"—are placed in a different category. By definition, these beliefs are accepted on faith and need not be subject to empirical test. Similarly, questions of morality and ethics cannot be evaluated scientifically, so we eliminate from further analysis statements such as "war is wrong under all circumstances" and "abortion is wrong."

Eventually, we are left with a number of items that are—or should be— questions of fact. Most students quickly acknowledge that their superstitions and paranormal beliefs stem from the *a priori* method or authority. The ideas simply "made sense," or someone had convinced them of their validity. The class discussion became much more interesting when we turned to the more widely accepted beliefs. Eighty-nine percent of the students said that the movement of electrons allows electric lights and appliances to function, but when I asked them how they knew, there was silence. None of them had ever directly observed an electron in action. At some point a teacher—an authority—had told them about electrons and electricity. The same is true for the notion that smoking causes lung cancer. Most of us accept these ideas as fact, but they have come to us by way of authority, not empirical test.

Other ideas may be logical in relation to some known facts, but not all the evidence is in. For example, under normal circumstances paper is much more biodegradable than plastic, leading to the widespread belief—held by over 70 percent of my students—that paper bags are better for the environment than plastic. However, most trash, including paper bags, ends up in large, sealed landfills that do not provide a good environment for degrading paper. More research is needed to determine the best practice, but it may be that plastic bags are a better option because they are less bulky. Until I see more evidence, I will continue to take paper bags over plastic, but the question is still an open one.[27]

Exercises such as this one demonstrate the importance of critical thinking. We all need to cultivate a healthy attitude of skepticism in our everyday lives—not the skepticism of someone who takes joy in deriding what he sees as the misguided delusions of those around him, but that of a respectful questioner. Astronomer Carl Sagan described the challenge of skepticism as the maintenance of the delicate balance between two conflicting attitudes: openness to new ideas and the critical evaluation of all ideas, old and new.[28] It is a prescription that is remarkably similar to Jonathan Baron's principles of good thinking.

If we are to discourage superstition and belief in the paranormal, it is important to teach the principles of critical thinking not only at the college level (where it has been effectively taught for many years), but in secondary and elementary schools.[29] Such material can easily be adapted for younger audiences. For example, given that we must obtain much of our information from various authorities, students could be taught to evaluate the authorities they encounter on television and elsewhere. They can learn how to determine whether the views of the authority are based on empirical inquiry (good), personal experience (not so good), or yet another authority (bad). Does the authority attempt to convince her audience by an appeal to the evidence or to her personal status and power? Does the authority have a vested interest in a particular view? What is the quality of the evidence given? More widespread instruction in this kind of analysis would have many desirable effects on our children.

Teach Decision Analysis

Recently some investigators have attempted to teach both children and adults how to make good decisions without being trapped by the kinds of cognitive biases and heuristics described in chapter 4. Unfortunately, the results have been rather mixed. For example, many business and medical students are taught to apply expected utility theory to decisions related to their professions, but it appears that few of them continue to use this approach after leaving school.[30] However, more promising findings have been produced by instructional programs for children. Although it is unclear how useful training in decision analysis will be, this area is deserving of more attention. Curricula that include this kind of material might help students make more rational decisions and avoid the pitfalls of sloppy thinking.

Promote Science Education

If we are to promote an appreciation for scientific thinking, we must teach science to young children. The United States is widely acknowledged to have the finest institutions of higher education in the world. Students come from all over the globe to attend our colleges and universities, yet our elementary and secondary schools do not enjoy a similar reputation. Increasingly, our top graduate programs in science and mathematics are being filled by foreign students who received better basic training in these subjects than their cohorts from the United States. From a purely economic point of view, greater emphasis on teaching science and mathematics is essential if we are to continue to be a competitive force in the technology marketplace, but better science education will also bring more general benefits. Many of those who accept paranormal ideas may do so in part because they are suspicious of science and scientists. Just as we often feel uneasy around people who are different from or, in some way, alien to us, the suspicion these people feel may come from lack of exposure. Science is difficult. It has its own language that is unintelligible to the uninitiated, and it relies heavily on yet another cryptic mode of communication: mathematics. As a result, many find it an easy subject to avoid, while others attempt it only to find the experience overwhelming and unrewarding. It is only natural that these people should turn to other methods of inquiry. The person who lacks an appreciation for both the process and products of science finds nonscientific thinking more appealing.

To instill greater interest in and understanding of science, it is important to teach it early. Understanding this, the National Science Foundation has, over the last ten years, steadily increased the proportion of its budget that is devoted to education and has continued to allocate over half of its education budget to the elementary and secondary grades.[31] The NSF provides funding for several science programs for children on the Public Broadcasting Service, such as *The Magic School Bus* and *Bill Nye the Science Guy*, and in 1993 it launched an ambitious initiative to improve science education in nine major urban areas. These and other similar efforts must be encouraged if we are to succeed in improving our understanding of science and promoting the use of scientific reasoning in the everyday world.

Improve the Public Image of Scientists

Science has a serious public-relations problem, and unfortunately it has been ever thus.[32] Due primarily to the traditional tension between science and religion, many unflattering portrayals of scientists can be found in literature, myth, and legend. Those who seek forbidden knowledge, hope to have influence over nature, or mimic God's creative powers are the subject of derision. Prometheus stole fire from the Gods and fashioned man out of clay. To punish him, the Gods gave him the first woman, Pandora, who, of course, was later seized by curiosity, opened her box, and released a multitude of woes upon the world. In *The Inferno*, Dante placed his representative of medieval science, the alchemist, in the final circle of hell. According to legend and as portrayed by Goethe, Marlowe, and Thomas Mann, Doctor Faust gave up his soul to Mephistopheles to satisfy his thirst for knowledge. And Mary Wollstonecraft Shelley created what is perhaps the classic symbol of science run amok in *Frankenstein*, the story of how Victor Frankenstein's quest to recreate life created a monster.[33]

This condemning view of science is still common in our contemporary literature and culture. As a young child growing up in the 1950s, I was fascinated with horror films; I still enjoy them on occasion. But at that time, the United States was steeped in the Cold War, and many of the great black-and-white horror classics of the decade either explicitly or implicitly blamed the unleashing of their terrifying antagonists on the atomic bomb. A scientist, though never the hero of the piece, was a standard character, but more often than not, his (the scientist was always a man) academic interest in the monster placed the populace at risk. The real hero of the piece was always a no-nonsense guy whose character was built more on brawn than on brains and who always got the girl. Similar roles appear in the films of the 1990s. For example, in *Jurassic Park*, the most successful movie of all time, the "monsters"—clones of prehistoric dinosaurs—were created by a scientist/businessman whose ideas led to several deaths. In a modest improvement over the films of my childhood, by the end of the movie the creator of Jurassic Park manages to recognize the error of his ways, and contrary to the old formula, the true heroes of the story are scientists—two archaeologists, a man and a woman.

New ideas, such as those inspired by scientific developments, are often aired and critiqued in our popular culture as part of a healthy process of public debate, and scientists sometimes deserve the criticism they get. But the popularization of science would be greatly enhanced by improving the prevailing images of the scientist. Part of the problem may be that the majority of the people who are most likely to write novels, plays, and film scripts were educated in the humanities, not in the sciences. Furthermore, the few scientists-turned-writers have used their scientific training as the source material for thrillers that further damage the image of science and scientists (e.g., Robin Cook, Michael Crichton). We need more screenplays and novels that present scientists in a positive light. In our current culture, television and film are particularly influential media, and it is likely that the introduction of more scientist-heroes would help to make science more attractive.

• • •

These are just a few ideas, and it is difficult to know how effective they would be. But it is important that we do what we can. The current social climate is so uncritically accepting of paranormal and pseudoscientific ideas that without some progress in the spread of scientific reasoning, we are in danger of being mired in irrationality. In our democratic society, we place a very high value on free speech. Everyone is entitled to his or her opinion, and rarely is one person's view given greater weight than another. But as Asimov said, "some ideas are better than others."[34] The future of our democratic society will be more secure if we help people find the good ideas.

Coda

During the time I spent researching and writing this book, I asked many people about their superstitions and paranormal beliefs. In most cases, their faces brightened as they told me colorful stories, often about rather personal episodes in their lives. And I loved hearing what they told me. As a behavioral scientist, I was curious about how their superstitions had begun and how they interpreted them now. As someone who simply loves a good story, I often found these personal narratives wonderfully entertaining. And far from diminishing my estimation of the storyteller, the stories seemed, more often than not, to give these people a dimension that endeared them to me.

When they had finished talking about their superstitions, some of these people would turn to me and ask, "Do *you* have any superstitions?" I always found this an uncomfortable moment—not because I wished to remain objectively distant from my subject matter and preferred not to say, but because I was forced to admit that I did not. Everyone probably holds some belief or engages in some action that, on close examination, is inconsistent with known scientific principles and therefore superstitious. But, as far as beliefs and actions of which I am consciously aware, I have no superstitions. This should not be an embarrassing confession to make, but at these moments, I often felt as if it were. Our culture is one that values belief and faith, and to some, the nonsuperstitious person seems somewhat cold and lacking in imagination. The believer gains a sense of innocence and wonder from an appeal to supernatural forces, whereas the nonbeliever seems incapable of granting exceptions to mundane logic.

But for me, this image is far from the truth.[35] Rejecting the paranormal may eliminate a potential source of solace and psychological support, but I do not feel deprived. I face the same uncertainties that others face, but I find comfort in understanding. Knowing how random processes operate and how to estimate probabilities does not improve my chances of obtaining an improbable reward, but it helps me live with whatever comes my way. If I receive the good outcome, I feel fortunate—not lucky. And if the outcome is not good, I am not surprised. Although the superstitious person may gain a sense of control from his rituals, I get a similar feeling from being able to think rationally about the circumstances I face. Even when I have no power over important events in my life, I gain a feeling of control from understanding them.

And I, too, have a sense of wonder. For me, discovering the workings of nature is a vibrant, satisfying experience that is both intellectual and emotional. To recognize the astronomical relationship between the Sun and the Earth, or to understand the optical phenomena that create its rosy light, does not strip the sunset of its beauty. Nor is it necessary to give the sunset supernatural meaning to be humbled by its magnificence. This book is a scientific exploration into an unusual form of human behavior. While it has exposed some of our natural weaknesses, it has also demonstrated our remarkable ability to reflect on our own natures, to understand ourselves. Human behavior can be studied scientifically, just as any other natural phenomenon, and we are enriched by the experience. When we recognize the power of human understanding, it is easy to choose science over magic, and the natural over the supernatural.

Notes

Preface

1. The best examples of earlier works on related subjects are Jahoda (1969) and Zusne and Jones (1989).
2. Gardner, J. (1977). *On Moral Fiction*. New York: Basic Books.

1 Believing in Magic

1. *Current Biography* (1990). Reichler (1990).
2. In fact, Wade's father, whose name, appropriately, is Winn Boggs, gave his son a copy of Williams's book *The Science of Hitting* at a time when the younger Boggs was experiencing a batting slump in high school (Williams & Underwood, 1971; Current Biography, 1990).
3. One of his most famous recipes is "Wade Boggs Lemon Chicken," which he believes has a particularly powerful effect on his hitting (Boggs, 1984).
4. *Current Biography* (1990). McCallum (1988). Curry (1994).

5. *Current Biography* (1990).

6. U.S. National Center for Health Statistics (1992).

7. Indeed, Jim Fixx's death due to a heart attack, suffered while on his daily run, has been attributed to a family history of serious heart disease.

8. When a team is behind and has not scored any runs in recent innings, players will often wear their caps backwards or in some other unusual fashion. It is believed that this practice will stimulate the team to rally and score more runs.

9. Kurtz and Fraknoli (1986) Gallup (1979).

10. Frazer (1922) *The Golden Bough*.

11. Evans (1967/1897).

12. Cranston (1988) *The miracle of Lourdes*.

13. Woodward (1990) *Making saints*.

14. Randi (1982) *The truth about Uri Geller*.

15. This and other examples in this section come directly from Frazer (1922).

16. Lienhardt (1979) *Social Anthropology*.

17. Rozin, Millman, and Nemeroff (1986) See also Rozin, Markwith, and Ross (1990).

18. Durkheim (1957/1915), page 23.

19. Durkheim (1957/1915), page 26.

20. Durkheim, p. 44.

21. Durkheim, p. 44.

22. Malinowski (1972/1925).

23. Oswalt (1972).

24. Malinowski (1972/1948).

25. Mauss (1972/1950).

26. Malinowski (1972/1948, pp. 139–140). reprinted by permission of the Bronislow Malinowski Trust.

27. Thomas (1971), p. 34.

28. Thomas (1971), p. 5. Reprinted by permission of the publisher.

29. Thomas (1971), p. 192.

30. Thomas (1971) p. 661.

31. Friedrick, Cronin, Riley, and Wyss (1987).

32. Rosellini (1993).

33. Mack (1994), page 15. These figures are based on a Roper Poll (Hopkins, Jacobs, and Westrum, 1991) that has been criticized for basing its estimates on a number of vague questions that are assumed to indicate abduction (e.g., having the sensation that someone was standing next to your bed as you slept).

34. Alcock (1981).

35. In the 1990 edition of *Books in Print* these topics appear separately as "occult sciences" and "psychical research," and in the 1994 edition, the titles were found under "occultism" (670 titles), "parapsychology" (486 titles), "astrology" (1117 titles), and a variety of other lesser categories (e.g., astral projection, clairvoyance, extrasensory perception, ghosts; a total of 585 titles). I am indebted to Susanne Dutton for this analysis.

36. Gallup (1979), p. 185.

37. *Variety* (1995, February 20–26).

38. Gallup (1978); Gallup and Newport (1990); McAneny (1995).

39. The other ten items and the percentages of respondents believing in them were: possession by the devil (49%), psychic or spiritual healing (46%), telepathy (36%), haunted houses (29%), extraterrestrial beings having visited Earth (27%), reincarnation (21%), telekinesis (moving or bending objects; 17%), channeling (11%), healing power of pyramids (7%), and healing power of rock crystals (4%) (Gallup & Newport, 1990)

40. Flexner (1987), *The Random House Dictionary of the English Language*, p. 1911.

41. In chapter 6 we will take a much closer look at the relationship between schizophrenia and superstition.

42. Marmor (1956), p. 119. Marmor's definition was based on one given in the *Encyclopedia Britannica* (14th ed.).

43. Holmyard (1957).

44. Ziskin (1981). As an example of the level of skepticism regarding psychological testimony, Ziskin reports the case of the "Alphabet Bomber." The jury found that the defendent was competent to stand trial, despite having heard from four defense psychiatrists that he was "psychotic, paranoid (or paranoid schizophrenic), suffered from delusions, had auditory halucinations and believed he was on trial for masturbating in public . . ." (p. 37). Of course, the jury may also have been expressing a sense of outrage about the crime and a desire to see the defendant stand trial.

45. Cormick (1984) Atlas (1985). Although the claim of levitation does not have adequate support.

46. Recently a number of writers (e.g., Dossey, 1993) have argued that scientific evidence supports the effectiveness of prayer in the treatment of a number of diseases. It is well known that meditation can lower blood pressure and may have other health benefits; thus, by extension, a sick person may be helped by prayer (Benson, 1984). However, other ideas about prayer are more controversial. For example, Dossey (1993) asserts that scientific evidence supports the idea that a sick person can be healed by the prayers of another person many miles away.

47. Cannon (1984).

48. This brief history and evaluation of parapsychology is drawn from Alcock (1981).

49. There are exceptions, of course. See, for example (Swann, 1991), *Everybody's guide to ESP: Unlocking the extrasensory power of your mind.*

2   The Superstitious Person

1. Regan (1988), p. 3.

2. Regan (1988), p. 301.

3. Reagan (1989), p. 49.

4. Quigley (1990), p. 11.

5. Reagan (1989), pp. 44–45. It should be noted that the death cycle, as stated, omits certain relevant facts. For example, both Thomas Jefferson and James Monroe were elected in zero years, yet they lived well beyond the end of their second terms in office. Conversely, Zachary Taylor died in office without being elected in a zero year. As we will see in chapter 4, this neglect of other relevant combinations of events is typical of many popularly held erroneous beliefs. Finally, with Mr. Reagan's survival of two full terms, the streak is broken, and perhaps the twenty-year presidential death cycle will now be relegated to the status of a quaint curiosity. For a written statement of the twenty-year death cycle, see Randles (1985).

6. Reagan (1989), p. 45.

7. Reagan (1989), p. 50. Reprinted with permission.

8. For eamples of superstitions among soldiers, see Stouffer et al. (1949), pages 188–189.

9. For those interested in reading about contemporary sports superstitions, I recommend McMallum (1988), from which the all the following examples but one are drawn. The George Seifert example is from Friend (1994).

10. Meserole (1990), page 142.

11. Hejza (1990).

12. Gmelch (1974).

13. Buhrmann and Zaugg (1981).

14. Buhrmann, Brown, and Zaugg (1982).

15. Gregory and Petrie (1975).

16. Hejza (1990)

17. I am indebted to Alta DeRoo for this anecdote.

18. Albas and Albas (1989).

19. Albas and Albas (1989), p. 607. Passages from Albas and Albas (1989) reprinted by permission of the Midwest Sociology Society.

20. Albas and Albas (1989), p. 608.

21. Albas and Albas (1989), pp. 609–610.

22. I am indebted to Susan Tien for this anecdote.

23. Cohen (1960), p. 53–60.

24. Cited in Jones (1980) p. 545.

25. Hayano (1978), Oldman (1974), King (1990).

26. Henslin (1967).

27. Henslin (1967), p. 320. Reprinted by permission of The University of Chicago Press.

28. In the case of student superstitions, very good students may be motivated less by the uncertainty of the outcome (although a good grade is never guaranteed) than a wish to "hedge their bets." Superstitions of this type will be addressed in chapter 3.

29. Becker (1975).

30. Hayano (1978), p. 480.

31. Oldman (1974).

32. Blum (1976), Blum and Blum (1974), Randall (1990), Randall and Dosrosier (1980), Tobacyk and Milford (1983), Tobacyk and Prichett (1988), Tupper and Williams (1986).

33. Tobacyk and Milford (1983).

34. Campbell and Beets (1978), Rotton and Kelly (1984), Sanduleak (1986).

35. Corrigan, Pattison, and Lester (1980).

36. Sanduleak (1986).

37. Bennett (1987) pages 27–28.

38. Bennett (1987) page 32.

39. Bennett (1987) page 32.

40. Epstein (1993).

41. Emery (1991, 1990), *Providence Journal Bulletin*, February 17, 1988, A1, A14, *Providence Journal Bulletin*, July 23, 1990, B2.

42. Gardner (1996); Mumford, Rose, and Goslin (1996).

43. Blum and Blum (1974).

44. Otis and Alcock (1982).

45. Wagner and Monnet (1979).

46. Pasachoff, Cohen, and Pasachoff (1970).

47. Eliot makes explicit mention of *The Golden Bough* in the notes to *The Waste Land*.

48. Jahoda (1968).

49. Salter and Routledge (1971).

50. Wilson (1988).

51. Gallup and Newport (1990).

52. Burhmann and Zaug (1981).

53. Schumaker (1987), p. 455.

54. Evans (1969), p. 5.

55. Robinson (1957), p. 665. Curry (1926).

56. Abrams et al. (1968), pp. 121–122. Text and notes reprinted by permission of the publisher.

57. Wechsler (1982),

58. Liebert and Spiegler (1982).

59. Sheldon is the perpetrator of the "Nude Posture Photo Scandal," which has

received much recent publicity (Rosenbaum, 1995). During the 1950s and 60s, freshman students at a number of Ivy League schools were photographed, proportedly to assess their posture, but in many cases to provide photographs of different body types for Sheldon's research. Much of the scandal stems from the fear (apparently justified) that many of the photos still exist (see Rosenbaum, 1995).

60. This summary and assessment of Sheldon's theory is from Liebert and Spiegler (1982) and Hall and Lindsey (1978).

61. McNemar (1946).

62. The authors of the recent controversial bestseller *The Bell Curve* estimate the hereditary component of intelligence at between 40 and 80 percent.

63. Gould (1981).

64. Sattler (1988).

65. Killen, Wildman, and Wildman (1974). Based on the author's reports, I calculated a *Cohen's d* of 0.63, indicating that the mean superstition scores were slightly more than half a standard deviation higher for the average IQ group.

66. Alcock and Otis (1980), Wierbicki (1985).

67. Messer and Griggs (1989).

68. McGarry and Newberry (1981).

69. Boshier (1973a, 1973b).

70. Wilson (1973), p. 259.

71. Tobacyk (1984), p. 31.

72. The concept of death threat is based on George Kelly's personal construct theory.

73. Tobacyk (1988), page 35. Reprinted by permission of the publisher.

74. Tobacyk (1984), page 32.

75. Lefcourt (1982), p. 58. Reprinted by permission of the author and the publisher.

76. Tobacyk and Milford (1983). Other studies include Tobacyk, Nagot, and Miller (1988), Randall and Desrosiers (1980), Scheidt (1973), and Allen and Lester (1994). For a rare conflicting finding (i.e., paranormal belief correlated with *internal* locus of control), see Eve and Harrold (1986).

77. McGarry and Newberry (1981), p 735.

78. Bandura (1977).

79. Wagner and Ratzeburg (1987).

80. Epstein (1994;1993)

81. Epstein (1991)

82. It should be noted that Epstein's scale of superstitious thinking includes some paranormal items that do not meet our definition of superstition. For example, one statement in the inventory is, "I believe in good omens." Belief in omens can be categorized as paranormal, but unless the the believer takes some action as a result of the omen, this belief does not meet our definition of a superstition. Nonetheless, the great majority of items reflect traditional, socially shared superstitions (e.g., "I have at least one good luck charm).

83. This is summarized from Epstein (1991), Table 3.2.

84. Epstein (1992), page 106.

85. Epstein's (1991) study is a notable exception.

86. Epstein (1988), Maccoby and Jacklin (1974).

3   Superstition and Coincidence

1. These stories about Bjorn Borg's family are taken from Kirkpatrick (1981).

2. For example, Stein (1967) lists only spatial meanings.

3. Hilgard (1987) p. 139; Pratt (1969).

4. Oxford University Press (1971), p. 3100. A note on the history of motion pictures: as early as 1880, British photographer Eadweard Muybridge was giving public exhibitions

of a device called the Zoöpraxiscope, which projected the movements of a running horse (Pratt, 1973). In 1881 and 1882, he entertained audiences in England and France with his invention. Theatrical films began to emerge just before the turn of the century, and the first feature length film (one hour or longer) in the world was the 1906 Austrialian production *The Story of the Kelly Gang* (Robertson, 1988). Germany produced its first feature film in 1911, a year following Wertheimer's abortive train ride.

5. This description of apparent motion is necessarily brief and omits many aspects of the research on this phenomenon. For a complete discussion of classical work in apparent motion, see Kolers (1972).

6. The Gestalt principle of proximity means "close but not touching," rather than true, complete contiguity.

7. As opposed to what the layperson calls learning. The schoolchild learns primarily through instruction rather than through direct experience. The earlier experience of others and our ability to respond to verbal direction saves students from having to learn everything for the first time.

8. Hilgard (1987), p. 47; Watson (1978).

9. Thorndike (1936) Hilgard (1987).

10. Thorndike (1936), p. 264.

11. It should be noted that under some circumstances these are not involuntary functions. Obviously, human respiration is often involuntary, but if we wish to, we can exert some control over it. Furthermore, biofeedback methods can be used to control heart rate, the electrical conductivity of the skin, and other "involuntary" functions.

12. Watson (1978).

13. Guthrie and Horton (1946).

14. A good early introduction to this topic is provided by Herrnstein (1966).

15. Epstein (1982), p. 99.

16. RBI = runs batted in. In Boggs's case there is the added problem that the meal and the game are not contiguous. Later in the chapter we will find one solution to this problem in the effects of reinforcement on longer sequences of behaviors; in chapter 4 we will see another.

17. Staddon and Simmelhag (1971); Timberlake and Lucas (1985).

18. Wagner and Morris (1987), p. 472.

19. The Wagner and Morris experiment included a number of control conditions and additional procedures, which are omitted here for simplicity.

20. Ono (1987).

21. Ono (1987), p. 265. Copyright by the Society for the Experimental Analysis of Behavior. Reprinted by permission of the author and the publisher.

22. See, for example, Holyoak, Koh, and Nisbett (1989).

23. Killeen's work is based on signal detection theory. For a complete description of his theory, see Killeen (1977, 1981).

24. Hacking (1975), p. 68.

25. Catania (1968).

26. Catania identifies a fourth form, *topographical superstition*, but it does not fit the definition of superstitious behavior adopted in this book. This last category is demonstrated when, like the cats in Guthrie and Horton's puzzle boxes, a very specific response form (or topography) emerges when any number of forms would work. Although Guthrie and Horton's cats behaved as if their specific responses are necessary, rather than merely sufficient, to open the door, the cats' responses did open the door. Therefore, strickly speaking these responses are not superstitious.

27. Morse and Skinner (1957).

28. Starr and Staddon (1982).

29. Kendrick (1992). Wilkinson (1993).

30. McCallum (1988).

31. Catania and Cutts (1963).

32. Catania and Cutts (1963), p. 207.

33. Vyse (1989; 1991) and Heltzer and Vyse (1994).

34. Vyse (1991), experiment one.

35. Vyse (1991), page 506.

36. Vyse (1989).

37. In fact, there were three groups in the experiment, but the third, which received points on every trip through the matrix, was merely an additional control group.

38. Vyse (1991), page 506, subject S9.

39. Falk (1986).

40. For a more complete explanation of the determinants of adjunctive behavior see Staddon (1977) or Falk (1977).

41. Wallace, Singer, Wayner, and Cook (1975).

4   Superstitious Thinking

1. This description of the 1990 Breeders' Cup draws heavily upon an article written for the *Los Angeles Times* by Bill Christine (1990)

2. Watson (1978).

3. One could argue that *not equal to* is more basic than the other two inequalities.

4. The best popular treatment of this topic is, of course, John Allen Paulos' (1988) book *Innumeracy*. Much of what follows is drawn or benefits from this work.

5. The typical roulette wheel has thirty-six numbers, half red and half black, plus one or two zeros. These zeros play an important role in keeping the odds slightly in favor of the house. For example, without the zeros, a bet on red would have a probability of .5 or even odds of 1–1. The zeroes, which are neither red nor black, keep the probabilities slightly in the house's favor. With two zeroes on the wheel, a bet on the red now has a probability of 18/38 or .47. Under this arrangement, the house will often loose the bet, but in the long run, it will win more than it loses.

6. Bakan (1960).

7. Neuringer (1982), Lopes and Oden (1987).

8. Page and Neuringer (1985).

9. Kahneman and Tversky (1972).

10. Gilovich, Vallone, and Tversky (1985).

11. Blackmore (1985).

12. For example, Koestler (1972) and Jung (1978a, 1978b).

13. Koestler (1972).

14. Although Freud's theory is much more influential in the mental health field, it, too, is based on many pseudoscientific assumptions. See Hines (1988) for a discussion of both Jung and Freud.

15. Jung (1978b), p. 438. Copyright (1978) by Princeton University Press. Reprinted by permission of Princeton University Press.

16. Diaconis and Mosteller (1989).

17. Fisher (1953), pp. 13–14, as quoted in Ruma (1989).

18. I actually received five chain letters, three delivered by the postal service and—in a new twist—two transmitted by electronic mail. Each of these letters was a version of the famous 'St. Jude' letter (Goodenough & Dawkins, 1994).

19. For a similar discussion of the effects of large numbers of rides on the chances of being stuck in an elevator, see Norman (1992), pp. 149–150.

20. Emery (1991).

21. Falk (1981), p. 20.

22. In the interest of simplicity, this discussion of the probabilities of complex events

glosses over several important points. In particular, intersections are calculated by the simple product of the individual probabilities only when the events in questions are independent (i.e., the occurrence or nonoccurrence of one event does not alter the probability of the other). In addition, probability of the union of two events is calculated by the sum of the individual probabilities only if they are mutually exclusive. If the events are not mutually exclusive (i.e., they could occur together), the probability of their union is calculated by the sum of the individual probabilities minus the probability of their intersections. For a more complete discussion of these probabilities, see a basic statistics text, such as Howell (1992).

23. Diaconis and Mosteller (1989) discuss the effects of near matches on the Birthday Problem.

24. For a simple discussion of the Birthday Problem, complete with easy-to-follow calculations, see Paulos (1988), pp. 25–28. For a more technical exegesis, see Diaconis and Mosteller (1989).

25. U.S. National Center for Health Statistics (1993). These figures actually mark a decrease in the relative rate of suicides. For example, in 1989, 55 percent of firearm deaths were suicides, and only 40 percent were homocides.

26. Firearms were the method in 60 percent of these suicides.

27. Media coverage of suicides is suspected to encourage teen suicide "clusters" (Coleman, 1987).

28. Combs and Slovic (1979) found that people's estimates of the frequencies of various causes of death are correlated with the amount of publicity these causes receive. Thus, death from cancer, diabetes, and emphysema are infrequently reported by the media, and research participants underestimate their likelihood. Conversely, death from drownings, fires, and homicides are more frequently covered, and their frequency is overestimated. This biased estimation of various risks is an example of the availability heuristic at work (see page 123). Combs and Slovic note that although one might blame biased reporting for misleading the public, it is also possible that public interest in these more catastrophic forms of death influence reporting practices. It goes both ways.

29. Simon (1990).

30. As an indication of this confusion, all three of the horses that died at the 1990 Breeder's Cup were recorded on the charts kept by *Daily Racing Form* as "fell"—despite the fact that only one of the three actually fell, in the usual sense of the word. Go For Wand broke down, fracturing a foreleg, and Mr. Nickerson had a heart attack. Only Shaker Knit actually fell as he collided with the faltering Mr. Nickerson. The categories used in Simon's (1990) analysis were: broke down, fell, DNF, lame, sore, pulled up, bled.

31. These probabilities come from an entertaining book called *What Are the Odds* by Les Krantz (1992).

32. In reality, this overall figure is only a rough approximation of Go For Wand's chances of a DNF from physical distress. For example, the best horses (like Go For Wand) run in "stakes" races, and the probability of a DNF is slightly lower for these events. For example, in 1990 this probability was .0034 or 1/294.

33. Fisher (1953).

34. The twenty-two Hebrew letters of the alphabet are each associated with a number, and numerical sums of words are part of the Hebrew Kabbala, an occult Jewish religion (see Falk, 1989).

35. This example, like the Birthday Problem, also entails the confusion of union versus intersection.

36. Hintzman, Asher, and Stern (1978) and Kallai (1985).

37. Lockie (1989), p. 1. It is interesting to note that the homeopathic principle, as stated by Lockie, hedges the bet. "May be" is not a very forceful phrase, but the less equivocal "is" would be harder to defend.

38. Lockie (1989), p. 416.

39. Barrett (1987) and Lockie (1989).

40. The statistically trained reader will recognize this as the principle of regression to the mean.

41. For an interesting study of a number of healers, see William Nolen's (1974) *Healing: A doctor in search of a miracle.* After examining hundreds of cases, he concluded that all could be explained by less than miraculous causes.

42. *Newsweek* (1987).

43. This figure and the surrounding discussion is due, in large part, to Hines (1988).

44. Hines (1988).

45. For a more extensive treatment of heuristics, biases, and the failings of human judgment and decision-making see Kahneman, Slovic, an Tversky (1982) and Nisbett and Ross (1980).

46. Holyoak and Nisbett (1988).

47. For example, Tversky and Kahneman (1974).

48. To simplify this example and produce a second dichotomous variable, quiz performance is conceived simply as pass/fail. In an actual case, raw quiz scores might be correlated with use or nonuse of the guide.

49. Correlations reported in this section are phi coefficients.

50. Phi for Table (c) is -.47.

51. Baron (1988).

52. Smedslund (1963).

53. Chapman and Chapman (1971).

54. Indeed, Chapman pointed this out in one of his early studies of illusory correlation (1967).

55. The phi coefficient for Figure 4.2 table (b) is +.36, which is not a statistically significant correlation.

56. We will return to Peirce later.

57. Glick and Snyder (1986).

58. Russell and Jones (1980).

59. Festinger, Reiken, and Schachter (1956).

60. Lord, Ross, and Lepper (1979).

61. The example given is drawn from Hines (1988).

62. See, for example, Broughton (1991), page 79.

63. This example also involves the social influences on superstition and paranormal belief, a topic to be addressed in the next chapter.

64. Cohen (1960).

65. Clotfelter and Cook (1989).

66. *Providence Journal Bulletin*, April 26, 1989.

67. Langer (1975).

68. This phrase suggests another way to calculate the probability of winning. The reciprocal of the number of possible combinations $\frac{1}{C_r^N}$ will produce the same result as the method that follows.

69. To keep things simple, I have ignored the fact that lesser prizes are given for matching fewer than six numbers. If all possible prizes were considered, the expected value of the ticket would reach the break-even point at a somewhat lower jackpot amount. However, it is safe to assume that most people who play Lotto are playing for the top prize. Few would buy a ticket if only the smaller prizes were offered. Finally, as we will learn in chapter 6, for the ticket to be worth $1, it is necessary for the jackpot to rise even higher than $12,913,583 because the diminishing marginal utility of money makes potential losses outweigh potential gains.

70. Clotfelter and Cook (1989), p. 9.

71. Alcock (1981), Hines (1988). For a dissenting view, see Broughton (1991).

72. Benassi, Sweeney, and Drevno (1979).

73. A note for psychologists: Benassi et al. (1979) reported an interaction between locus of control and involvement, such that active participants who were internals had greater confidence in their PK abilities; whereas, externals and inactive participants reported lower confidence.

74. Langer and Roth (1975). For the sake of simplicity, several details of this study are omitted.

75. Rothbaum, Weisz, and Snyder (1982).

76. Seligman (1975).

77. Langer and Rodin (1976).

78. Taylor (1983).

79. Taylor and Brown (1988).

80. Taylor (1989).

81. Friedland, Keinan, and Regev (1992).

82. Of course, participants were never shocked.

83. Keinan (1994).

84. During the war, families waited out the missle attacks in a room in their home that was sealed against gas. This particular superstition is a good example of the concept of contagion.

85. From Snyder and Shenkel (1975). Reprinted with permission from *Psychology Today*, copyright © 1975 (Sussex Publishers, Inc.).

86. Meehl (1956).

87. Snyder and Shenkel (1975).

88. Goodman (1968).

89. Ironically, no astrologer's interview can compare with the amount of data collected in a typical psychological assessment. The obvious implication of this research is that the elaborate methods of the clinical psychologist enhance the Barnum effect and make it more likely clients will believe their evaluations are accurate.

90. Glick, Gottesman, and Jolton (1989).

91. This is known as "blind" administration, and when both the experimenter who gives the pill and the participant who takes it do not know whether it is a placebo or the active drug, the experiment is said to be "double-blind." Double-blind methods are considered the most reliable because the expectancies of neither party—the giver or the taker—can affect the results of the experiment.

92. Rawlinson (1985).

93. Kirsch (1985).

94. Kirsch and Weixel (1988). The most interesting and surprising result of this study was that the typical blind administration method (telling the participants that they might be receiving either placebo or drug) produced very different results than deceptive administration, in which the participants are told they are drinking caffeinated coffee when they are not. Deliberately lying to the coffee drinkers (which is a better simulation of real-life placebo administration) produced much stronger effects that were, in most cases, in the opposite direction of the typical blind administration method.

95. Kirsch (1985), p. 1192.

96. Kirsch (1985). For a similar view see Barker (1990).

97. Hines (1988).

5   Growing Up Superstitious

1. Goldberg (1992b).

2. Goldberg (1992a).

3. Rivenburg (1992).

4. This section on recapitulation is drawn from Gould (1977).

5. Or, as it is more often stated, "Ontogeny recapitulates phylogeny."

6. Gould (1977), pp. 126–135.

7. Hall (1904), p.202.

8. For the sake of simplicity, however, I will refer to them as superstitions and paranormal beliefs.

9. Opie and Opie (1959), p. 128.

10. Opie and Opie (1959), p. 126.

11. Opie and Opie (1959), p. 125.

12. Opie and Opie (1959), p. 122. This and the other passages from Opie and Opie (1959) in this chapter are reprinted by permission of Oxford University Press.

13. Opie and Opie (1959). p. 209.

14. Opie and Opie (1959), p. 222.

15. Opie and Opie (1959), p. 221. Heard in Sheffield.

16. Opie and Opie (1959), p. 222.

17. Opie and Opie (1959), p. 222.

18. Often the wells need to be emptied of change on a regular basis. The contributions of those making wishes are sometimes used for charitable fundraising.

19. Opie and Opie (1959), pp. 206–208.

20. Opie and Opie (1959),p. 310.

21. Opie and Opie (1959), p. 311.

22. Opie and Opie (1959), p 312.

23. Opie and Opie (1959), p. 226.

24. Opie and Opie (1959), p. 227. I understand that this examination is not quite as pivotal point in a British child's career as it was in the 1950's, when the Opies were writing.

25. Ginsburg and Opper (1988), pp. 1–3.

26. For a more complete description of Piaget's theory, see Ginsburg and Opper (1988).

27. Piaget and Inhelder (1956)

28. Piaget (1960), chapter 3.

29. Piaget (1960), page 93. This and the following passages from Piaget (1960) are reprinted by permission of Routledge, Chapman & Hall Ltd.

30. Piaget (1960), page 108.

31. Piaget (1960), page 118.

32. Piaget (1960), page 139. Interestingly, Piaget's descriptions of magical thinking in children are more often based on the recollections of his collaborators and other adults than on interviews with children.

33. It should be noted that the Opies were folklorists who studied superstitions shared by groups of children. As a result, the beliefs they reported were, in most cases, socially communicated features of the society of school children. As a developmental psychologist, Piaget was less interested in beliefs acquired from a larger group than he was in those that sprung directly from the child's immature reasoning. Yet his examples and those of the Opies share an acceptance of the magical participation between actions and things.

34. Piaget (1960), page 141.

35. Piaget (1960), page 145.

36. Piaget (1960), page 146.

37. Piaget (1960), page 147.

38. Piaget (1960), pages 157–158.

39. Sugarman (1987).

40. Lesser and Paisner (1985).

41. Piaget and Inhelder (1975).

42. Bernstein, Roy, Srull, and Wickens (1993), page 61.

43. Higgins, Morris, and Johnson (1989), experiment one. The description of this experiment is simplified but, I hope, true to its essential features.

44. Higgins, Morris, and Johnson (1989), page 310.

45. Lest we think that only children can be led astray by false instructions, see Baron and Galizio (1983) and Kaufman, Baron, and Kopp (1966).

46. This technique is known as shaping. To establish new behavior, the parent or teacher waits for the beginning piece of the behavior to occur and reinforces it with praise or some other reinforcer. As the child continues to engage in similar behavior, the parent reinforces successive approximations of the final, desired response.

47. James (1890), p. 408.

48. Meltzoff and Moore (1977; 1983; 1989)

49. Bandura and Walters (1963).

50. Bandura, Ross, and Ross (1961).

51. Leibert and Sprafkin (1988).

52. Bandura (1986).

53. Bandura and Walters (1963), Bandura (1977; 1986).

54. Higgins, Morris, and Johnson (1989), experiment two. As in the description of experiment one above, several details have been omitted interest of brevity.

55. Pole, Berenson, Sass, Young, and Blass (1974). As noted in chapter 2, these two studies, both of which used walking under a ladder as their operational definition of superstition, appear to be the only published investigations of overt superstitious behavior in unsuspecting participants.

56. It should be noted that the Pole et al. (1974) study differs from Higgins et al. (1989) in a number of important ways. It is a study of adults, not children; it involved the imitation of nonsuperstitious behavior; and, most importantly, it is an example of imitation but not social learning. All of the participants knew how to exit the building before the beginning of the experiment, but in some cases they imitated the choice of exit modeled by the confederate.

57. A different viewpoint is presented by Poggie, Pollnac, and Gersuny (1976). The authors studied the use of taboos among fisherman from Point Judith, Rhode Island, and Stonington, Connecticut, and found that sailors used more taboos when they went on longer, riskier fishing trips and that fishermen who grew up in fishing families were less likely to use taboos. Poggie, Pollnac, and Gersuny concluded that their findings supported Malinowski's (1948) traditional view that superstitions are caused by anxiety and therefore did not support a social learning hypothesis.

58. Latané (1981).

59. Latané and Darley (1970).

60. Asch (1955).

61. Actually, Asch (1955) found a ceiling at seven opposing confederates, but others have found conformity to be a monotonic increasing function of opposing group size (see Latané 1981).

62. Kiesler and Kiesler (1969), page 2.

63. Asch (1955).

64. Erikson (1968).

65. Brown, Clasen, and Eicher (1986).

66. Schachter (1951).

67. Milgram (1974).

68. In most versions of the experiment, the participants were all male, but in one replication with female participants (Milgram [1974] experiment eight) the results were virtually identical.

69. Milgram (1974) pages 30–31.

70. Brown (1986).

71. Piaget (1932/1965).

72. Tisak (1986).

73. Laupa (1991).

74. Singer (1973) and Singer and Singer (1990).

75. Singer (1973).

76. Singer and Singer (1990) page 19.

77. Hugget (1975), page 15. The other explanations offered for the superstitiousness of actors include their being "high strung, nervous, optimistic, apprehensive, sensitive, and credulous," their common "hopes, fears, insecurity, and tension," and because "poverty, neglect, and frustration alternate in an actor's life with affluence, fame, and fulfillment."

78. Robert Sternberg (1988) has identified six major elements that make up our popular conception of creativity, two of which are *lack of conventionality* (free spirit, unorthodox) and *questioning spirit* (questions societal norms, truisms, assumptions). When applied to the question of imagination and belief in superstition, these dimensions lead to the opposing predictions I have postulated.

6   Is Superstition Abnormal, Irrational, or Neither?

1. This passage is from an article written by Stephen Weiner entitled "When weird isn't fun: Notes on magical thinking." The article was orginally published in the San Francisco–area mental health newsletter *Update*, probably in the 1980s, but neither my efforts nor Mr. Weiner's produced an exact reference.

2. American Psychiatric Association (1994).

3. American Psychiatric Association (1994), p. xxi.

4. American Psychiatric Association (1994), p. xxi. Copyright 1994 American Psychiatric Association. Reprinted with permission.

5. Other popular models of behavior include the psychodynamic model, the behavioral model, and the cognitive model (see Rosenhan and Seligman [1989]).

6. Rosenhan and Seligman (1989), p. 5–17.

7. American Psychiatric Association (1994); Rosenhan and Seligman (1994). It should be noted that the *DSM-IV* also lists *obsessive-compulsive personality disoder*, code 301.6. (American Psychiatric Association, 1994, p. 669–673). Because this category is a personality disorder rather than a mental disorder, it describes a stable feature of the individual that has been present since adolescence or early adulthood. In addition, although personality disorders lead to distress or impairment, obsessive-compulsive personality disorder is described as less severe than obsessive-compulsive disorder. For example, the personality disorder is distinguished by the absence of true compulsions such as the hoarding of many useless objects. Instead, the criteria for obsessive-compulsive personality disorder emphasize a preoccupation with orderliness, perfectionism, and control.

8. Swedo and Rapoport (1989).

9. Rapoport (1989a), p. 82.

10. Rapoport (1989a), p. 75.

11. Rapoport (1989a), p. 5.

12. Laughlin (1967).

13. The Howard Hughes material is drawn from Rosenhan and Seligman (1989) and Rapoport (1989a). The Samuel Johnson material is from Rapoport (1989a).

14. McKeon and Murray (1987).

15. Rapoport (1989), p. 160.

16. Leonard, Goldberger, Rapoport, Cheslow, and Swedo (1990) and Leonard (1989).

17. Leonard et al. (1990), p. 22.

18. Leonard et al. (1990), p. 20.

19. Rosenhan and Seligman (1989), p. 692.

20. Rosenhan and Seligman (1989), p. 694.

21. Rosenhan and Seligman (1989).
22. American Psychiatric Association (1994) and Rosenhan and Seligman (1989).
23. Gottesman (1991).
24. Gottesman (1991).
25. Gottesman (1991).
26. Gottesman (1991).
27. American Psychiatric Association (1994).
28. Fujioka and Chapman (1984).
29. American Psychiatric Association (1994), p. 629.
30. American Psychiatric Association (1994), p. 645.
31. Eckblad and Chapman (1983).
32. The complete Magical Ideation Scale is presented below. The answers indicative of magical ideation are indicated. Copyright © (1983) by the American Psychological Association. Reprinted with permission.

   1. Some people can make me aware of them just by thinking about me (T).

   2. I have had the momentary feeling that I might not be human (T).

   3. I have sometimes been fearful of stepping on sidewalk cracks (T).

   4. I think I could learn to read others' minds if I wanted to (T).

   5. Horoscopes are right too often for it to be a coincidence (T).

   6. Things sometimes seem to be in different places when I get home, even though no one has been there (T).

   7. Numbers like 13 and 7 have no special powers (F).

   8. I have occasionally had the silly feeling that a TV or radio broadcaster knew I was listening to him (T).

   9. I have worried that people on other planets may be influencing what happens on earth (T).

   10. The government refuses to tell us the truth about flying saucers (T).

   11. I have felt that there were messages for me in the ways things were arranged, like store windows (T).

   12. I have never doubted that my dreams are the products of my own mind (F).

   13. Good luck charms don't work (F).

   14. I have noticed sounds on my records that are not there at other times (T).

   15. The hand motions that strangers make seem to influence me at times (T).

   16. I almost never dream about things before they happen (F).

   17. I have had the momentary feeling that someone's place has been taken by a look-alike (T).

   18. It is not possible to harm others merely by thinking bad thoughts about them (F).

   19. I have sometimes sensed an evil presence around me, although I could not see it (T).

   20. I sometimes have a feeling of gaining or losing energy when certain people look at me or touch me (T).

   21. I have sometimes had the passing thought that strangers are in love with me (T).

   22. I have never had the feeling that certain thoughts of mine really belonged to someone else (F).

   23. When introduced to strangers, I rarely wonder whether I have known them before (F).

   24. If reincarnation were true, it would explain some unusual experiences I have had (T).

   25. People often behave so strangely that one wonders if they are part of an experiment (T).

   26. At times I perform certain little rituals to ward off negative influences (T).

   27. I have felt that I might cause something to happen just by thinking too much about it (T).

   28. I have wondered whether the spirits of the dead can influence the living (T).

   29. At times I have felt that a professor's lecture was meant especially for me (T).

   30. I have sometimes felt that strangers were reading my mind (T).

33. Bailey, West, Widiger, and Freiman (1993); Ecblad and Chapman (1983).

34. George and Neufeld (1987).

35. Chapman, Chapman, Kwapil, Eckblad, and Zinser (1994).

36. It should be noted that in the Chapman et al. (1994) study, this group was high on both the Magical Ideation Scale and Perceptual Aberration Scale, a questionnaire that measures "grossly schizophreniclike distortions in the perception of one's own body." Using a gross count of psychotic histories ten years later, it is impossible to determine what part of the effect is due to magical ideation alone; however, other analyses in the study do point to a separate relationship between magical ideation and psychotic behavior.

37. Tobacyk and Wilkinson (1990). Williams and Irwin (1991).

38. Williams and Irwin (1991)

39. Personal communication (August 5, 1994).

40. Baron (1994), p. 30–31.

41. Elster (1986).

42. Baron (1994).

43. These characteristics of poor thinking are from Baron's search-inference framework (1994), p. 31. Reprinted by permission of Cambridge University Press.

44. von Neumann and Morgenstern (1944); Baron (1994).

45. Frank (1991), p. 182.

46. Baron (1994), chapter 17.

47. Table 6.3 is from, and Tables 6.4 and 6.5 are based on Baron (1994) pp. 315–319. Reprinted by permission of Cambridge University Press.

48. Attempts are always being made to validate paranormal phenomena. One of the most interesting involves an ESP phenomena called the Ganzfeld Effect. A well-respected social psychologist, Daryl Bem, recently stated his belief in this mind-reading technique in an article published in a prestigious psychological journal (Bem, 1994; Bem & Honorton, 1994); however, others are skeptical (Hyman, 1994).

49. This approach is patterned after Multiattribute Utility Theory (MAUT) as described by Baron (1994), pp. 341–346.

50. Albas and Albas (1989).

51. Rather than saying that superstitions have a zero probability of affecting events, it is probably more accurate to say that they have an extremely small (something like 1/1,000,000,000), but non-zero, probability of being valid. When the potential gains are infinite, even this small a probability can produce substantial gains.

7   A Magical View of the World

1. I am indebted to Tom Ryan for this anecdote.

2. Opie and Opie (1959).

3. It is important to note that contiguity is not the only way that operant conditioning can occur. Indeed, conditioning can result when contiguity is absent but responding is still correlated with high levels of reinforcement. For fuller discussion of the question of correlation versus contiguity in operant conditioning, see Mazur (1994).

4. See Baron (1994) p. 44–47.

5. Seligman (1975). A recent study (Matute, 1994) suggests that there are some methodological problems with laboratory studies of learned helplessness in humans and, more important to us, that superstitious behavior may be a hedge against the development of learned helplessness. Conditions that produce learned helplessness in animals tend to produce superstitious behavior in humans.

6. In a small pilot study of normal college students, Tuck (1995) found that reports of childhood rituals and superstitions were associated with higher levels of both current mag-

ical ideation and current obsessive-compulsive disorder symptoms. When all three variables were examined simultaneously in a multiple regression, only the relationship between childhood superstitions and obsessive-compulsive symptoms was significant. However, this was a retrospective study conducted on a small non-clinical population, and, as a result, we must await further research to know whether the findings have any bearing on a potential relationship between childhood superstitions and obsessive-compulsive disorder.

7. Willoughby (1979). The definition of substance abuse given in the American Psychiatric Association's (1994) *DSM-IV* is quite similar to Willoughby's system. See American Psychiatric Association (1994), pp. 181–183.

8. Willoughby (1979), p. 49.

9. Willoughby (1979), chapter 5.

10. Barbero, Steiner, and Sheaffer (1992); Tuerkheimer and Vyse (in press).

11. Emery (1995).

12. King (1990).

13. American Medical Association (1993), p. 306. Reprinted with permission.

14. Rosa (1994).

15. Mackey (1995).

16. The recent publication of a journal called *Alternative Therapies* represents a similar problem for consumers of medical information. The journal describes itself as "peer-reviewed" and includes an extensive editorial board filled with M.D.s and Ph.D.s from many reputable academic institutions, but it also contains many nonscientific articles about fringe therapies. It is very professional journal in appearance, similar to the *Journal of the American Medical Association*, but in a recent editorial, the executive editor argued that the stringent, double-blind procedures common to reputable medical research are too rigid for the study of alternative therapies (Dossey, 1994). It appears that this new journal is aimed at lending respectability to alternative medical techniques by aping the appearance of an authoritative publication while presenting research based on less rigorous methodologies. Journals such as this make it extremely difficult for interested professionals and laypeople to separate the reputable from the disreputable in medical treatment.

17. According to Topolnicki and MacDonald (1993), almost one million people filed for bankruptcy in 1992, accounting for $21.5 billion in debt.

18. Waldman and Thomas (1990).

19. Sweat and Drum (1993).

20. The department is known as the Office of Alternative Medicine of the NIH. Jones (1987).

21. Much of this presentation of Peirce's methods of fixing knowledge comes from Kerlinger (1986), pp. 6–7, and Rosenthal and Rosnow (1991), pp. 8–9.

22. Cohen and Nagel (1934).

23. Rosenthal and Rosnow (1991), p. 9.

24. It should be noted that one of the most elaborate examples of rationalism in the behavioral sciences is the use of statistics. Statistical methods provide the criteria for making probabilistic decisions about whether a hypothesis is true or false, and furnish a rationale for generalizing the results obtained from a small sample of people to the entire population (all individuals of that type).

25. A number of the items on my classroom questionnaire are patterned after questions from the Paranormal Belief Scale by Tobacyk and Milford (1983); however, unlike the Tobacyk and Milford scale, students must respond either "true" or "false."

26. Jahoda (1968); Wagner and Monnet (1979).

27. Tierney (1996).

28. Sagan (1987) p. 41–42.

29. Langer and Chiszar (1993).

30. Baron (1994) page 350.

31. Zurer (1994).

32. For further examples of the contemporary negative images of science, see Park (1995).

33. Published in 1818, the full title of Mary Shelley's novel is *Frankenstein or the Modern Prometheus*. The author's husband, Percy Bysshe Shelley, published *Prometheus Unbound* in 1820.

34. Asimov (1989).

35. These concluding remarks are inspired, in part, by a speech that James Randi, professional magician and skeptic, often uses to end his public lectures.

References

Abrams, M. H., Donaldson, E. T., Smith, H., Adams, R. M., Monk, S. H., Ford, G. H., & Daiches, D. (1968). *The Norton Anthology of English Literature*. Vol. 1. New York: Norton.

Albas, D, & Albas, C. (1989). Modern magic: The case of examinations. *The Sociology Quarterly* 30, 603–613.

Alcock, J. E. (1981). *Parapsychology: Science or magic?* Oxford: Pergamon.

Alcock, J. E., & Otis, L. P. (1980). Critical thinking and belief in the paranormal. *Psychological Reports* 46, 479–482.

Allen, J., & Lester, D. (1994). Belief in paranormal phenomena and external locus of control. *Perceptual and Motor Skills* 79, 226.

American Medical Association (1993). *Reader's Guide to Alternative Health Methods*. Chicago: Author.

American Psychiatric Association (1994). *Diagnostic and Statistical Manual of Mental Disorders ,4th Edition*. Washington, DC: Author.

American Psychological Association (1992). Ethical principles of psychologists and code of conduct. *American Psychologist*, 47, 1597–1611.

Anonymous (1990, August). Wade Boggs. *Current Biography* 51, 6–10.

Asch, S. E. (1955). Opinions and social pressures. *Scientific American* 193, 31–35.

Asimov, I. (1966). *Understanding physics*. NY: Walker.

Asimov, I. (1989, March/April). The never-ending fight. *The Humanist*, 7–8, 30.

Atlas, J. (1985, April 22). Maharishi U. *The New Republic*, 13–16.

Bailey, B., West, K. Y., Widiger, T. A., & Freiman, K. (1993). The convergent and discriminant validity of the Chapman scales. *Journal of Personality Assessment* 61, 121–135.

Bakan, P. (1960). Response-tendencies in attempts to generate binary series. *American Journal of Psychology* 73, 127–131.

Bandura, A. (1977a). Self-efficacy: Toward a unifying theory of behavioral change. *Psychological Review* 84, 191–215.

Bandura, A. (1977b). *Social learning theory*. Englewood Cliffs, NJ: Prentice Hall.

Bandura, A. (1986). *Social foundations of thought and action: A social cognitive theory*. Englewood Cliffs, NJ: Prentice Hall.

Bandura, A., Ross, D., & Ross, S. A. (1961). Transmission of aggression through imitation of aggressive models. *Journal of Abnormal Social Psychology* 63, 575–582.

Bandura, A., & Walters, R. H. (1963). *Social learning and personality development*. New York: Holt, Rinehart and Winston.

Barbero, Y., Steiner, R., & Sheaffer, R. (1995). Psychic's predictions (surprise!) fizzle for 1991. *The Skeptical Inquirer* 16, 239–240.

Barker, R. A. (1990). *They call it hypnosis*. Buffalo, NY: Prometheus Books.

Baron, A., & Galizio, M. (1983). Instructional control of human operant behavior. *The Psychological Record* 33, 495–520.

Baron, J. (1994). *Thinking and deciding* (2nd ed.). New York: Cambridge University Press.

Barrett, S. (1987). Homeopathy: Is it medicine? *Skeptical Inquirer* 12, 56–62.

Becker, J. (2975). Superstition in sport. *International Journal of Sport Psychology* 6, 148–152.

Bem, D. J. (1994). Response to Hyman. *Psychological Bulletin* 115, 25–27.

Bem, D. J., & Honorton, C. (1994). Does psi exist? Replicable evidence for an anomalous process of information transfer. *Psychological Bulletin* 115, 4–18.

Benassi, V. A., Sweeney, P. D., & Drevno, G. E. (1979). Mind over matter: Perceived success at psychokinesis. *Journal of Personality and Social Psychology* 37, 1377–1386.

Bennett, G. (1987). *Traditions of belief: Women, folklore, and the supernatural today*. London: Penguin Books.

Benson, H. (1984). *Beyond the relaxation response*. New York: Times Books.

Bernstein, D. A., Roy, E. J., Wickens, C. D., Srull, T. K. (1993). *Psychology*. Boston: Houghton Mifflin.

Blackmore, S. (1985). Belief in the paranormal: Probability judgements, illusion of control, and the chance baseline shift. *British Journal of Psychology* 76, 459–468.

Blum, S. H., & Blum, L. H. (1974). Do's and don'ts: An informal study of some prevailing superstitions. *Psychological Reports* 35, 567–571.

Boggs, W. (1984). *Fowl tips*. Wakefield, RI: Narragansett Graphics.

Boshier, R. (1973a). An empirical investigation of the relationship between conservatism and superstition. *British Journal of Social and Clinical Psychology* 12, 262–267.

Boshier, R. (1973b). Conservatism and superstitious behaviour. In G. D. Wilson (ed.), *The psychology of conservatism* (149–159). London: Academic Press.

Broughton, R. S. (1991). *Parapsychology: The controversial science*. New York: Ballantine.

Brown, R. (1986). *Social Psychology* (2nd ed.). New York: Free Press.

Brown, B. B., Clasen, D. R., & Eicher, S. A. (1986). Perceptions of peer pressure, peer conformity dispositions, and self-reported behavior among adolescents. *Developmental Psychology* 22, 521–530.

Bruce, V., & Green, P. R. (1990). *Visual perception: Physiology, psychology, and ecology* (2nd ed.). Hove, UK: Lawrence Erlbaum.

Buhrmann, H., Brown, B., & Zaugg, M. (1982). Superstitious beliefs and behavior: A comparison of male and female basketball players. *Journal of Sport Behavior* 5, 175–185.

Buhrmann, H. G., & Zaugg, M. K. (1981). Superstitions among basketball players: An investigation of various forms of superstitious beliefs and behavior among competitive basketballers at the junior high school to university level. *Journal of Sport Behavior* 4, 163–174.

Campbell, D. E., & Beets, J. L. (1978). Lunacy and the moon. *Psychological Bulletin* 85, 1123–1129.

Cannon, A. S. (1984). *Popular beliefs and superstitions from Utah*. Salt Lake City: University of Utah Press.

Catania, A. C. (1968). Glossary. In A. C. Catania (ed.), *Contemporary resarch in operant behavior* (327–349.). Glenview, IL: Scott, Foresman.

Catania, A. C., & Cutts, D. (1963). Experimental control of superstitious responding in humans. *Journal of the Experimental Analysis of Behavior* 6, 203–208.

Chapman, L. J. Illusory correlation in observational report. *Journal of Verbal Learning and Verbal Behavior* 6, 151–155.

Chapman, L. J., & Chapman, J. P. (1971, November). The results are what you think they are. *Psychology Today*, 18–22.

Christine, B. (1990, October 28). Tragedy overshadows glory at Breeders' Cup. *Los Angeles Times* 109, C1, C17.

Clotfelter, C. T., & Cook, P. J. (1989). *Selling hope: State lotteries in America*. Cambridge, MA: Harvard University Press.

Cohen, J. (1960). *Chance, skill, and luck: The psychology of guessing and gambling*. Baltimore: Penguin.

Cohen, M., & Nagel, E. (1934). *An introduction to logic and scientific method*. New York: Harcourt.

Coleman, L. (1987). *Suicide clusters*. Boston: Faber and Faber.

Combs, B., & Slovic, P. (1979). Newspaper coverage of causes of death. *Journalism Quarterly* 56, 832–849.

Cordes, H. (1993, January/February). A new age of miracles? *Utne Reader*, 22–24.

Cormick, J. M. (1984, January 2). Utopian thinking in Iowa. *Newsweek*, 31.

Cranston, R. (1988). *The miracle of Lourdes*. New York: Image Books.

Curry, J. (1994, March 15). Boggs is beyond compare, and he's the first to say so. *New York Times* 143, L15.

Diaconis, P., and Mosteller, F. (1989). Methods for studying coincidences. *Journal of the American Statistical Association* 84, 853–861.

Dossey, L. (1994). How should alternative therapies be evaluated? *Alternative Therapies* 1, 6–10, 79–85.

Dossey, L. (1993). *Healing words: The power of prayer and the practice of medicine*. San Francisco: HarperSanFrancisco.

Durkheim, E. (1957/1915). *The elementary forms of the religious life*. London: George Allen.

Eckblad, M., & Chapman, L. J. (1983). Magical ideation as an indicator of schizotypy. *Journal of Consulting and Clinical Psychology* 51, 215–225.

Ellis, A., & Grieger, R. (1977). *Handbook of rational-emotive therapy*. New York: Springer.

Elster, J. (1986). Introduction. In J. Elster (ed.), *Rational choice*. New York: New York University Press.

Emery, C. E., Jr. (1995). Telephone psychics: Friends or phonies? *Skeptical Inquirer* 19, 14–17.

Emery, C. E., Jr. (1991). Chain letter weighs heavily on top journalists. *Skeptical Inquirer* 16, 24–25.

Emery, C. E., Jr. (1991). Pell aide hears code in backwards speeches. *Skeptical Inquirer* 15, 351–353.

Emery, C. E., Jr. (1990, October 20). The flip side of Simone is "enormous." *Providence Journal-Bulletin*, A1.

Epstein, C. F. (1988). *Deceptive distinctions: Sex, gender, and the social order.* New Haven: Yale University Press.

Epstein, R. (1982). Editor's note. In R. Epstein (ed.), *Skinner for the classroom: Selected papers* (99–100). Champaign, IL: Research Press.

Epstein, S. (1991). Cognitive-experiential self theory: Implications for developmental psychology. In M. Gunnar & L. A. Sroufe (eds.), *Self-processes and development.* Minnesota symposia on child psychology, vol 23. (79–123). Hillsdale, NJ: Erlbaum.

Epstein, S. (1993). Implications of cognitive-experiential self-theory for personality and developmental psychology. In D. C. Funder, R. D. Parke, C. Tomlinson-Keasy, & K. Widaman (eds.), *Studying lives through time: Personality and developmental psychology* (399–438). Washington, DC: American Psychological Association.

Epstein, S. (1994). Integration of the cognitive and the psychodynamic unconscious. *American Psychologist* 49, 709–724.

Erikson, E. H. (1968). *Identity: Youth and crisis.* New York: Norton.

Evans, E. C. (1969). *Physiognomics in the ancient world.* Philadelphia: The American Philosophical Society.

Evans, H. R. (1967/1897). The mysteries of modern magic. In A. A. Hopkins, *Magic: Stage illusions and scientific diversions.* New York: Benjamin Blom.

Eve, R. A., & Harrold, F. B. (1986). Creationism, cult archaeology, and other pseudoscientific beliefs: A study of college students. *Youth & Society* 17, 396–421.

Falk, J. L. (1977). The origin and functions of adjunctive behavior. *Animal Learning and Behavior* 5, 325–335.

Falk, J. L. (1986). The formation and function of ritual behavior. In T. Thompson and M. D. Zeiler (eds.), *Analysis and integration of behavioral units* (pp. 335–355). Hillsdale, NJ: Lawrence Erlbaum.

Falk, R. (1981). On coincidences. *Skeptical Inquirer* 6, 18–31.

Falk, R. (1989). Judgement of coincidence: Mine versus yours. *American Journal of Psychology* 102, 477–493.

Festinger, L., Riecken, H. W., & Schachter, S. (1956). *When prophecy fails.* New York: Harper & Row.

Fisher, R. A. (1953). *The design of experiments* (6th ed.). Edinburg: Oliver & Boyd.

Flexner, S. B. (1987). *Random house dictionary of the English language* (2nd ed.). New York: Random House.

Frank, R. H. (1991). *Microeconomics and behavior.* New York: McGraw-Hill.

Frazer, J. G. (1922). *The golden bough.* London: Macmillan.

Friedland, N., Keinan, G., & Regev, Y. (1992). Controlling the uncontrollable: Effects of stress on illusory perceptions of controllability. *Journal of Personality and Social Psychology* 63, 923–931.

Friedrick, O., Cronin, M., Riley, M., & Wyss, D. (1987, December 7). New age harmonies. *Time*, 62–72.

Friend, T. (1994, January 12). 49er tension is high where Seifert roams. *New York Times* 143, B12.

Fujioka, T. A. T., & Chapman, L. J. (1984). Comparison of the 2-7-8 MMPI profile and the perceptual aberration-magical ideation scale in identifying hypothetically psychosis-prone college students. *Journal of Consulting and Clinical Psychology* 52, 458–467.

Gallup, G. (1978, June 15). Surprising number of Americans believe in paranormal phenomena. The Gallup Poll. Wilmington, DE: Scholarly Resources.

Gallup, G. H. (1979). The Gallup Poll. Wilmington, DE: Scholarly Resources.

Gallup, G. H., & Newport, F. (1990, August 6). Belief in the psychic and paranormal widespread among Americans. *Gallup News Service 55*, 1–7.

Gardner, M. (1995). Claiborne Pell: The senator from outer space. *Skeptical Inquirer* 20(2), 12–15.

George, L., & Neufeld, R. W. (1987). Magical ideation and schizophrenia. *Journal of Consulting and Clinical Psychology 55*, 778–779.

Gilovich, T. Vallone, R., & Tversky, A. (1985). The hot hand in basketball: On the misperception of random sequences. *Cognitive Psychology 17*, 295–314.

Ginsburg, H. P., & Opper, S. (1988). *Piaget's theory of intellectual development* (3rd ed.). Englewood Cliffs, NJ: Prentice Hall.

Glick, P., Gottesman, D., & Jolton, J. (1989). The fault is not in the stars: Susceptibility of skeptics and believers in astrology to the Barnum effect. *Personality and Social Psychology Bulletin 15*, 572–583.

Glick, P., & Snyder, M. (1986, May/June). Self-fulfilling prophecy: The psychology of belief in astrology. *The Humanist 46*, 20–25, 50.

Gmelch, G. (1974). Baseball magic. In J. Spradley and D. McCurdy (eds.) *Conformity and conflict* (346–352). Boston: Little Brown.

Goldberg, P. (1992a, April 6). The Dodgers owe big to a lucky cap. *Los Angeles Times*, B5.

Goldberg, P. (1992b). *This is next year*. New York: Ballantine.

Goodenough, O. R., & Dawkins, R. (1994). The 'St. Jude' mind virus. *Nature 371*, 23–24.

Goodman, L. *Linda Goodman's sun-signs*. New York: Bantam.

Gottesman, I. I. (1991). *Schizophrenia genesis: The origins of madness*. New York: W. H. Freeman.

Gould, S. J. (1977). *Ontogeny and phylogeny*. Cambridge, MA: Harvard University Press.

Gould, S. J. (1981). *The mismeasure of man*. New York: Norton.

Gregory, C. J., & Petrie, B. M. (1975). Superstitions of Canadian intercollegiate athletes: An inter-sport comparison. *International Review of Sport Sociology 10*, 59–68.

Guthrie, E. R., & Horton, G. P. (1946). *Cats in a puzzle box*. New York: Rinehart & Co.

Hall, C. S., & Lindsey, G. (1978). *Theories of personality* (3rd ed.). New York: Wiley.

Hall, G. S. (1904). *Adolescence: Its psychology and its relations to physiology, anthropology, sociology, sex, crime, religion, and education*. New York: D. Appleton.

Hayano, D. (1978). Strategies for the management of luck and action in an urban poker parlor. *Urban Life 7*, 475–488.

Hejza, T. (1990, September). Superstitious minds. *Vine Line 5*, 10.

Heltzer, R. A., & Vyse, S. A. (1994). Problem solving and intermittent consequences: The experimental control of superstitious beliefs. *The Psychological Record 44*, 155–169.

Henslin, J. M. (1967). Craps and magic. *American Journal of Sociology 73*, 316–330.

Herrnstein, R. J. (1966). Superstition: A corrollary of the principles of operant conditioning. In W. K. Honig (ed.), *Operant behavior: Areas of research and application* (33–51). New York: Appleton-Century-Crofts.

Higgins, S. T., Morris, E. K., & Johnson, L. M. (1989). Social transmission of superstitious behavior in preschool children. *The Psychological Record 39*, 307–323.

Hilgard, E. R. (1987). *Psychology in America: A historical survey*. San Diego: Harcourt Brace Jovanovich.

Hines, T. (1988). *Pseudoscience and the paranormal*. Amherst, NY: Prometheus Books.

Hintzman, D. L., Asher, S. J., & Stern, L. D. (1978). Incidental retrieval and memory for coincidences. In M. M. Gruneberg, P. E. Morris, & R. N. Sykes (eds.), *Practical aspects of memory* (61–68). London: Academic Press.

Holyoak, K. J., Koh, K., Nisbett, R. E. (1989). A theory of conditioning: Inductive learning with rule-based default hierarchies. *Psychological Review 96*, 315–340.

Holyoak, K. J., & Nisbett, R. E. (1988). Induction. In R. J. Sternberg, & E. E. Smith (eds.), *The psychology of human thought* (50–91). Cambridge: Cambridge University Press.

Holmyard, E. J. (1957). *Alchemy*. Harmondsworth, Middlesex: Penguin.

Hopkins, B., Jacobs, D., & Westrum, R. (1991) *Unusual personal experiences: An analysis of the data from three national surveys*. Las Vegas: Bigelow Holding Company.

Howell, D. C. (1992). *Statistical methods for psychology*. Boston: PWS-Kent.

Huggett, R. (1975). *Supernatural on stage: Ghosts and superstitions of the theatre*. New York: Taplinger.

Hyman, R. (1994). Anomaly or artifact? Comments on Bem and Honorton. *Psychological Bulletin* 115, 19–24.

Jahoda, G. (1968). Scientific training and the persistence of traditional beliefs among West African university students. *Nature* 220, 1356.

Jahoda, G. (1969). *The psychology of superstition*. London: Allen Lane / The Penguin Press.

James, W. (1890). *The principles of psychology*. New York: Holt, Rinehart & Winston.

Jennings, D. L., Amabile, T. M., & Ross, L. (1982). Informal covariation assessment: Data-based versus theory-based judgement. In D. Kahneman, P. Slovic, & A. Tversky, *Judgment under uncertainty: Heuristics and biases* (211–230). Cambridge: Cambridge University Press.

Jones, L. (1987). Alternative therapies: A report on an inquiry by the British Medical Association. *Skeptical Inquirer* 12, 63–69.

Jones, W. (1880). *Credulities past and present*. London: Chatto and Windus.

Jung, C. G. (1978a). On synchronicity. In C. G. Jung, *Collected Works*, vol. 8 (520–531). Princeton: Princeton University Press.

Jung, C. G. (1978b). Synchronicity: An acausal connecting principle. In C. G. Jung, *Collected Works*, vol. 8 (419–519). Princeton: Princeton University Press.

Kahneman, D., & Tversky, A. (1972). Subjective probability: A judgement of representativeness. *Cognitive Psychology* 3, 430–454.

Kahneman, D., Slovic, P., & Tversky, A. (1982). *Judgment under uncertainty: Heuristics and biases*. Cambridge: Cambridge University Press.

Kallai, E. (1985). *Psychological factors that influence the belief in horoscopes*. Unpublished master's thesis, The Hebrew University, Jerusalem. (Cited in Falk, 1989.)

Kaufman, A., Baron, A., & Koff, R. E. (1966). Some effects of instructions on human operant behavior. *Psychonomic Monograph Supplements* 1, 243–250.

Keinan, G. (1994). Effects of stress and tolerance of ambiguity on magical thinking. *Journal of Personality and Social Psychology* 67, 48–55.

Kelly, G. (1955). *The psychology of personal constructs*. New York: Norton.

Kendrick, A. (1992). *Superstitious beliefs and personality among college students*. Unpublished manuscript. Department of Psychology, Connecticut College, New London, CT.

Kerlinger, F. N. (1986). *Foundations of behavioral research* (3rd ed.). New York: Holt, Rinehart, and Winston.

Kiesler, C. A., & Kiesler, S. B. (1969). *Conformity*. Reading, MA: Addison-Wesley.

Killeen, P. R. (1977). Superstition: A matter of bias, not detectability. *Science* 199, 88–90.

Killeen, P. R. (1982). Learning as causal inference. In M. L. Commons and J. A. Nevin (eds.), *Quantitative Analyses of Behavior: Discriminative Properties of Reinforcement Schedules* (89–112). Cambridge, MA: Ballinger.

Killeen, P., Wildman, R. W., and Wildman, R. W. II (1974). Superstitiousness and intelligence. *Psychological Reports* 34, 1158.

King, K. M. (1990). Neutralizing marginally deviant behavior: Bingo players and superstition. *Journal of Gambling Studies* 6, 43–61.

Kirkpatrick, C. (1981, June 22). The beard has begun. *Sports Illustrated* 54(26), 46, 51, 53, 54, 57.

Kirsch, I. (1985). Response expectancies as a determinant of experience and behavior. *American Psychologist* 11, 1189–1202.

Kirsch, I., & Weixel, L. J. (1988). Double-blind versus deceptive administration of a placebo. *Behavioral Neuroscience* 102, 319–323.

Koestler, A. (1972). *The roots of coincidence*. London: Hutchinson.

Kolers, P. A. (1972). *Aspects of motion perception*. Elmsford, NJ: Pergamon.

Krantz, L. (1992). *What the odds are: A-to-z odds on everything you hoped or feared could happen*. New York: HarperCollins.

Kurtz, P., & Fraknoi, A. (1986). Scientific tests of Astrology do not support its claims. In K. Frazier, *Science confronts the paranormal* (219–221). Buffalo, NY: Prometheus.

Langer, E. J. (1975). The illusion of control. *Journal of Personality and Social Psychology* 32, 311–328.

Langer, E. J., & Rodin, J. (1976). The effects of choice and enhanced personal responsibility for the aged: A field experiment in an institutional setting. *Journal of Personality and Social Psychology* 34, 191–198.

Langer, E. J., & Roth, J. (1975). Heads I win, tails it's chance: The illusion of control as a function of the sequence of outcomes in a purely chance task. *Journal of Personality and Social Psychology* 32, 951–955.

Lange, P., & Chiszar, D. (1993). Assessment of critical thinking courses. *Perceptual and Motor Skills* 77, 970.

Latané, B. (1981). The psychology of social impact. *American Psychologist* 36, 343–56.

Latané and Darley (1970). *The unresponsive bystander: Why doesn't he help?* New York: Appleton-Century-Crofts.

Laughlin, H. P. (1967). *The neuroses*. Washington, DC: Butterworth.

Laupa, M. (1991). Children's reasoning about three authority attributes: Adult status, knowledge, and social position. *Developmental Psychology* 27, 321–329.

Lavater, J. C. (1792) *Essays on physiognomy: Designed to promote the knowledge and the love of mankind*. London: John Murray, Henry Hunter, & Thomas Holloway.

Lefcourt, H. M. (1982). *Locus of control: Current trends in theory and research* (2nd ed.). Hillsdale, NJ: Erlbaum.

Leonard, H. L. (1989). Childhood rituals and superstitions: Developmental and cultural perspective. In J. L. Rappoport (ed.), *Obsessive-compulsive disorder in children and adolescents* (289–309). Washington, DC: American Psychiatric Press.

Leonard, H. L., Goldberger, E. L., Rapoport, J. L., Cheslow, D. L., & Swedo, S. E. (1990). Childhood rituals: Normal development or obsessive-compulsive symtoms? *Journal of the American Academy of Child and Adolescent Psychiatry* 29, 17–23.

Lesser, R., & Paisner, M. (1985). Magical thinking in formal operational adults. *Human Development* 28, 57–70.

Liebert, R. M., & Spiegler, M. D. (1982). *Personality: Strategies and issues*. Homewood, IL: Dorsey.

Liebert, R. M., & Sprafkin, J. (1988). *The early window* (3rd ed.). New York: Pergamon.

Lienhardt, R. G. (1979). *Social anthropology*. Oxford: Oxford University Press.

Lockie, A. (1989). *The Family Guide to Homeopathy*. New York: Prentice-Hall.

Lopes, L. L., & Oden, G. C. (1987). Distinguishing between random and nonrandom events. *Journal of Experimental Psychology: Learning, Memory, and Cognition* 13, 392–400.

Lord, C. G., Ross, L., & Lepper, M. R. (1979). Biased assimilation and attitude polarization. *Journal of Personality and Social Psychology* 37, 2098–2109.

Maccoby, E. E., & Jacklin, C. N. (1974). *The psychology of sex differences*. Stanford, CA: Stanford University Press.

Mack, J. E. (1994). *Abduction: Human encounters with aliens*. Accord, MA: Wheeler.

Mackey, R. B. (1995). Discover the healing power of therapeutic touch. *American Journal of Nursing* 95(4), 26–34.

Malinowski, B. (1972/1948). *Magic, Science and Religion*. New York: Doubleday.

Marmor, J. (1956). Some observations on superstitions in contemporary life. *American Journal of Orthopsychiatry* 26, 119–130.

Maturi, R. (1990, February). Why you should hate the Mets. *Changing Times*, 41–43.

Matute, H. (1994). Learned helplessness and superstitious behavior as opposite efects of uncontrollable reinforcement in humans. *Learning and Motivation 25*, 216–232.

Mauss, M (1972/1950). *A general theory of magic.* London: Routledge & Kegan Paul.

McAneny, L. (1995, January). It was a very bad year: Belief in hell and the devil on the rise. *Gallup Poll Monthly,* 14–15.

McCallum, J. (1988, February 8). Green cars, black cats, and lady luck. *Sports Illustrated 68,* 86–94.

McGarry, J. J., Newberry, B. H. (1981). Beliefs in paranormal phenomena and locus of control: A field study. *Journal of Personality and Social Psychology 41,* 725–736.

McKeon, J., & Murray, R. (1987). Familial aspects of obsessive-compulsive neurosis. *British Journal of Psychiatry 151,* 528–534.

McNemar, Q. (1946). Opinion-attitude methodology. *Psychological Bulletin 43,* 289–374.

McTigue, M. (1992). *Acting like a pro.* Cincinnati: Betterway Books.

Meehl, P. E. (1956). Wanted—a good cookbook. *American Psychologist 11,* 262–272.

Meltzoff, A.N., & Moore, M.K. (1977). Imitation of facial and manual gestures by human neonates. *Science 198,* 75–78.

Meltzoff, A.N., & Moore, M.K. (1983). Newborn infants imitate adult facial gestures. *Child Development 54,* 702–709.

Meltzoff, A. M., & Moore, M.K. (1989). Imitation in newborn infants: Exploring the range of gestures imitated and the underlying mechanisms. *Developmental Psychology 25,* 954–962.

Messer, W. S., & Griggs, R. A. (1989). Student belief and involvement in the paranormal and performance in introductory psychology. *Teaching of Psychology 16,* 187–191.

Milgram, S. (1974). *Obedience to authority.* New York: Harper & Row.

Morse, W. H., & Skinner, B. F. (1957). A second type of superstition in the pigeon. *American Journal of Psychology 70,* 308–311.

Mumford, M. D., Rose, A. M., & Goslin, D. A. (1995, September). *An evaluation of remote viewing: Research and applications.* Washington, DC: The American Institutes for Research.

Neuringer, A. Can people behave "randomly"?: The role of feedback. *Journal of Experimental Psychology: General 115,* 62–75.

Newsweek (1987, June 1). Preying on AIDS patients, 52–54.

Nisbett, R., & Ross, L. (1980). *Human inference: Strategies and shortcomings of social judgment.* Englewood Cliffs, NJ: Prentice-Hall.

Nolen, W. A. (1974). *Healing: A doctor in search of a miracle.* New York: Random House.

Norman, D. A. (1992). *Turn signals are the facial expressions of automobiles.* Reading, MA: Addison-Wesley.

Oldman, D. (1974). Chance and skill: A study of roulette. *Sociology 8,* 407–426.

Ono, K. (1987). Superstitious behavior in humans. *Journal of the Experimental Analysis of Behavior 47,* 261–271.

Opie, I., & Opie, P. (1959). *The Lore and Language of School Children.* London: Oxford University Press.

Oswalt, W. H. (1972). *Other peoples, other customs.* New York: Holt, Rinehart, Winston.

Otis, L. P., & Alcock, J. E. (1982). Factors affecting extraordinary belief. *The Journal of Social Psychology 118,* 77–85.

Oxford University Press (1971). *The compact edition of the Oxford English dictionary.* Glasgow: Author.

Page, S., & Neuringer, A. (1985). Variability is an operant. *Journal of Experimental Psychology: Animal Behavior Processes 11,* 429–452.

Park, R. L. (1995, July 9). The danger of voodoo science. *New York Times,* E15.

Pasachoff, J. M., Cohen, R. J., and Pasachoff, N. W. (1971). Belief in the supernatural among Harvard and West African university students. *Nature, 232,* 278–279.

Paulos, J. A. (1988). *Innumeracy: Mathematical illiteracy and its consequences.* New York: Hill and Wang.

Piaget, J. (1960/original French, 1926). *The child's conception of the world.* London: Routledge & Kegan Paul.

Piaget, J. (1965/1932). *The moral judgement of the child.* London: Routledge & Kegan Paul.

Piaget, J., & Inhelder, B. (1975/original French, 1951). *The origin of the idea of chance in children.* New York: Norton.

Piaget, J., & Inhelder, B. (1956/original French, 1948) *The child's conception of space.* New York: Norton.

Poggie, J. J., Pollnac, R. B., & Gersuny, C. (197). Risk as a basis for taboos among fishermen in southern New England. *Journal for the Scientific Study of Religion* 15, 257–262.

Pole, J., Berenson, N., Sass, D., Young, D., & Blass, T. (1974). Walking under a ladder: A field experiment on superstitious behavior. *Personality and Social Psychology Bulletin* 1, 10–12.

Pratt, C. C. (1969). Wolfgang Köhler 1887–1967 [Introduction]. In W. Köhler, *The task of gestalt psychology.* Princeton, NJ: Princeton University Press.

Pratt, G. C. (1973). *Spellbound in darkness: A history of the silent film.* Greenwich, CT: New York Graphic Society.

Quigley, J. (1990). *What does Joan say? My seven years as White House astrologer to Nancy and Ronald Reagan.* New York: Pinnacle Books.

Randall, T. M., & Desrosiers, M. (1980). Measurement of supernatural belief: Sex differences and locus of control. *Journal of Personality Assessment* 44, 493–498.

Randi, J. (1982). *The truth about Uri Geller.* Buffalo, NY: Prometheus.

Randles, J. (1985). *Beyond explanation: The paranormal experiences of famous people.* Manchester, NH: Salem House.

Rapoport, J. L. (1989a). *The boy who couldn't stop washing: The experience and treatment of obsessive-compulsive disorder.* New York: Dutton.

Rapoport, J. L. (1989b). *Obsessive-compulsive disorder in children and adolescents.* Washington, DC: American Psychiatric Press.

Rawlinson, M. C. (1985). Truth-telling and paternalism in the clinic: Philosophical reflections on the use of placebos in medical practice. In L. White, B. Tursky, & G. E. Schwartz (eds.), *Placebo: Theory, research, and mechanisms* (403–418). New York: Guilford.

Reagan, N. (1989). *My turn.* New York: Random House.

Regan, D. T. (1988). *For the record.* San Diego: Harcourt Brace Jovanovich.

Reichler, J. L. (1990). *The baseball encyclopedia.* New York: Macmillan.

Rivenburg, R. (1992, May 13). Kids won't step on cracks—or give up their superstitions. *New York Times*, E1, E5.

Robertson, P. (1988). *The Guinness book of movie facts and feats.* Middlesex, UK: Guinness Publications.

Robinson, F. N. (1957). *The works of Geoffrey Chaucer* (2nd ed.). Boston: Houghton-Mifflin.

Rosa, L. A. (1994). Therapeutic touch. *Skeptic* 3, 40–49.

Rosellini, L. (1993, March 23). The case of the weeping Madonna. *U. S. News and World Report*, 46–55.

Rosenbaum, R. (1995, January 15). The great ivy league nude posture photo scandal: How scientists coaxed America's best and brightest out of their clothes. *New York Times Magazine*, 26–31,40, 46, 55–56.

Rosenhan, D. L., & Seligman, M. E. P. (1989). *Abnormal Psychology* (2nd ed.). New York: W. W. Norton.

Rosenthal, R., & Rosnow, R. L. (1991). *Essentials of behavioral research: Methods and data analysis* (2nd ed.). New York: McGraw-Hill.

Rothbaum, R., Weisz, J. R., & Snyder, S. S. (1982). Changing the world and changing the self: A two-process model of perceived control. *Journal of Personality and Social Psychology* 42, 5–37.

Rotton, J., & Kelly, I. W. (1985). Much ado about the full moon: A meta-analysis of the lunar-lunacy research. *Psychological Bulletin* 97, 286–306.

Rozin, P., Markwith, M., & Ross, B. (1990). The sympathetic magical law of similarity, nominal realism and neglect of negatives in response to negative labels. *Psychological Science* 1, 383–384.

Rozin, P., Millman, L., & Nemeroff, C. (1986). Operation of the laws of sympathetic magic in disgust and other domains. *Journal of Personality and Social Psychology* 50, 703–712.

Russell, D., & Jones, W. H. (1980). When superstition fails: Reactions to disconfirmation of paranormal beliefs. *Personality and Social Psychology Bulletin* 6, 83–88.

Sagan, C. (1987). The burden of skepticism. *Skeptical Inquirer* 12, 38–46.

Salter, C. A., & Routledge, L. M. (1971). Supernatural beliefs among graduate students at the University of Pennsylvania. *Nature* 232, 278–279.

Sanduleak, N. (1986). The moon is acquitted of murder in Cleveland. In K. Frazier, *Science confronts the paranormal* (235–241). Buffalo, NY: Prometheus.

Sattler, J. M. (1988). *Assessment of children* (3rd ed.). San Diego: Author.

Schachter, S. Deviation, rejection, and communication. *Journal of Abnormal and Social Psychology* 46, 190–207.

Scheidt, R. J. (1973). Belief in supernatural phenomena and locus of control. *Psychological Reports* 32, 1159–1162.

Schumaker, J. F. (1987). Mental health, belief deficit compensation, and paranormal beliefs. *Journal of Psychology* 121, 451–457.

Seligman, M. E. P. (1975). *Helplessness: On depression, development, and death.* San Francisco: Freeman.

Sheldon, W. H. (1940). *The varieties of human physique: An introduction to constitutional psychology.* New York: Harper & Brothers.

Simon, M. (1990, December). Incidence of breakdowns. *Thoroughbred Times*, 18–20.

Singer, J. L. (1971). *The child's world of make-believe: Experimental studies of imaginative play.* New York: Academic Press.

Singer, D. G., & Singer, J. L. (1990). *The house of make-believe: Children's play and developing imagination.* Cambridge, MA: Harvard University Press.

Skinner, B. F. (1948). "Superstition" in the pigeon. *Journal of Experimental Psychology* 38, 168–172.

Skinner, B. F. (1972). A case history in scientific method. In B. F. Skinner, *Cumulative record. A selection of papers* (3rd ed.), (101–124). New York: Appleton-Century-Crofts.

Smeldslund, J. (1963). The concept of correlation in adults. *Scandinavian Journal of Psychology* 4, 165–173.

Snyder, C. R., & Shenkel, R. J. (1975, March). Astrologers, handwriting analysts, and sometimes psychologists use the P. T. Barnum effect. *Psychology Today*, 52–54.

Staddon, J. E. R. (1977). Schedule-induced behavior. In W. K. Honig and J. E. R. Staddon, *Handbook of operant behavior* (125–152). Englewood Cliffs, NJ: Prentice-Hall.

Staddon, J. E. R., & Simmelhag, V. L. (1971). The "superstition" experiment: A reexamination of its implications for the principles of adaptive behavior. *Psychological Review* 78, 3–43.

Starr, B. C., & Staddon, J. E. R. (1982). Sensory superstion on multiple interval schedules. *Journal of the Experimental Analysis of Behavior* 37, 267–280.

Steiger, B., & Hansen-Steiger, S. (1990). *Hollywood and the supernatural.* New York: St. Martin's Press.

Stein, J. (Ed.). (1967). *The Random House dictionary of the English language*. New York: Random House.

Sternberg, R. J. (1988). *The triarchic mind: A new theory of human intelligence*. New York: Viking.

Stouffer, S. A., Lumsdaine, A. A., Lumsdaine, M. H., Williams, R. M., Smith, M. B., Janis, I. L., Star, S. A., & Cottrell, L. S. (1949). *The American soldier (vol. 2): Combat and its aftermath*. Princeton, NJ: Princeton University Press.

Sugarman, S. (1987). *Piaget's construction of the child's reality*. Cambridge: Cambridge University Press.

Swann, I. (1991). *Everybody's guide to natural ESP: Unlocking the extrasensory power of your mind*. Los Angeles: Tarcher.

Sweat, J. A., & Durm, M. W. (1993). Psychics: Do the police really use them? *Skeptical Inquirer* 17, 148–158.

Swedo, S. E., & Rapoport, J. L. (1989). Phenomenology and differential diagnosis of obsessive-compulsive disorder in children and adolescents. In J. L. Rapoport (ed.), *Obsessive-compulsive disorder in children and adolescents* (13–32). Washington, DC: American Psychiatric Press.

Taylor, S. E. (1983). Adjustment to threatening events: A theory of cognitive adaptation. *American Psychologist* 38, 1161–1173.

Taylor, S. E. (1989). *Positive illusions: Creative self-deception and the healthy mind*. New York: Basic Books.

Taylor, S. E., & Brown, J. D. (1988). Illusion and well-being: A social psychological perspective on mental health. *Psychological Bulletin* 103, 193–210.

Thomas, K. (1971). *Religion and the decline of magic*. NY: Scribner's.

Thorndike, E. L. (1936). Edward Lee Thorndike. In C. Murchison (ed.), *A history of psychology in autobiography* (vol. 3), (263–270). Worcester, MA: Clark Universiy.

Tierney, J. (1996, June 30). Recycling is garbage. *The New York Times Magazine*, 24–29, 44, 48, 51, 53.

Timberlake, W., & Lucas, G. A. (1985). The basis of superstitious behavior: Chance contingency, stimulus substitution, or appetitive behavior? *Journal of the Experimental Analysis of Behavior* 46, 15–35.

Tisak, M. S. (1986). Children's conceptions of parental authority. *Child Development* 57, 166–176.

Tobacyk, J. (1985). Paranormal beliefs, alienation, and anomie in college students. *Psychological Reports* 57, 844–846.

Tobacyk, J. (1984). Death threat, death concerns, and paranormal belief. In F. R. Epting & R. A. Neimeyer (eds.), *Personal meanings of death: Applications of personal construct theory to clinical practice* (29–38). Washington: Hemisphere.

Tobacyk, J., & Milford, G. (1983). Belief in paranormal phenomena: Assessment instrument development and implications for personality functioning. *Journal of Personality and Social Psychology* 44, 1029–1037.

Tobacyk, J. J., Nagot, E., Miller, M. (1988). Paranormal beliefs and locus of control: A multidimensional examination. *Journal of Personality Assessment* 52, 241–246.

Tobacyk, J., & Shrader, D. (1991). Superstition and self-efficacy. *Psychological Reports* 68, 1387–1388.

Tobacyk, J. J., & Wilkinson, L. V. (1990). Magical thinking and paranormal beliefs. *Journal of Social Behavior and Personality* 5, 225–264.

Topolnicki, D. M., & MacDonald, E. M. (1993, August). The bankruptcy bonanza! *Money* 22, 82–5.

Tuck. B. (1995). *The relationship of childhood superstition to magical ideation and obsessive compulsive symptoms in adulthood*. Unpublished paper, Department of Psychology, Connecticut College, New London, CT.

Tuerkheimer, A. M., & Vyse, S. A. (in press). *The Book of Predictions: Fifteen years later. The Skeptical Inquirer.*

Tversky, A., & Kahneman, D. (1974). Judgment under uncertainty: Heuristics and biases. *Science* 185, 1124–1131.

U. S. National Center for Health Statistics (1988). *Vital statistics of the United States, 1986.* Washington, DC: U. S. Government Printing Office.

von Neumann, J., & Morgenstern, O. (1944). *Theory of games and economic behavior.* Princeton, NJ: Princeton University Press.

Vyse, S. A. (1989, August). *Behavioral stereotypy and problem solving: Some correlates of general, specific, and superstitious rule statements.* Address presented by invitation at the annual convention of the American Psychological Association, New Orleans, LA.

Vyse, S. A. (1991). Behavioral variability and rule-generation: General, restricted, and superstitious contingency statements. *The Psychological Record* 41, 487–506.

Wagner, G. A., & Morris, E. K. (1987). "Superstitious" behavior in children. *The Psychological Record* 37, 471–488.

Wagner, M. W., & Monnet, M. (1979). Attitudes of college professors toward extra-sensory perception. *Zetetic Scholar* 5, 7–16.

Wagner, M. W., & Ratzeburg, F. H. (1987). Hypnotic suggestibility and paranormal belief. *Psychological Reports* 60, 1069–1070.

Waldman, S., & Thomas, R. (1990, May 21). How did it happen? *Newsweek* 115(21), 27–32.

Wallace, M., Singer, G., Wayner, M. J., & Cook, P. (1975). Adjunctive behavior in humans during game playing. *Physiology and Behavior* 14, 651–654.

Wason, P. C. (1960). On the failure to eliminate hypotheses in a conceptual task. *Quarterly Journal of Experimental Psychology* 12, 129–140.

Watson, R. I. (1978). *The great psychologists* (4th ed.). Philadelphia: Lippincott.

Wechsler, J. (1982). *A human comedy: Physiognomy and caricature in the 19th century Paris.* London: University of Chicago Press.

Wierzbicki, M. (1985). Reasoning errors and belief in the paranormal. *The Journal of Social Psychology* 125, 489–494.

Wilkinson, C. (1993). *Superstitious beliefs and personality among college students.* Unpublished manuscript, Department of Psychology, Connecticut College, New London, CT.

Williams, L. M., & Irwin, H. J. (1991). A study of paranormal belief, magical ideation as an index of schizotyty and cognitive style. *Personality and Individual Differences* 12, 1339–1348.

Williams, T., & Underwood, J. (1971). *The science of hitting.* NY: Simon and Schuster.

Willoughby, A. (1979). *The alcohol troubled person.* Chicago: Nelson Hall.

Wills, G. (1987). *Reagan's America: Innocents at home.* Garden City, NY: Doubleday.

Wilson, G. D. (1973). A dynamic theory of conservatism. In G. D. Wilson (ed.), *The psychology of conservatism.* London: Academic Press.

Wilson, L. (1988, September). The aging of Aquarius. *American Demographics* 10, 34–39.

Woodward, K. (1990). *Making saints: How the Catholic Church determines who becomes a saint, who doesn't, and why.* New York: Simon and Schuster.

Ziskin, J. (1981) *Coping with psychiatric and psychological testimony Vol. 1* (3rd ed.). Venice, California: Law and Psychology Press.

Zurer, P. S. (1994, August 15). NSF stakes millions on sweeping reform of science, math education. *Chemical & Engineering News* 72, 25–31.

Zusne, L., & Jones, W. H. (1989). *Anomalistic psychology: A study of magical thinking.* Hillsdale, New Jersey: Lawrence Erlbaum Associates.

Index